TAKING CHANCES:

Abortion
and the
Decision
Not to
Contracept

TAKING

CHANCES:

Abortion
and the
Decision
Not to
Contracept

Kristin Luker

University of
California Press
Berkeley
Los Angeles
London

University of California Press
Berkeley and Los Angeles, California
University of California Press, Ltd.
London, England
Copyright © 1975, by
The Regents of the University of California
First Paperback Edition, 1978
ISBN: 0-520-03594-1
Library of Congress Catalog Card Number: 74-22965
Printed in the United States of America

2 3 4 5 6 7 8 9 0

Contents

Preface

The study of contraceptive risk-taking among women had its genesis in the summer of 1969, when, in the course of a two-month period, three different women presented themselves to the contraceptive clinic where I was working as an intake interviewer. Ostensibly, these three women were coming in for contraceptive care, but the screening interview soon revealed that their real concern was a fear that they were pregnant; they had come to the clinic both to test that fear and to begin the process of arranging for an abortion should their fears prove valid. What distinguished these three women from most others who come to contraceptive clinics was that each of them had experienced an induced therapeutic abortion within the previous six months.

Not only the fact of having had an abortion, but the whole social and personal styles of these women challenged what Peter McHugh has called "the rules of plausibility" about abortion. They were white, middle class, and had at least one child already; they had been given contraceptive follow-up attention after the first abortion; they presented no grossly obvious psychological abnormalities; and yet they had engaged in behavior which made them willing to consider a second therapeutic abortion within a six-month period. Although the liberalized California therapeutic abortion law had been in effect for almost two years, the behavior of these women cast into doubt the "things that everybody knows" about legal abortion, both as a means of fertility control and as a social and psychological experience. For example, in 1969 it was still generally thought that abortion was an expensive, traumatic, socially upsetting, and painful way to end a pregnancy; yet here were three women who had twice engaged in behavior that was likely to subject them to this painful and traumatic experience. Similarly, because abortions were thought to be so undesirable, it was assumed that almost any woman would prefer to use contraception rather than seek an abortion; yet none of these three women had used the contraception prescribed for them after the first abortion. Finally, because these assumptions about the social and psychological undesirability of abortions were so generally accepted, the presence of three women who could subject themselves to not one but two abortions in a short period of time meant one of two things: either there existed striking examples of deviance from the "laws of plausibility" about abortion, or the "laws of plausibility" needed re-examining.

What made the case more puzzling was that the behavior of these three women could not be readily explained away. They were not young, they were not poor, they were not from racial minorities, they were not single women angling for husbands, and they were not Catholic—all of which are factors associated in the minds of laymen and professionals with the non-use of contraception and subsequent unwanted pregnancies. Of course, that left the possibility that these three were disturbed women, acting out their own psychic conflicts in an idiosyncratic but self-destructive way. Although the psychic functioning of these particular women remains an unknown so far as this study is concerned (and might possibly be "crazy" in some clinical sense of the word), as a ready explanation for their behavior it did not work: as they sat in the intake interview office, they appeared to be normal, well-adjusted, suburban housewives, different in no readily definable or visible ways from other women coming through that suburban family planning clinic. Most important, there were too many of them. One, and perhaps even two women in their position could have been dismissed as anomalies, rare exceptions that prove the rule. But to meet in eight short weeks three such women, who had apparently done what the rules of plausibility suggest is the unthinkable, began to raise the suspicion that "what everybody knows" about abortion might not be so. At the very least, a significant subcategory existed.

So this is a book about women and men, about sex and contraception. At first glance, this would appear to be obvious: after all, the word "abortion" appears in the title of the book, and a quick glance through the table of contents should reveal that this book is about taking a chance on getting pregnant. But there is a hidden agenda in this Preface, as there is in the book itself.

First, this book assumes that women *and* men take chances with contraception, that women *and* men become pregnant, and that women *and* men seek abortions or other solutions to their unwanted pregnancies. Second, it assumes that contraception is intimately related to sexuality. In logic alone, these premises simply express obvious biological facts, but in our social experience they have been obscured and almost forgotten as time and technology play their roles in the practice of contraception. Throughout the book we will attempt to demonstrate how scientists (and to a large extent the public as well) have come to act *as if* only women get pregnant and *as if* the disconnection of "modern" birth control (the pill and the IUD) from intercourse means that contraception is disconnected from sexuality.

In a sense, this is a political book. Although it does not explicitly set out to analyze the value commitments of contraceptive researchers, family planning agencies, medical practitioners, and policy makers, it will expose some of those values in the process of demonstrating that "what everybody knows" about unwanted pregnancy is not necessarily so. In fact, one of the main goals of this book will be to suggest how our values—about sexuality, about contraception, and even about the nature of women—have in fact helped create the social realities in which we presently find ourselves. If it can be shown that much of our thinking on sex, abortion, and contraception has been based not on fact but on value judgments, perhaps we can come to see problems in these areas in a different light.

I would like to add that this book is not intended as a "hatchet job" of any sort. Although it will demonstrate how certain social and research assumptions have tended to make women suffer for the fact of being female, no wicked conspiracies are hinted at. I believe it will be more worthwhile, for sociologists and feminists alike, to accept a more difficult challenge: to analyze why people of goodwill, working in the presumed best interests of all of us, have helped create social realities which are oppressive to women.

Acknowledgments

In what I suspect is almost always the case with an intellectual undertaking, this book represents the time, support, and thought of many people. I remain continually surprised at the amount of time and effort people are willing to spend in order to read manuscripts, make suggestions, offer advice,and volunteer data. I am indebted to all those people, in ways that I can never express. There are a few people, however,without whose help this book would not have been written. I can never repay them fully, but I would like to thank them here:

First, my thesis committee at Yale—Wendell Bell, August Hollingshead, and Patricia Jette—for patience above and beyond the reasonable; Lincoln Day,who taught me, with all the joy of the born teacher, to love sociology as he does; Anselm Strauss, who rescued me from the deserts of survey research; Jacqueline Wiseman, who showed me by example the standards of excellence for committed scholars, creative feminists, and unflagging friends; and Diane Horowitz, who single-handedly pulled this research out of the Slough of Despair with wit, insight, and her own remarkable work in the sociology of sexual and reproductive behavior.

Next, Laura Tow, who tabulated, cross-tabulated, and then cross-tabulated again, proving that friendship and statistics are not necessarily incompatible; John Clausen, who taught me, again by example, the creative use of qualitative data in building a living sociology; Claude Fischer, who helped solve the dilemma of naming this book; Kingsley Davis and Judith Blake, who think rigorously and write lucidly, and demand those skills of others; and Planned Parenthood/World Population—in particular, E. P. Stevenson, Dottie Gibson, Dr. Don Minkler, Dr. Leonard Laskow, and Dr. Sadja Goldsmith—for their generous giving of time and information and their endless tolerance of an inquisitive sociologist.

Next, Dr. Harold Van Maren, for sharing with me the insights gained from his extensive work in the field of therapeutic abortion; the Booth Memorial Home and the Florence Crittendon Homes, for permitting me to interview women who do not seek abortions; the California State Department of Health, and in particular Dr. Edwin Jackson and Beth Berkov; and The Program in Social Structure and Personality (USPHS training grant MH-08268), for postdoctoral support to rethink and extend this research.

And finally, my heartfelt thanks to those women who permitted me to enter their lives, who told me of their pain and showed me their strength, and whose remarkable cooperation made this study possible—the women of the Abortion Clinic.

K. C. L.

1

The Scope of
the Problem:
The "Abortion
Revolution"

In California in 1971-1972, more than two out of ten pregnancies were terminated by abortion, the ratio being 286 abortions to every 1,000 live births. There were 103,687 induced therapeutic abortions in California in 1971 (up from 65,369 in 1970), and the rate per 1,000 women aged 15 to 44 was 24.2. This compared with a California live birth rate of 74.7 births per 1,000 women. Figures such as these have prompted some experts to speak of an "abortion revolution."[1]

Two things are clear about abortion in California. First, it is a rapidly growing phenomenon. In simple numbers, abortions have increased twenty-fold since 1968, the first full year after liberalization of the state abortion law. (All figures refer to California residents only.) More important, abortion *rates*, which are a much better measure of actual behavior, have increased accordingly.[a] (Admittedly, there were changes in the age structure during this period of time, as women born in the postwar baby boom became old enough to get pregnant and have abortions; but these changes were not nearly large enough to account for such a dramatic increase in abortion.)[2]

Second, abortion in California is rapidly becoming a de facto method of birth control. Whether this phenomenon represents a rational,

---

a. Abortion ratios (abortions per 1,000 live births as above) have two independent sources of variation: the numerator and the denominator. Since both can (and do) vary independently, dramatic shifts may appear without any change in the overall *probability* of abortion. As a hypothetical example, assume that at T_1 there are 1,000 live birhts and 333 abortions. The ratio is thus (roughly) 3:1. Assume then at T_2, the number of live births drops to 600, but the abortions remain stable at the 333 figure. The ratio suddenly becomes 2:1, without any real change in *incidence* of abortion. This is analogous to the situ-

planned alternative to contraception, or whether, as we shall argue later, it is the result of social pressures which make contraception unwieldy, it is clear that neither social scientists, family planning experts, nor the medical profession expected it, and that the majority of the American public still does not accept it. Most Americans favor abortion only when the pregnancy presents a threat of life or health to the prospective mother, and very few support abortion on demand.[3] Although the most recent Gallup poll on this question (1973) has shown important shifts in public opinion, it is safe to say that the norms dictating when it is appropriate to seek an abortion are still much more conservative than the actual behavior of women in California.[4]

In the abstract, what is happening in California should not be surprising: abortion as a method of birth control is both ancient and widespread. Georges Devereux, for example, suggests that abortion occurs in virtually every society, and Kingsley Davis points out that for whole societies as well as for individual families, abortion is one of the most frequent responses to population pressure.[5] Currently, as a worldwide phenomenon, induced abortion is one of the most important methods of fertility control. Social systems as different as those in the Eastern European countries, Japan, and much of Latin America (where abortion is officially forbidden) rely primarily on abortion for population control. In Eastern Europe, for example, abortions in some countries in recent years outnumbered live births,[6] and it is primarily through the use of induced abortion that Japan cut her birth rate in half in less than twenty years.[7] In Latin America, where facts are harder to collect because abortion is illegal, Daniel Callahan states that abortion is the single most important method of fertility control; Mariano Requena has estimated the abortion ratio per 1,000 pregnant women ranges from 117 in Bogota to 246 in Buenos Aires.[8] (California figures using a comparable base of 1,000 pregnant women would be about 357.)[9]

If these were the only terms of comparison, the frequency of induced

---

ation in the United States where overall live births are declining. Thus abortion *rates* (abortions per 1,000 women aged 15-44, the reproductive years) are preferable, as they are more accurate although they entail additional census information.

abortion in California should not come as a surprise. What makes it surprising is the fact that California, unlike any of the countries mentioned, has both a technologically developed society and a population with high levels of contraceptive expertise. Both the Eastern European countries and Latin America have minimal levels of contraception; in the Socialist countries this is partly because the production of contraceptives is assigned a low social and economic priority, and in Latin America it is largely because organized opposition by the religious hierarchy has made contraception generally unavailable.[10] Japan, which would appear at first glance to be nearly comparable to California in terms of technological development, differs primarily for historical reasons. Before and during the Second World War, contraception was forbidden in Japan as a matter of state policy.[11] Thus at the end of the war Japanese society, suffering from economic disorganization and the virtual destruction of most of its industry, confronted a pressing need to curb its high birth rate but had little experience with contraceptive techniques. Abortion became popular under these conditions of crisis, and it apparently remains popular because it is cheap, easily obtained, and lacks formalized opposition. Various attempts have been made in Japan since the late 1960s to introduce contraceptives as an alternative to abortion, but they have met with only moderate success.

In a last attempt at comparison, it might be assumed that the Scandinavian countries are most similar to California: both are technologically developed, have relatively high levels of contraceptive expertise, and share a common Judeo-Christian ethic; and both have what on paper appear to be liberal laws about abortion. But this resemblance is only superficial. In practice, the Scandinavian countries view abortion primarily as a humanitarian measure designed to protect a woman's life and health; fertility control is only an accidental corollary. In all of the Scandinavian countries, for example, various "gatekeeping" institutions determine which women may legitimately obtain abortions. As a consequence, the abortion to live-birth ratio in most Scandinavian countries is low compared to that of California.[12] (There is, however, a substantial rate of illegal abortion, since women found ineligible for legal abortions often leave the country, usually for Poland, to obtain low-cost illegal abortions.)[13]

In contrast, although California technically had a set of similar "gatekeeping" institutions until 1973 (when two Supreme Court decisions made such institutions illegal),[b] these "gatekeepers" exercised relatively little control over who was "eligible" for an abortion: in 1970, over 90 percent of all applications were approved and most of the rest were withdrawn or revoked by the pregnant women themselves.[14] The authority of these institutions was thus apparently more formal than real.

California, then, represents an anomaly: it is one of the few areas in the world which has a high level of technological development, a high standard of living, and a high level of contraceptive expertise in the population (see Chapter Two) and yet relies significantly on abortion as a de facto method of fertility control. Of course, California is anomalous in so many other ways (it has the second highest suicide rate in the United States, for example, and the second highest estimated rate of alcoholism)[15] that one might suspect its abortion rate to be simply another manifestation of the state's general "anomie" or its frontier heritage. It appears more likely, however, that California is in fact the first clear example to emerge of a heretofore unsuspected but universal relationship between the availability of contraception and the use of abortion. (See Appendix One for a discussion of the possible limits of the universality of this relationship.)

First let us examine the general assumption that abortion becomes a significant method of fertility control only when contraception is not readily available. The relationship of contraception and abortion under differing conditions of access is shown in typological form in Figure 1.

When access to contraception is restricted (shown by a minus sign in the figure), abortion becomes the primary method of fertility control, either overtly (open access, hence legal abortion) or covertly (lack of open access, hence illegal abortion). When access to contraception is relatively unrestricted (a plus sign), the tendency until recently, even in the presumably "liberal" Scandinavian countries, has been to restrict

b. These were decided on the same day and, in a sweeping decision, hold in effect that abortion is a matter between a woman and her doctor during the first trimester. *Roe v. Wade,* 410, U.S. 113, 93 Supreme Court 705; and *Doe v. Bolton,* 410 U.S. 179, 93 Supreme Court 739 (1973).

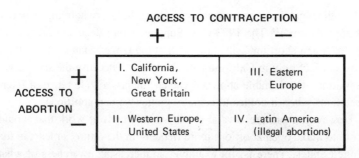

FIGURE 1. Relationship of contraception and abortion under differing conditions of access.

the access to abortion, and specifically to oppose "open abortion" or "abortion on demand." For historical reasons, cells two, three, and four have represented the status quo since the Second World War—three and four representing the overt or tacit acceptance of abortion in contraceptively limited societies such as Eastern Europe and Latin America, and cell two representing the situation in the rest of Europe and the United States. These historical reasons appear to be related to the technological status of both abortion and contraception, and to the pronatalist ethos which has held sway in the Western Hemisphere since the end of the Second World War. Although necessarily speculative, it seems reasonable that the restriction of abortion in contraceptively sophisticated societies (cell two) has been in part based on the assumption that when women have the option of prior contraception, abortion should be reserved only for those few cases where circumstances compensate for the non-use or failure of contraception. In other words, if a woman can prevent pregnancy, she must, and abortion should be a "back-up" for only a chosen few.

Only within the last five years has open access to both contraception and abortion (cell one) been an empirical reality. At the present time, only Great Britain (including Wales), California, and New York offer relatively unimpeded access to both. (For purposes of this argument, an "open" abortion situation exists when there are no "gatekeeping institutions" and abortion is a matter between a woman and her doctor, or when the "gatekeepers" routinely approve the overwhelming majority of applications.)[16] The 1973 U.S. Supreme Court decisions legally set up an "open abortion" situation in all of the United States, but so far it exists in fact only in California and New York, because the same legal definition of acceptable abortions can encompass a wide range of interpretations when it comes to actually giving women abortions.

However, there are several society-wide trends at work that would seem to make open abortions more frequent in the future, at least in the United States. There is, for example, an increasing awareness of what are broadly called "women's issues" and an increasing acceptance of the fact that complete control over pregnancy is fundamental to the achieving of further liberation for women. Second, the traditional pronatalist ethos is being gradually replaced by a concern about over-population and a growing antinatalist movement. As part of this, there seems to be a feeling that restrictive abortion, which Judith Blake has called "one of the more repressive of pronatalist policies," is ill-suited to a nation with a real concern for curbing population growth.[17] Finally, there is an increasing tendency in the courts to place matters of reproductive choice under the protection given to other rights of privacy. This reverses previous legal policy to the effect that the state had a "compelling interest" in the reproductive lives of its citizens. Perhaps because of the decline of pronatalism, the current judicial tendency is to deny that such a "compelling interest" exists.[c]

California appears to be a test case of what happens when access to abortion is made more available in a contraceptively sophisticated population. This relationship in other circumstances has proved to be both baffling and unpredictable. In Japan, for example, the introduction of contraceptive services has had little effect on the overall incidence of

c. In *Bours v. United States,* 229 F. 960 (1915), the Seventh Circuit Court of Appeals held that the Comstock Laws indicated "a national policy of dis-countenancing abortion as inimical to the national life." In *Babbitz v. McCann* (U.S.D.E., March 5, 1970), in contrast, the court held that "in our opinion, the state does not have a compelling interest even in the normal situation to require a woman to remain pregnant during the early months following her conception." And "when measured against the claimed rights of an embryo, four months or less, we hold that the mother's right transcends that of such an embryo."

abortion.[18] While this may be idiosyncratic and due to the same unique historical circumstances that led Japan to adopt abortion in the first place, it appears to indicate that in the absence of other compelling motivations, the introduction of contraception in a society where abortion is readily available, inexpensive, safe, and efficient, will have little effect on the incidence of abortion. In short, there are no empirical grounds for assuming that women have an à priori preference for contraception over abortion.

In the example of Latin America, Requena found that the introduction of contraception actually *raised* the incidence of illegal abortion, at least in the short run. This result was unexpected and unwelcome, particularly since the contraceptive programs had been accepted by officials as a necessary evil designed to combat the high rate of illegal abortion.[19] It was even more surprising because abortions in Latin America are not only illegal, but medically dangerous and often fatal. Requena explained the rise by arguing that when access to contraception is provided it legitimizes the desire to limit family size, which leads to acceptance of abortion as a back-up method in case of failure. This may well be the general model in populations where access to both contraception and abortion are restricted: increasing the access to contraception where illegal abortion is the primary method of fertility control may have at least the short-term effect of legitimizing increased access to abortion, even when that access is formally taboo. Requena predicts that this effect will level off in the long run.

Thus although it is sketchy, there is some research that predicts what increased access to abortion will do to the relationship between abortion and contraception under two very different conditions—when abortion is readily available but contraception is not, and when neither abortion nor contraception is available. But what happens in the third case, when contraception is readily available but abortion is not? What effects will increased access to abortion have on the actual incidence of abortion?

Because of the assumption in contraceptively sophisticated societies that most women will prefer to prevent pregnancies rather than interrupt them, it has generally been thought until now that increased access to abortion would merely legalize illegal abortions, or legitimize the aborting of "marginal" pregnancies that could not be terminated under the restrictive laws of the past (for example, pregnancies to single women, pregnancies where rape or incest was involved, or pregnancies with a high likelihood of fetal deformity due to exposure of the mother to drugs like Thalidomide or diseases like rubella).

The legal and social legacy of abortion in the United States, as well as the current economic realities of obtaining an abortion in California, would tend to support this expectation. Abortion, after all, has been virtually illegal since the Comstock Laws of 1873,[d] and although almost every state has grounds for legal abortions to save the life (and in some states the health) of the mother, these laws have in the past been strictly interpreted. Until recently, for example, most hospitals have had formal or informal quotas of abortions to live births that kept the incidences low.[20] Until the recent liberalization of abortion laws, it was not unusual for a woman to have to accept obligatory sterilization as part of the bargain for a legal abortion; if *this* pregnancy were a threat to her life or health, the doctors could say, the same would be true of any subsequent pregnancies.[21] In fact, sterilization requirements were more or less tacitly designed to limit the use of abortion to extreme cases and to minimize its use as a fertility control measure. Thus the law forbade the use of abortion except to save life or health, and the medical profession typically defined those cases very narrowly.

The medical taboo on abortion was certainly no stronger than the public taboo. In the 1962 Gallup poll 16 percent of the respondents disapproved of terminating a pregnancy even when it was a threat to the mother's health (although this condition, strictly speaking, is legal grounds for abortion in most states); 29 percent disapproved even when the child might be born deformed, and 74 percent disapproved when the reason for abortion was that the family did not have enough money to support another child.[22] In the 1965 National Fertility Study, 11 percent disapproved of abortion even when the mother's life was in danger, and 42 percent disapproved even when the pregnancy occurred as a result of

d. The Comstock laws forbade sending material on both contraception and abortion through the mails. The first prohibition of the *act* of abortion was in the New York Revised Statutes of 1829. For a historical overview of abortion laws, see Hall (ed.), *Abortion in a Changing World* (New York: Columbia University Press, 1970), pp. 127, 136. See also S. Polsky, "Legal Aspects of Abortion," *Seminars in Psychiatry*, Vol. 2 (1970), pp. 246-257.

rape; 84 percent disapproved when the reason for abortion was that the woman was unmarried, 87 percent disapproved when the reason was that the family could not afford another child, and 91 percent disapproved when the reason was that the family did not want another child. It is significant that discretionary abortions (when the family cannot afford a child, when the woman is unmarried, when the couple has all the children they want) were almost universally condemned.[23]

This legacy of a century of harsh laws did not end with the liberalization of abortion laws in several states (New York, California, Alaska, Hawaii, and Colorado) between 1967 and 1970. By 1969, public opinion on abortion had been only slightly changed by the public debate surrounding liberalization in these states. One out of ten Americans (13 percent) still felt that abortions should not be legal even when the health of the mother was in danger; one out of four (25 percent) disapproved of abortion even when the child might possibly be born deformed; and over two-thirds of those questioned (68 percent) disapproved of abortion performed because the family could not afford another child.

In addition to the fact that abortion is still contrary to the public mores (and Blake has noted that this disapproval is *more* marked among young people according to the Gallup polls taken between 1960 and 1970), abortions are also expensive and cumbersome to obtain. In the San Francisco Bay Area in 1971, the average abortion price was over three hundred dollars, and often the price went as high as seven hundred dollars. (By 1973, after the study was completed, the price had fallen to one hundred and fifty dollars.) In addition, a woman (or her doctor) had to file for permission with the therapeutic abortion board of a hospital accredited by the Joint Commission on Accreditation of Hospitals. (As noted, this was largely a formality because virtually all petitions were approved; but the procedure took both time and effort, and there was always the *possibility* that a petition could be denied.) Although systems in various hospitals differed, it was not unusual for a hospital to demand a psychiatric evaluation prior to the abortion, and performance of the abortion was often made contingent on this evaluation.

It seems as if common sense would lead women who have open access to contraception to avoid such an expensive and normatively taboo way of controlling fertility as abortion, especially when they must submit to some degree of social control and personal investigation in order to obtain it. But this is not the case in the state of California. The 103,000 therapeutic abortions given to California residents in 1971 cannot be entirely accounted for by previously illegal abortions made visible, nor by contraceptive failures.[e] Nor were these abortions last-ditch attempts on the part of contraceptively ignorant women to plan their families: California women are at least as contraceptively sophisticated as the American population as a whole, if not more so.[24] More evidence is provided by the fact that almost a quarter of the women seeking abortions at the clinic where this study was made had previously been clients of a related family planning clinic in the area. In addition, virtually every woman in this study had *some* contraceptive skills and over half had used at some time the most effective contraceptive currently available, the pill. (A more detailed description of contraceptive use is given in Chapter Two.)

Some small part of the twenty-fold increase in therapeutic abortion from 1968 to 1971 can possibly be accounted for by the legalization of previously illegal abortions and by the increasing tendency of women to abort marginal pregnancies which would have been carried to term in earlier years. Among these marginal pregnancies are those involving contraceptive failure, rape, unwed motherhood, and fetal deformities. However, there is clearly something else going on. California women seem to be making a de facto choice of abortion as a method of fertility control. Why women who have easily available, inexpensive, efficient, and presumably convenient contraceptives within their reach should turn to an expensive, at times humiliating, and often traumatic procedure to end a pregnancy, especially in a social context which severely

e. While exact data is hard to come by, because abortion was until recently illegal, the consensus in the field is that the increased incidence of therapeutic abortion includes other than the mere legalization of otherwise illegal abortions. Included are pregnancies which would otherwise be carried to term, a higher rate of conceptions possible after abortion than after full term delivery, and reduced motivation to use contraceptives. See C. Tietze, "Abortion on Request: Its Consequences for Population Trends and Public Health," *Seminars in Psychiatry,* Vol. 2, pp. 375-381, and E. C. Moore, "Induced Abortion and Contraception," *Studies in Family Planning,* Vol. 53, pp. 7-8.

disapproves of discretionary abortions, is the question we shall explore in this study.[f]

To explore the question thoroughly, we must overcome several difficulties. Precisely because of the official sanction against abortion until recently, statistics about abortions are largely sketchy, of questionable validity, or nonexistent, and research as a consequence has been limited. Even with the coming of more liberalized laws in California and more accurate statistics about the parameters of the "abortion revolution," what these statistics really mean is far from clear. In California, at the same time the more liberal law was passed, the state legislature passed a resolution calling for more accurate surveillance of the abortion situation. In compliance with the resolution, the State Department of Public Health has kept records on all therapeutic abortions since the 1967 liberalization. These records list age of mother, race, "gravity" (number of previous pregnancies), marital status, residence, and length of pregnancy at termination. Additionally, they note whether the woman paid for the abortion through insurance, privately, or through Medi-Cal (medical care to the indigent) and thus give a rough measure of social class and income.

Although these figures provide invaluable data for discussing the abortion situation as a whole and making generalizations about large-scale changes and trends, they tell us very little about why the frequency of abortion is so high in California. What they do make very clear is something else—that many of the common-sense notions about what abortion means simply do not hold for this particular population of abortion-seeking women.

For example, it is often assumed that abortion is something most likely to happen to the very young woman, presumably too young to seek out and effectively use contraception. In reality, more abortions

f. It is vital to emphasize that we do not consider abortions necessarily "expensive, humiliating, and often traumatic." Indeed, in a country such as Japan where abortions are both inexpensive and commonplace, abortion need not be either humiliating or traumatic. Presently, however, as we shall demonstrate in Chapters Three and Five, abortion still suffers from a "stigma effect" which results from a well-intentioned desire on the part of abortion personnel to help women "understand" their "self-destructive" behavior.

are given in California to women aged twenty to twenty-four than to women aged fifteen to nineteen. To put it more precisely, the abortion *rate* per 1,000 women twenty to twenty-four years old is higher than the rate for a comparable number of fifteen to nineteen-year-olds.[25] (This distinction is important because some observers have noted that the abortion *ratio*—abortions per live births—is higher in the younger age group, but this is an artifact of having so few live births to form the denominator of the ratio.)

These figures also refute the common assumption that abortions are given mostly to unmarried women who would otherwise have illegitimate births. Only half of the abortions in 1971 were performed on unmarried women, and the remaining half were almost equally divided between married women on the one hand and separated, widowed, divorced, and "other" women on the other. When it is remembered that a fairly high percentage of American wives are already pregnant when they marry (and presumably marry because they are already pregnant), the stereotype of the frightened girl attempting to hide a stigmatized pregnancy by abortion is hardly an adequate explanation.[26]

Nor do these statistics support the common assumption that abortion is a last ditch "back-up" method used primarily by poor women and "welfare mothers," who are assumed to have less access to contraception than wealthier women. Although the assumption about access to contraception is valid (at least according to the 1960 Growth of American Families Study), the assumption about poverty is not: only a little over a third of the women having abortions in 1971 had them paid for by Medi-Cal (medical care to the indigent), and almost two-thirds of them paid for their abortions themselves.[27] Moreover, there is some evidence to suggest that this figure *over*represents what could truly be called "poor" or welfare women. Many of these women were not on the welfare rolls prior to their abortions and left Medi-Cal status immediately after receiving them. Some part of these Medi-Cal figures, then, are accounted for by young middle-class women who could neither pay for their abortions themselves nor turn to their families or partners for financial help. Thus truly "poor" women probably account for even less than a third of the abortions in the state.

Finally there is the assumption, encountered primarily in the professional literature, that a substantial number of abortions are explained by the "exhausted mother syndrome": women with children too closely spaced together can become too exhausted or too harried to use a contraceptive effectively; when faced with another pregnancy, the burden of caring for yet another child seems intolerable to them, and they become candidates for abortion. This may well describe why abortions are sought by a certain group of women, but it cannot be a very significant causal factor in the state as a whole. In 1971, only one abortion out of five was given to a woman with four or more pregnancies (which is not the same as four or more children, because the earlier pregnancies may have terminated in stillbirths, miscarriages, and prior abortions).[28] And so, however accurate the syndrome may be in accounting for abortions among women with higher-order births, it cannot explain other abortions, which are in the large majority.

In fact, each one of these common-sense notions probably explains why certain women seek abortion. It would be surprising if they did not. The point here is that no single one of them can adequately account for the incidence of abortion in California, and that even taken together they cannot account for the "abortion revolution." Obviously, these statewide statistics are provocative because they eliminate easy answers and highlight the original question I have posed: why do women who can presumably use freely available methods of contraception end up having unwanted pregnancies which result in induced abortions?

The conclusions this study presents should be considered within the context of the methodologies used. A brief review of the research methods used in this investigation follows here; the more technical description of research design and methodology may be found in Appendix One.

Because the nature of abortion has changed so dramatically in recent years, it is clearly not feasible to undertake a study that would "control" for the variables thought to be significant in the earlier literature. Nor can a secondary analysis of the newer statewide data be undertaken at this point, because that data is too limited in scope. Rather, since abortion in California represents a whole new problem, which we have defined as the relationship between contraception and abortion in an open-access situation, my research methodology is designed to perform two tasks: first, to define and document the structure of this relationship; and second, to outline the important social variables that bear on it.

In order to accomplish both these tasks the following steps were taken. First, a single abortion clinic was chosen as a case study, using the statewide data as a background to establish the limits of generalizability. Second, a survey was taken of the records of all women using the clinic, so that general statements about abortion-seeking women could be developed. Finally, a sampling of individual women was made, and the women interviewed, in order to identify and analyze what the relationship of abortion to contraception meant to them—to translate statistical assumptions into social facts as described by the women themselves. Thus every step of the research strategy was aimed at making the analysis less general and more complete.

The first step in the research was to gain access to an abortion clinic that was serving a representative range of abortion-seeking women. This was provided through the generous support of Planned Parenthood/ World Population, which permitted research entrée to one of their West Coast abortion facilities, which I shall call the Abortion Clinic (all names in this study are fictitious). This clinic was opened in Northern California in the spring of 1970 with a fairly concrete service goal in mind: to provide low-cost abortion services to those women who could not afford the fees charged by private practitioners at the time (which averaged about four hundred dollars, although fees up to seven hundred were not unheard of) and who were not eligible for Medi-Cal, the State of California's medical care to the indigent program. Fees at the Abortion Clinic were three hundred dollars (later reduced to two hundred and fifty dollars) and some loans were available. Thus this clinic had a fairly varied clientele. In age the women ranged from 15 to 45; in marital status from single, to married, separated, widowed, and divorced; in education from less than a high school degree to postgraduate degrees; in "gravity" (previous pregnancies) from one to seven; and in ethnicity from black, to white, Mexican-American, Oriental (both Japanese-Americans and Chinese-Americans), and American Indian. In religious orientation this population had almost exactly the same proportions of Protestants, Catholics, Jews, Buddhists, and "others" as metropolitan Northern California as a whole.

The second step in the research was to examine the voluminous medical records of the first five-hundred women seen through the Clinic. (For reasons unrelated to this research, the Clinic closed soon after the research was completed and the total number of women seen through the Clinic numbered only 660. The time series analysis of these first five-hundred records, then, represents over 80 percent of all the women seen through the Clinic.) These five-hundred records were coded for almost thirty variables, including race, age, marital status, employment status, education, contraception ever used, contraception used immediately preceding the pregnancy, date of last menstrual period, contraception prescribed post-abortion, and pregnancy history. Once again, Planned Parenthood generously made research assistance and funds available for this stage of the project. These data were coded onto cards and a series of cross-tabulations and simple statistical validations was undertaken. (See Appendix Two for details on this aspect of the research.)

As the third step, fifty women undergoing abortions at the Clinic were interviewed in a series of in-depth, semi-structured interviews, and the responses were recorded verbatim. These interviews lasted on the average of one hour, but some went on for considerably longer. In several instances, conjoint interviews involving either the husband or the lover of the pregnant woman were undertaken as well. Moreover, ten women undergoing therapeutic abortions under the care of a private practitioner in the San Francisco Bay Area were included for purposes of comparison. Interviews were also undertaken with a limited number of unwed mothers in the same geographic area, but these interviews are not included in this series. Thus qualitative data from sixty interviews was made available for analysis.

This particular research design has several advantages. (The drawbacks are discussed in Appendix One.) It permits maximum flexibility in the generation of hypotheses, because the hypotheses under consideration can be constantly reconsidered and redefined with each new addition of information. This technique, which Glaser and Strauss have developed under the general term of "grounded theory,"[29] is admirably suited for pilot research aimed at theory generating rather than theory testing, and it appears most appropriate for use in research situations like this one, where valid empirical data are limited and the broad outlines of the phenomenon are not known.

This design has a second and equally important advantage: it takes in and analyzes as significant data the perceptions of the pregnant women themselves. As we shall have ample opportunity to demonstrate later, this is a radical departure from most contraceptive and abortion-oriented research. In large part, research on these women and the delivery of services to them has been carried out by people who have never had an unwanted pregnancy—the majority of them, in fact, are incapable of having an unwanted pregnancy because they are men.

Without attempting to resolve the knotty problems of institutional sexism in research and the delivery of services, and the even more complicated issues of "value-free" and "value-laden" sociology, it is sufficient to say that two separate and distinct "definitions of the situation" have arisen around unwanted pregnancies. The prevailing and "outsider" position is that any pregnancy which is unwanted should have been prevented, or at least should have a history of attempts at prevention. If no attempts were made to prevent it, then the female (rarely does this analysis extend to the male half of the couple) is at best irrational and at worst pathological. There is an important but little-noted flaw in this reasoning. It assumes that women know at the outset what the eventual results of their contraceptive risk-taking will be: that over the long run 80 percent of all women exposed to intercourse without contraception will become pregnant.[30]

If women thought about their pregnancies using the same "definition of the situation" as the one taken for granted by most researchers and policy makers, the sort of open-ended research proposed in this study would not be necessary. But the fact is that they do not. In making decisions about contraception they try to attain many goals, only one of which is not getting pregnant. They are usually aware of the odds of pregnancy (as noted, roughly 80 percent), but for them individually the chances are zero or one: either they get pregnant or they do not. One simply cannot translate an 80 percent chance of pregnancy *over the long run* into being 80 percent pregnant, so the risk-taking is very different for them than for statisticians.g By the time pregnancy occurs, however, the cost accounting has changed: the odds have suddenly become 100 percent. It is at this point that women face the prevailing definition of the situation—that any pregnancy which was not actively prevented is irrational and inexplicable—and thus begin to feel that they must be either irrational or confused about what they really want.

Whether or not these women are neurotic or irrational people is not germane to this study; they may well be, but there is no à priori reason for assuming that the distribution of "normal" to "abnormal" is any different in this particular population than in the population at large. What *is* germane to this study, however, is that their behavior leading up to the unwanted pregnancy is both reasonable and logical given their *own* definition of the situation, which can and will be outlined and analyzed below. But just as the thinking of researchers and policy makers lacks important information—how women themselves define the situation—the women's "rational" view lacks an important piece of information as well: over the long run, most of them will become pregnant.

No effective policy can be created and no meaningful services offered without both views of the situation: of client and service agency, of woman and concerned professional. Until researchers, contraceptive clinics, and public health officials can recognize and respond to the social and structural assumptions that women act on in dealing with contraception, unwanted pregnancy will continue to remain an "irrational act" beyond the reach of intervention.

g. See Chapter Five for a fuller discussion of the subjective aspects of probability. In addition, it should be noted that the 80 percent pregnancy figure is based on a "law of large numbers" which draws on clinic data for pregnancy rates. The current population of women under study, however, were often unmarried, had sporadic sexual exposure, varying degrees of fertility, and were having intercourse with men whose fertility may have varied from day to day. Over the long run of multiple exposure to intercourse, with a large sample of women, these factors will tend to become less salient, but estimating the likelihood of pregnancy to any individual from a specific act of intercourse is a statistician's nightmare, and women find it no easier. Here, and in the rest of this book, we shall use the term "fertility" to refer to the *potential* of bearing children (and consequently "fecundity" for the accomplished fact). Although this is the reverse of accepted demographic usage, it does conform to medical terminology, and more important, to the terminology used by the women themselves.

CHAPTER

2

Contraceptive
Risk-Taking:
A Theoretical
Overview

There are at present two prevailing theories
about why women have unwanted pregnancies. The first, most often
discussed by family planning agencies and their supporters, suggests
that women have unwanted pregnancies because they lack the contraceptive expertise to prevent them. The second, favored by psychologists
and psychiatrists, particularly of the psychoanalytic school, suggests
that women have the contraceptive skills to prevent pregnancies but
encounter psychological resistance to using them. In this chapter we
shall examine the empirical evidence for each of these theories, and
offer some conclusions about their adequacy as true explanations of
abortion.

The first, which we may call the contraceptive ignorance theory,
dates at least from the early part of this century and the efforts of
Margaret Sanger. Mrs. Sanger attracted volunteers for her nascent
American Birth Control League by describing the agonizing death of
one Sadie Sachs from a septic abortion, to which she was driven,
according to Mrs. Sanger, by her inability to control by contraception
births which she could neither afford nor support.[1] Mrs. Sanger argued
eloquently that contraception was withheld from all but the privileged
few by Federal laws (notoriously the Comstock Laws), middle-class
hypocrisy, and ignorance. In 1965, a good half-century after Mrs.
Sanger's crusade, the contraceptive ignorance of all but the privileged
few was still being cited as a major determinant of unwanted births.[2] It
is true, of course, that formal and informal taboos against the dissemination of birth-control information did (and do) exist. Until a surprisingly recent Supreme Court decision, for example, anti-contraceptive
laws, although virtually never enforced, remained on the books in
several states.[3] Many welfare agencies, as another example, maintained

tacit policies with their clients which effectively precluded the presentation of any official contraceptive information to the poor.[4] And there can be no doubt that as recently as the late 1960s there was a considerable reluctance on the part of doctors to prescribe birth control devices, particularly in heavily Catholic communities.[5]

David Kennedy has shown that in order to attract converts to her cause, the charismatic Mrs. Sanger was willing to embroider the truth a bit, often claiming vast and abysmal ignorance of contraception in the United States.[6] (She was hardly unique in this; social reform movements aimed at changing normative standards have a general tendency to exaggerate the scope of the problem in order to enlist members.)[7] She once claimed, for example, that she had to travel to France in order to find any birth control information whatsoever.[8] In fact, the Index Catalogue of the Library of the Surgeon General's Office, a reference work widely available for more than a decade prior to Mrs. Sanger's crusade, listed two full pages of books and articles on the prevention of contraception, which described such methods as the "condom, vaginal douching, suppositories, tampons, and the cervical pessary."[9]

Although the evolution of Mrs. Sanger's organization into Planned Parenthood paralleled its transformation from a radical social reform movement into a widely respected social institution,[10] the emphasis on contraceptive ignorance as a primary cause of unwanted births has persisted. Bumpass and Westoff, for example, in a study widely quoted in official family planning literature, have suggested that almost a fourth of all American births are unwanted and could be avoided by a population using completely effective contraception.[11] Oscar Harkavy and others have asserted that in the late 1960s there were at least five million women in need of Federally assisted birth-control programs.[12] Both these assertions stress the taboos on the dissemination of birth-control information as primary causes of contraceptive ignorance, and assume that contraceptive ignorance is a primary cause of unwanted births.

Neither of these assumptions, however, is critically tenable. As Blake has shown, public approval of birth control has been considerable for more than a quarter of a century.[13] In a 1937 Gallup poll, 66 percent of the men and 70 percent of the women interviewed approved of birth control. By 1964 the percentages were 89 percent and 86 percent respectively.

It is true, of course, as others have noted, that when there is a discrepancy between official normative standards and privately held opinions, a wide range of behavior can result—from deviance, to the creation of new patterns more consonant with private opinions, to ritualistic observance of the formal norms.[14] The practice of birth control in the United States appears to provide another pattern: widespread private deviance from official norms, but general public support of them. Although it cannot be fully analyzed in this study, it is possible that historically, disapproval of birth control has been the position of a vocal and articulate minority, a position tacitly tolerated but never fully accepted by the larger majority.[15]

That the presumed real-life taboo on birth control has had little effect on actual contraceptive behavior in American life can be amply demonstrated. As early as 1936, *Fortune* magazine reported that the supplying of birth-control devices was a $250,000,000-a-year business.[16] At the same time, the Gallup polls quoted above (1937 and 1964) indicate that abstract acceptance of birth control has been fairly widespread. "Knowledge, Attitude, and Practice" studies (known as KAP studies) in the United States have demonstrated repeatedly that acceptance in practice far exceeds acceptance as a matter of expressed principle. Freedman found in 1955 that 95 percent of all fecund American couples used contraception, or planned to use contraception once ideal family size was attained.[17]

An analysis of the first five hundred medical records of women who sought abortions at the Abortion Clinic studied here demonstrated this same pattern of widespread contraceptive acceptance and use. Over half of the women seen at the Clinic had used a prescription method of birth control (primarily anovulent pills) at some point in the past, and 86 percent had used some method of birth control. Only 14 percent had never used any method and an additional 11 percent had used the less effective methods of douching, withdrawal (coitus interruptus), and rhythm. The remaining 20 percent were condom and foam users.

In terms of clinical effectiveness, Christopher Tietze has estimated that the rates of accidental pregnancy are approximately 1 percent with the anovulent pills, approximately 3 percent with the intrauterine devices,[18] 14.9 percent with the condom, 15 percent with the diaphragm, 16 percent with withdrawal, 34.5 percent with the rhythm method, and 37.8 percent with douching.[19] Of the women coming into the Clinic, then, fully half had skills to avoid pregnancy with 99 percent effectiveness; 20 percent had skills in the 85 percent effective range; and 14 percent had skills ranging from 84 effective to 62 percent effective.[20]

It could be argued that if we combine this last group of women, 14 percent with skills adequate to avoid pregnancy only from 62 to 84 percent of the time, with the 11 percent of women who had no contraceptive skills whatsoever, we have 25 percent of the clinic population whose experience upholds, at least in part, the theory of contraceptive ignorance as a major cause of unwanted pregnancy. In order to support this assumption, however, it would be necessary to demonstrate that these women truly lacked access to contraceptive skills and information—that they were in fact contraceptively ignorant rather than unable or unwilling to act on the information they possessed. Although the clients of the Abortion Clinic are not a perfectly representative sample of all women having abortions in the Northern California area, they seem to provide evidence that a lack of proven contraceptive expertise does not necessarily represent either an inability to obtain contraception or a true contraceptive ignorance.

The majority of women seen at the Clinic displayed "some" or "much" birth-control information when interviewed by trained social workers;[21] and, as we shall demonstrate later in this study, they were aware of the risks involved in not using contraception or in using relatively ineffective methods. Many had made tentative gestures toward improving their skills, and virtually all of them knew how to obtain birth control information and material. And so, although there may be scattered individuals who are contraceptively ignorant, as a whole the Clinic population refutes the thesis that unwanted pregnancies result from a lack of contraceptive skills.

There is one important exception to this conclusion, however, which should be noted here. Older women in this study (those over thirty) were significantly more likely to use only those methods on the less effective end of the scale or to have used no method at all (see Figure 2). This appears to reflect their entrance into a new phase in the family building process. As a rule, they began their sexual careers approximately ten to fifteen years ago (assuming that typical American marriage patterns apply) and are thus likely to have married young,[22] to have had their children soon after marriage,[23] and to have wanted larger

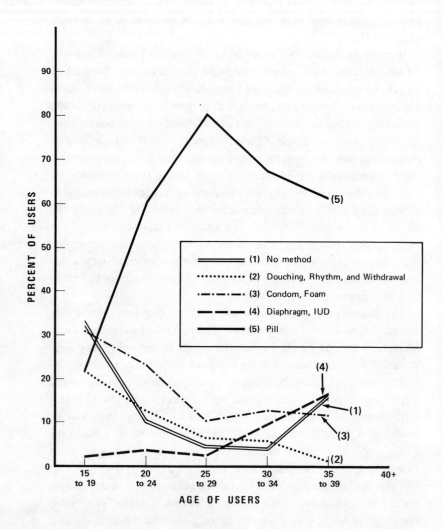

FIGURE 2. Most effective contraception ever used by age and by percent of users.

families than the younger women seen through the Clinic.[24] Because the more effective methods (the pill and the IUD) did not become widely available until the latter part of the 1960s, these women probably continued to use the method of contraception that worked fairly well for them throughout the major part of their child-bearing years, and hence had no impetus to change methods.[a] In particular, it appears that these lesser methods were used primarily to *time* births, and that mistakes in timing were usually taken in stride. As one respondent said in her interview:

R: We said we'd like to have our first child after five years. There was a laugh because all three guys in grad school came in with children in the first year.

With increasing age and some degree of freedom from children, however, the contraceptive needs of these older women shifted from timing births to avoiding them, and it was here that the less effective methods eventually failed. In terms of this study, these women were in a sense contraceptively ignorant (if we stretch the meaning of the term somewhat) because they were unaware of the new contraceptive risk to which their changed sociological position exposed them. But except for this special group of older women (who comprise a mere 11 percent of all the women seen), the contraceptive skills of the Clinic clients were more than adequate to refute the theory of contraceptive ignorance.

Pregnancy occurred in this population of women not because they lacked the skills to avoid it, but because they did not use those skills or used them only inconsistently. Over 40 percent of the women seen at the Clinic had used no method at all since the last menstrual period (the fertile period during which pregnancy occurred) and 26 percent had used a method inconsistently, sometimes in conjunction with the rhythm method. An additional 13 percent had used the rhythm method exclusively, but in both cases we must consider rhythm an inconsistent method, since for most women it represented nothing more than a vague

a. Oral contraceptives were first field tested in Puerto Rico in 1956, and in Haiti in 1957. In 1960, the first oral contraceptives were made available in the United States. Searle Reference and Resource Program, *A Prescription for Family Planning* (New York: 1841 Broadway, 1964), pp. 27-33. However, 1965 was the first time that pill use was more frequent than other methods. See U.S. Bureau of the Census, *Current Population Reports*, "Fertility Indicators: 1970."

awareness of "safe days" and an attempt to schedule intercourse during those days. Thus almost 80 percent of the women seen at the Clinic showed erratic or nonexistent contraceptive use. For the 20 percent who reported consistent use of a method, there was still underuse of skills, because most used a method less effective than the most effective method they had ever used. Only 6 percent reported consistent use of the highly effective prescription methods.

In addition, there is some evidence that the consistency of use reported in these figures is somewhat inflated, gathered as it is from the contraceptive use reported to the abortion agency. Women were asked at two different times about their contraceptive patterns prior to the pregnancy: once by a trained social worker, and once by the examining physician. All of the social workers were women, and most of the examining physicians were men, the ratio of men to women physicians being approximately seven to one. The replies to these two different sets of questions were entered on two different forms, and when the two replies were tallied for all women, there appeared a small but consistent tendency to exaggerate the consistency of contraception reported to the physician and to describe a somewhat more erratic pattern of use to the social worker. In addition, the approximately 10 percent of the women who were interviewed by the author reported an even lower level of consistency, probably because the interviews took place after the abortion had been performed, and because the interviewer was known to be detached from the organization.[25] The reasons for the different levels of consistency—among which could be a desire to provide a socially appropriate "presentation of self," a concern that the abortion would not be granted if contraceptive use was proved to be irresponsible,[b] and a differential "presentation of self" to different roles and

b. This was not an irrational fear. Although virtually all abortion petitions in the two years covered by this research (1971-1972) were granted, the hospital therapeutic abortion board had the right to deny any abortion petition it saw fit. Also, as we shall demonstrate later, the personnel of the abortion clinic (whose recommendations were the basis of the hospital board's decision) subtly stigmatized women for becoming pregnant. Thus the fear that the abortion might not be granted was a perfectly accurate "definition of the situation," although it failed to realize the *degree* to which the staff were committed to reducing unwanted births.

sexes—are not clear; but it does appear that the figures here probably exaggerate consistency of contraceptive use.

This pattern of non-use or erratic use of contraception naturally urges consideration of the second prevailing theory about the cause of unwanted pregnancy, which we may call the "intrapsychic conflict" theory—that women have adequate skills to prevent pregnancy but for a variety of psychological and psychoanalytic reasons have resistances against using them. For example: "Women are ambivalent about pregnancy throughout most of their reproductive lives. Psychic conflict regarding contraception is to be anticipated, as conscious and unconscious reasons for and against its use exist simultaneously."[26] Or again: "Throughout a larger part of their procreative period, most women are ambivalent about becoming pregnant—an ambivalence which helps them to adjust to the monthly uncertainty. What happens when we give a woman confidence that she will not become pregnant? . . . The conflict between wanting to be fertile and not wanting a child can be great."[27]

This area of inquiry is most generally called research on "contraceptive conflict," by which is meant the failure to use adequate contraception to prevent any pregnancy which is neither planned nor wanted. But what constitutes adequate contraception, and what constitutes a planned and wanted pregnancy, are not clearly defined in this literature. As Blake has noted, it is extremely difficult to determine after the fact what is an unwanted pregnancy.[28] Too often there is a tendency to assume that any pregnancy that is unplanned is also unwanted. In the body of literature under review, unwanted pregnancies have usually been defined by a case-study approach, using as a population either unwed mothers (usually from maternity homes) or women seeking therapeutic abortions.

Apart from the problem that these sample populations are not representative of the whole universe of women with unwanted pregnancies, there is also evidence that they represent a skewed population of women. First, women in maternity homes, although easily accessible to the researcher, often tend to disproportionately represent the undereducated and psychologically less adequate woman who lacks alternatives to her unwed pregnancy.[29] Second, women seeking legal abortions during the years when most of this literature was produced were also a highly skewed population; the restrictive laws prevalent in the United States until recently demanded that a woman present and prove severe psychological disorganization in order to qualify for a therapeutic abortion.[30] Since it was not uncommon to demand surgical sterilization as a corollary of the abortion, this population was probably biased in favor of the more desperate. In addition, both unwed mothers and women seeking abortions were "deviant," particularly in terms of the pronatalist ethos of the era, and it is not possible to separate the psychological effects of such deviance from prior psychological organization which may have caused it. As one author asks, "are these women different because they are pregnant, or are they pregnant because they are different?"[31] In short, psychologistic explanations in support of the contraceptive conflict theory are severely weakened by the unrepresentative populations of unwanted pregnancies that have been available to researchers.

Another problem in this literature is the difficulty of defining exactly what behavior constitutes a volitional or chosen failure of contraceptive skills. The problem occurs for two reasons. First, the various contraceptive techniques themselves differ widely in effectiveness: douching after intercourse will fail to prevent pregnancy in about a third of the cases, for example, while oral birth control pills will fail less than 1 percent of the time.[32] Thus "method failure" rates vary widely. Second, the various contraceptive methods differ greatly in their potential for ineffective use. An IUD, once put in place by a physician, is rarely removed by the woman herself. Anovulent pills, even when not taken daily, tend by their hormonal action to provide a "margin of error" that lessens the risk of pregnancy.[33] Both of these methods, therefore, have low "user failure" potentials. The other methods, however (douching, withdrawal, foam, condoms), have relatively high user failure potentials: they must be used consistently at each intercourse (which takes planning each time) and very close to the actual time of intercourse, when emotional stress is likely to make user failure even more probable.[34]

It is often hard to determine, however, whether it is the method or the user that has failed, because any contraceptive failure depends on both the *intent* of the user (a psychological variable) and the *effect* of the method (a technological variable). Also, this assessment is usually undertaken on the assumption that women can choose freely from among the various contraceptive methods, that they are aware of the probabilities of pregnancy associated with each method, and that the choice of a high-risk method therefore demonstrates some measure of contraceptive gambling in itself. And since this body of literature is a product of the psychologically and psychoanalytically oriented researchers, it shows a notable tendency to discount stated intent in favor of observed effect. At its least tenable, it tends to discount intent entirely, and to assume a reasoning that verges on the tautological: there is no such thing as an unwanted pregnancy, because if a woman gets pregnant she must have wanted to.[c] This happens partly because effect, in the form of an unwanted pregnancy, is much easier to measure than intent (particularly after the fact), and partly because psychologistic and psychoanalytic researchers, ever sensitive to the irrational and subconscious aspects of behavior, are prone to be skeptical about the rational and conscious components of statements by women about their contraceptive intent. Unwanted pregnancies, in the context of the pronatalist ethos that characterized much of the 1950s and 1960s, tend to be seen as the product of user failure, and the conflict tends to be seen as primarily, if not uniquely, intrapsychic.

At its least careful, the intrapsychic conflict theory leads to viewing unwanted pregnancies and the contraceptive behavior which leads to them as neurotic, deviant, and unrealistic.[d] As one author has noted, in our culture deviance in the form of unwed pregnancy represents "a distorted and unrealistic way out of inner difficulties and is thus comparable to neurotic symptoms on the one hand and delinquent behavior on the other."[35] Even with the passing of the strongly pronatalist ethos of the past two decades and with the increasing awareness of social

c. For example, "we may speculate that although the woman consciously did not wish to become pregnant, the fact that she did, suggests that unconsciously she may have wanted to." Z. Alexander Aarons, "Therapeutic Abortion and the Psychiatrist," *American Journal of Psychiatry,* Vol. 124, No. 6 (December 1967), p. 747.

d. For example: "The very fact that a woman cannot tolerate a pregnancy, or is in intense conflict about it, is an indication that the pre-pregnancy personality of this woman was immature and in that sense can be labeled psychopathological." May E. Romm, "Psychoanalytical Considerations," in Rosen (ed.), *Therapeutic Abortion* (New York: The Julian Press, 1954), p. 210.

forces on the part of writers in this field, there is still a tendency to see contraceptive conflict as primarily an intrapsychic process, and usually a somewhat neurotic process at that: "A physician who accepts proffered statements for the whole truth is soon confounded by the apparent irrational action of some patients in their misuse or rejection of the prescribed contraceptives and by the unreasonable and inconsistent explanations as to why none of the various methods are utilizable. . . . It is obvious that behavior in contraceptive use does not always conform to apparently rational, externally voiced attitudes and that conflicted psychological forces, conscious and unconscious, are extremely influential."[36]

There are at least four reasons why the psychic conflict theory of unwanted pregnancy cannot fully explain why women do not use the contraceptive skills they have. First, as we have noted, there are the methodological weaknesses involved in examining primarily deviant unwanted pregnancies, unwed pregnancies, and the rare therapeutic abortion performed prior to the recent liberalization of laws. These weaknesses have been made more serious by the inability or unwillingness of researchers to carefully define the differential components of contraceptive conflict, contraceptive failure, and unwanted pregnancy, and by their willingness to assume that most, if not all, unwanted pregnancies result from user failure rather than method failure.

This first reason is closely connected with a second one: writers focusing on the intrapsychic level of action have largely ignored the social and demographic aspects of contraceptive behavior, so that their conclusions tend to be both culture-bound and value-laden. Devereux, for example, in a cross-cultural analysis of abortion, notes that the two most frequently aborted pregnancies are the first and the third—the first because it triggers crises of maturity in the parents, and the third because it evokes unresolved sibling rivalries.[37] This may be true, of course, but it ignores another significant fact: even in the most primitive societies, the first and third births are understood to be watersheds in the family-building process—the first because it is the beginning of family building, and the third because it produces one child more than the number biologically necessary to replace the parents.[38] Without a critical examination of the "givens" implicit in psychologistic thinking, and a demand for some kind of external verification, there is a tendency to present as immutably human and universal certain values which are in fact socially variable, variable over time, and variable from culture to culture.[e]

Third is a problem common to all psychological explanations of social events: a primarily intrapsychic theory of cause cannot account for changes over time, and for variations by race, class, and area, unless it assumes that psychic functioning also changes and varies along those parameters. As an example, almost three out of every ten pregnancies in California now end in legal induced abortions.[39] Thus induced abortions can no longer be called deviant, at least in the strict statistical sense, and a purely intrapsychic explanation (one which ignores social and demographic factors) cannot account for a phenomenon of such frequency unless it assumes mass neurosis.

Fourth, and finally, the intrapsychic theory of contraceptive conflict is unscientifically misogynist, for it views women who fail to protect themselves contraceptively as qualitatively different from people who fail to protect life or health in other ways. There is no mistaking the moralistic tone of disapproval sometimes taken toward women who do not effectively use contraception to prevent pregnancies they do not want, nor the clear assumption that this ineffectiveness is a product of inadequate personality organization. For example: "Compulsive sexuality—engaging in sexual intercourse without regard to the consequences to oneself or the partner—has to do with abnormally strong feelings of need for fusion with another and hatred for oneself and others. The result is often a destructive life pattern based on sexuality, usually without pleasure, with consequences of illegitimate pregnancy, abortion, and venereal disease, and without human closeness or even adequate relationships."[40] This implies that "engaging in sexual intercourse without regard to the consequences to oneself or the partner" is psychologically distinct from other kinds of human behavior

e. As an example of variability over time, in 1973 the Harris Survey found that 52 percent of all Americans favored the recent Supreme Court decision that abortion was a matter between a woman and her doctor. This is a dramatic shift in opinion since 1969, when 13 percent of all Americans disapproved of abortion even to save the life of the mother, and 68 percent disapproved of abortion when the reason for wanting it was that the family could not afford another child. See Judith Blake, "Abortion and Public Opinion: the 1960-1970 Decade."

engaged in without regard to consequences, such as cigarette smoking, skiing, or failing to fasten safety belts in an automobile.[f] Do behaviors like these have connotations of virility and devil-may-careness which make them risks of a socially different nature? And would it smack of *ad hominem* argument to suggest that we are more likely to hear a critical tone toward unwanted pregnancy being taken by researchers who are biologically incapable of taking that risk? Perhaps, but the distinctive tone of much research on contraceptive conflict is still noteworthy.

What both the contraceptive ignorance theory and the intrapsychic conflict theory have in common are a variety of assumptions about unwanted pregnancy. Both theories, for example, assume that the two important dimensions of unwanted pregnancy are information (specifically contraceptive information) and rationality, and there appears to be a consensus as to the definitions of these terms, although they are not always strictly followed in the literature. In general, the consensus is based on the difference between intent and effect noted earlier. Contraceptive ignorance, for example, is seen as a purely technical dimension which describes the presence or absence of contraceptive skills which are technologically adequate to prevent pregnancy with a high degree of effectiveness. Rationality, on the other hand, is defined as the presence of a body of thinking which defines a goal (such as the prevention of pregnancy) defines appropriate means to achieve the goal (such as the use of contraception), and then uses the means in an effort to achieve the goal.[41]

Thus contraceptive ignorance is defined by the effect of given skills, and rationality is defined by the intent of the user. Using this definition, a woman in a preliterate society who wears an amulet to prevent pregnancy is rational in pursuing what her culture defines as appropriate means to achieve the desired goal of preventing pregnancy; she is, however, ignorant (contraceptively speaking) because the amulet is not technologically effective in preventing pregnancy. In contrast, a

---

f. In Chapter Five, we shall examine the "social nature of risk" in some detail. As a point of comparison, serious injury or death occurs to approximately 50 per 100,000 skiers, and approximately 5 per 100,000 abortion-seeking women. The skiing figures are from the National Safety Council, and the abortion figures are from Planned Parenthood/World Population.

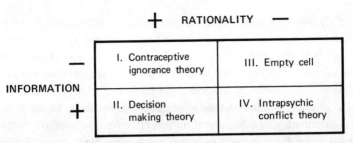

FIGURE 3. Theoretical dimensions of unwanted pregnancy.

middle-class American woman who wears an amulet to prevent pregnancy while knowing that it is technologically ineffective is irrational, by this definition, because she is aware that the wearing of an amulet is not an appropriate means to prevent pregnancy. She may not necessarily be ignorant contraceptively, since she may well have had an extensive history of using highly effective contraceptive skills in the past.

The role of these two dimensions in the prevailing thinking about unwanted pregnancy is demonstrated in Figure 3, which presents a typology of theories of pregnancy along the parameters of information and rationality. Cell one in this typology represents the contraceptive ignorance theory, which is based on the assumption that women are rational (they are aware of means to a goal and use those means) but ignorant (the means are not effective). Thus information is not present, but rational action is.

Cell three is an empirically empty cell, which implies the absence of both information and rational action. It could be filled by a theory positing that women have unwanted pregnancies because they are neither informed nor rational, but at the present time, no such theory appears to exist. Logically, it would be possible to have such a theory by arguing for a hypothetical primitive tribe where no effective contraceptive skills exist and where no means, however ineffective, are conceptualized at all for the prevention of pregnancy. Empirically, however, even the Trobrianders, a tribe which allegedly does not connect intercourse with fecundation, reportedly have a variety of rituals for controlling the occurrence of pregnancy.[g]

g. Bronislaw Malinowski, in *The Sexual Life of Savages in Northwestern Melanesia* (London: Routledge, 1929), said that the Trobrianders believe only

Cell four represents the intrapsychic conflict theory, which assumes that women have the necessary information and skills to prevent pregnancy, but choose not to use them. In some variants of this theory, the tacit assumption is that women know that the information is available in the society as a whole, and know the relative technological effectiveness of each method. For these women, then, failing to seek out information or using one of the less effective contraceptive methods is the same thing, in terms of intent, as choosing not to use skills previously acquired.

Cell two (which will be developed at length in Chapter Five) represents the theory to be set forth in this study—that women are both informed and rational. It will be argued that unwanted pregnancy is the end result of an informed decision-making process; and more important, that this process is a rational one, in which women use means appropriate to their goals. That pregnancy occurred anyway, for the women in this study, is because most of them were attempting to achieve more diffuse goals than simply preventing pregnancy.

When the two traditional theories of the occurrence of unwanted pregnancy are considered as ideal types within a typology, it is clear that they have several other features in common beyond the reliance on information and rationality as parameters. They are both, for example, "scientific" in their assumption that the problem of unwanted pregnancy occurs because of a lack of information in the system.[42] In the earlier contraceptive ignorance theory, it was assumed that this lack of information was strictly contraceptive in nature; but with the spread of contraceptive information into the society as a whole, the more recent

vaginal dilation or perforation is necessary (pp. 154-155) and the "physical fatherhood is unknown" (p. 171). R. F. Fortune, in *The Sorcerers of Dobu*, has shown that the lack of connection between intercourse and conception occurs in other tribes besides the Trobrianders. Malinowski's assertion led to an acrimonious debate in the journal *Man*, where A. C. Rentoul argued that the Trobrianders *did* use methods to control conception, and hence connected intercourse and pregnancy. Alex C. Rentoul, "Physiological Paternity and the Trobrianders," *Man*, Vol. 31, Art No. 162 (1931). Malinowski dismissed Rentoul's evidence as "one of the typical myths which circulates among the semi-educated white residents." (Rentoul was a Resident Magistrate.) Malinowski, "Pigs, Papuans, and Police-Court Perspective," *Man*, Art. 44 (1932).

intrapsychic conflict theory assumes that it is a lack of information about the "real" motivations surrounding unwanted pregnancy which leads to intrapsychic conflict.[43]

One consequence of this kind of "scientific" theory is that the solution to the problem is also presumed to be informational: add more information to the system by increasing the resources spent on the contraceptive education and counseling of women. Closely connected to this assumption that the problem is one of information is the placing of responsibility for the problem on the individual woman, rather than on the system *as a system*. Because it is assumed either that the individual is not aware of contraceptive information that exists within the system, or that she is unwilling to use that information for idiosyncratic reasons, her unwanted pregnancy is viewed primarily as an individual and psychological problem rather than as a structural and social problem.[44] It is only when unwanted pregnancy in general is seen as a cause of the larger problem of overpopulation that social-structural explanations are even advanced.[h]

The logical result of a model that perceives the problem of unwanted pregnancy as informational and individual is that resources are spent to increase the amount of information in the system, either through contraceptive education plans or through counseling (and the resources spent on this task are far from insignificant in the United States).[i] If, however, the problem is not resolved and if women continue to have unwanted pregnancies, then either the model or the participants in the model must be rejected. At the present time, it is the participants who are most frequently rejected. The failure of the model is explained by

h. Kingsley Davis, for example, has made a thorough-going criticism of the tendency of population policy makers to see overpopulation as solely a medical and technological problem. He draws attention to the obvious fact that birth and birth planning (either pro-natalist or anti-natalist) are highly socially controlled aspects of human behavior, and hence "social" problems. Consequently, he argues for a social-structural viewpoint and describes the lack of such viewpoints to date. See Davis, "Population Policty: Will Current Programs Succeed?", *Science*, 158 (1967), pp. 730-739.

i. Oscar Harkavy says that in 1967, 10 million dollars in federal funds became available to finance "identifiable family planning programs." ("Family Planning and Public Policy," *Science*, Vol. 162, No. 25, July 1969, p. 369.) This is, of course, merely the tip of the iceberg.

defining the women who continue to have unwanted pregnancies as being outside the system. In the contraceptive ignorance theory these "outside" women have supposedly not yet learned the contraceptive skills that the rest of America has long since put into common practice; in the intrapsychic conflict theory the "outside" women are self-destructive and neurotic, persisting in patterns of behavior that are counterproductive. Again, it is only when the issue of overpopulation is raised that these basic assumptions are challenged. In other words, the continuation of unwanted pregnancies is in part a function of the way they are conceptualized. Since individual women are assumed to be the "cause," remedies for the problem tend to be piecemeal, individualistic, and ultimately unsuccessful.

This study will challenge these assumptions at all structural levels and will hypothesize a third and alternative theory of unwanted pregnancy: unwanted pregnancy results from "contraceptive risk-taking" behavior which is the result of conscious decision making.

A "decision-making theory" of unwanted pregnancy has many advantages. First, it sees contraceptive risk-taking as an orderly social process that is open to analysis, rather than an intrapsychic enigma that must be dealt with on the same terms as other "irrational actions."[45] Second, it makes intervention possible. If contraceptive risk-taking decisions are based, as decision-making theory assumes, on what amounts to a cost-benefit analysis by the individual, then the costs and benefits, once outlined, can be changed by contraceptive programs or larger population policies that correspond more closely to the costs and benefits perceived by the individual.[46] (It will be argued later in this study that the majority of contraceptive programs are not effective in preventing abortions for certain women precisely because they respond not to the "definition of the situation" experienced by risk-taking women, but to institutional needs instead.) Third, considering contraceptive risk-taking as a decision-making process permits us to borrow analytical tools from the literature on decision making, and opens up the possibility of applying larger social theory in our analysis of this behavior. Finally, placing contraceptive risk-taking within the more general process of decision making under risk conditions permits us to examine it in the same way as other risk-taking behaviors, such as failing to fasten safety belts in cars, cigarette smoking, and risk-taking in sports. The assumption that there are many ways in which even the most well-adjusted individuals habitually take chances with their health and safety, and that most persons take some risks in their lives eventually, eliminates the basis for the misogynist and morally critical tone that characterizes much psychologistic writing on this subject.

In general, the literature on decision making under conditions of risk assumes that the individual is aware of the decision-making process, perceives both penalties ("costs") and payoffs ("benefits") to be experienced with any given line of action, and weighs the differential costs against the probabilities of benefit in order to make a decision.[47] To date, by far the most frequent method of testing the development of decision-making strategies by individuals has been the laboratory testing of betting behavior. It has generally been assumed that in this simulated setting, because money is used, both the costs and the utilities are uniform for all individuals—that is, that winning or losing a dollar has the same meaning for all bettors. More recent research, however, has suggested that despite the apparent social consensus on the value of any given amount of money, individuals differ in their assignment of value. Children from poorer homes, for example, are significantly more likely to visually perceive coins as larger than children from wealthier homes.[48] Another piece of recent research suggests that there are at least two distinct modes of bettor behavior, one group of individuals preferring a small but steady payoff (low risk, low gain) and another preferring the unlikely but spectacular payoff (high risk, high gain).[49]

The suggestion that costs and utilities in a decision can be a very personal matter is an important modification of decision-making theory. It is particularly important in the context of contraceptive risk-taking behavior, because it has generally been assumed that contraception is not "costly," especially when compared to an unwanted pregnancy, and that an unwanted pregnancy has few if any rational benefits.[50] If it is assumed that contraception is uniformly beneficial, and that any pregnancy which is other than planned and wanted has no benefits of any consequence to normal, well-adjusted women, it is clear that the decision not to use contraception (particularly when viewed from an ad hoc position after a pregnancy has occurred) is irrational and self-destructive. If, on the other hand, it is assumed that contraception often has social, emotional, financial, and physical costs which are reason-

able in the context in which they occur, and that pregnancies, including
those which ultimately end in abortions, have benefits which are conscious, social, and equally reasonable given the context in which they
occur, then the decision not to use contraception can be seen as a
weighing process between a series of fairly well-defined costs and
benefits.

Another aspect of the theory of decision making under conditions of
risk defines the difference between "risk" and "uncertainty," a difference that plays a significant part in women's decisions to take risks with
contraception. In classical decision-making theory, a "risk" is a probability of known magnitude: there is a consensus as to the likelihood of
a given event. An "uncertainty," on the other hand, is a probability of
unknown magnitude.[51] Thus for women, getting pregnant is an "uncertainty," while for statisticians, physicians, and family planners it is a
"risk" of known probability. This difference means that women will
make different decisions about the use of contraception than would
statisticians, physicians, and family planners. The logic of women's
decisions is examined in the next two chapters, "The Costs of Contraception" and "The Benefits of Pregnancy."

CHAPTER
3
The Costs of
Contraception

The ideological position of many physicians and family planners is that the strictly biological "costs" of abortion make contraception an automatically preferable method of fertility control. Nevertheless, as we have noted, a wide variety of cultures use induced abortion as a primary method of fertility control; and when done with modern medical techniques, it is both safe and successful. Moreover, the probability of death from a therapeutic abortion in the United States today is lower than the probability of death from a full-term pregnancy. Thus in terms of sickness and death, induced abortion in a hospital is roughly as safe as the use of anovulent pills.[1]

It is only when social factors are considered that the weight of costs swings so dramatically against abortion, making contraception the apparently more "rational" choice. Abortions have socially defined costs that individual women must pay. The most obvious of these is financial: in Northern California at the time of the study, for example, the average abortion cost well over three hundred dollars, and although the costs for privately prescribed pills can run up to one hundred dollars a year, there are several low-cost clinics for the delivery of contraception in the area, and contraception is almost always routinely covered in medical insurance plans.

In comparison, at the low-cost Abortion Clinic we studied, the price for an abortion was still a full three hundred dollars (although it later dropped to two hundred and fifty dollars). Additionally, the inclusion of abortion in medical insurance plans is still in flux, and depends upon the marital status of the policyholder, the official diagnosis of her need for an abortion, the geographic area in which she finds herself, and the formal or informal policies of the insurance carrier.

As a second example of the socially structured costs exacted from women seeking abortions, women at the time of this study were required to undergo psychiatric examinations in order to certify that continuation of the pregnancy would be a threat to their mental health; in these examinations they would be questioned about their sex lives, partners, attempts at contraception, and "real" motivations for pregnancy. Although three other provisions outlined in the law provided grounds for abortion—a threat to physical health, the occurrence of rape, and incest—the number of women choosing these grounds was small (less than 5 percent of the total number of women seeking abortion in the state).[2] This is understandable because relatively few physiological conditions call for abortion, and because a claim of rape or incest had to be stated in a formal complaint entered with the District Attorney's office.[3] Thus most women in the state presented "a threat to mental health" as their reason for seeking an abortion, and were required to be interviewed by a therapist to validate that claim.

In our Abortion Clinic, that interview was largely a ritual step in terms of "earning" the right to get an abortion; most of the staff therapists stated that they reassured a woman at the start of her interview that the abortion would be approved as a matter of course. Nonetheless, we should remember that women seeking abortions here had to undergo a degree of social intervention and invasion of personal privacy not usually necessary for obtaining contraception.

A third example of the social costs of abortion is the disapproval expressed through the psychiatric labeling process: women seeking abortions are viewed negatively as "having problems," whereas women who come to contraception clinics are seen as prudent and "future-oriented" people.[4] In part this stems from the theoretical problems outlined in Chapter Two. When outsiders (such as the Abortion Clinic personnel) look at risk-taking after the advent of pregnancy, the risk-taking that led to the pregnancy is defined as "self-destructive" because it resulted in an unwanted outcome. Thus the therapists in the Clinic saw their job as helping the women understand why they had engaged in such "irrational" behavior. But such "understanding" is not free of cultural biases: Table 1, for example, cross-tabulates the psychiatric diagnosis (the label necessary for the abortion) assigned to each woman with marital status. Diagnoses were from the Diagnostic and Statistical Manual of Mental Disorders of the American Psychiatric Association,[5] and in all, twenty-one different psychiatric labels were represented, although one diagnosis ("transient situational

TABLE 1

Cross-Tabulation of Psychiatric Diagnosis by Marital Status

	Depressive Neurosis	Personality disorders	Transient Situational Disturbance	Other
Single	11% (34)	13% (41)	67% (215)	8% (30)
Married	10% (11)	6% (6)	74% (77)	10% (13)
D/W/S	12% (8)	20% (13)	48% (32)	20% (13)

X^2 = 16.06
p ⩽ = .02
(6 d.f.)

disturbance") accounted for 65 percent of the diagnoses in the five hundred medical records surveyed. (Neuroses accounted for 15 percent of the remaining diagnoses and personality disorders for another 16 percent.) Since "transient situational disturbance" by definition implies some statement about social events, it is less negative than the labels "neurosis" and "personality disorder," which refer exclusively to intrapsychic functioning.

As Table 1 shows, women going through the Clinic experienced what Edwin Lemert has called "labeling phenomena" on the basis of marital status.[6] Married women, for example, were more likely to be diagnosed as having transitional situational disturbances and less likely to be diagnosed as having personality disorders. On the other hand, separated, widowed, and divorced women (only a small number were widowed) were much more likely to be diagnosed as having personality disorders and less likely to be diagnosed as having transient situational disturbances. Single women play an intermediate role between the two other marital categories. We suspect that this difference occurs because a woman's social category triggers certain assumptions in the minds of those who put labels on her as she goes through an abortion clinic. Formerly married women, for example, are thought to have "known better" than to get pregnant, and currently married women tend to have their pregnancies defined as the result of "contraceptive failure." (Implicit in this is an assumption that risk-taking by people who can have illegitimate pregnancies is more "neurotic" than risk-taking by people who cannot; and that single women can be forgiven their ignorance, whereas formerly married women can not.)

A non-random distribution of the labels imposed at the Abortion Clinic shows that almost a third of the women going through the Clinic were viewed by the staff as "sick" people, and the likelihood of being defined as "sick" was significantly greater if the women were in a marital category socially defined as "less acceptable" for seeking an abortion. For many women, then, receiving negative social labeling and feeling its consequences were an integral part of getting an abortion.

Of course, it is possible that psychiatric functioning at the time of an abortion may vary with marital status, and that the diagnoses presented here are indeed valid and not a function of the labeling process. The bulk of the evidence presented in the current study, however, suggests that this is not the case.

A final cost of abortion evoked by the social structure is that abortion as a primary method of fertility control runs counter to the socialization of most women. Although abortion is now legal, available, and proclaimed to be normatively acceptable, all the women in this study (as all American women in general) were brought up in a social milieu in which abortion was illegal and normatively proscribed. Many women described the feelings of "culture lag" that the dramatic changes in abortion availability have made. As one said: "It's hard for me to imagine I would ever get one. I never thought I would be the type. I have such memories of women in high school who had to go to Tijuana and the kinds of women they were, and what it did to them." And so, however hard it is to define clinically, some remaining sense of abortion as "wrong" and illegal must be included in the social costs of abortion.

The costs to the individual exacted by the social structure have been examined in some detail here because current thinking has tended to make the choice between abortion and contraception an open and shut one. The agreement that contraception is far preferable to abortion verges on consensus among physicians, family planning experts, and health officials. Often, however, their thinking tends to view abortion as *intrinsically* undesirable for medical, biological, or psychological reasons. When it is realized, however, that the costs attendant on abortion are primarily social in their origin, it is easy to see how women who fail to contracept, get pregnant, and seek abortions may have a different perspective on the "costs" of their various decisions.

Nowhere is this discrepancy more noticeable than in the traditional thinking about the costs of contraception. The traditional or "outsider" assumption that abortion is intrinsically undesirable goes along with an assumption that contraception has virtually no intrinsic costs. It is sometimes grudgingly admitted that some contraceptives, in particular the pill, may have some undesirable side effects which could be accounted as "costs," but when these costs are weighed against the possibility of pregnancy, they are assumed to be very small indeed. And there is the crux of the problem: "experts" do their own "cost accounting." They weigh the probability of pregnancy (which is a known probability to them) against potential costs of contraception, and then, given the high probability of pregnancy, discount the legitimacy of the costs connected with contraception. Women, on the other hand, for whom pregnancy is a risk of unknown magnitude (and one of unknown "utility," in the decision-making sense of the word), have nothing to weigh against the current costs they are experiencing. In direct contrast to the experts, women weigh the *actual* costs of contraception against a discounted risk of pregnancy.

It is important to note that there may be costs to contraception beyond the ones analyzed here.* Other sample populations might well report other patterns. But the goal of this study is to provide a theoretical framework which can then be expanded by researching the decision making of women who find themselves in a wide variety of social situations.

In our study, four major categories of costs associated with contraception emerged: costs imposed by the larger social and cultural meanings of contraception; costs deriving from the structural problems of contraception; costs associated with maintaining contraceptive activity over time; and costs related to the medical and biological aspects of contraception.

SOCIAL AND CULTURAL MEANINGS OF CONTRACEPTION

For better or worse, intercourse and the reproduction of human beings is an activity subjected to a high degree of social control. Whether it is

---

*In particular, other research has suggested that the cost accounting of poor and minority women may be very different.

argued that social control of sexual activity stems from a need to keep women in circulation so as to promote other forms of social cooperation (Lévi Strauss), or for basic libidinal reasons (Freud), or because any society must control sexual activity as a component of the reproduction of the species (Davis), it is clear that sex is a social act surrounded by a multitude of taboos and sanctions.[7] Contraception, which is directly related to sexual activity (as in the chemical and mechanical methods of birth control) or indirectly related (as in the use of the pill or the IUD) therefore carries with it many of the same social taboos and meanings as intercourse itself, and like intercourse itself, these meanings are emotionally charged.

Within this category of social and cultural meanings of contraception, four themes occur: that contraception means acknowledging intercourse; that contraception means planning intercourse; that continuing contraception over time means that socially a woman is sexually available; and that contraception means that sexual activity is planned and cannot be spontaneous.

Costs of acknowledging intercourse. Acknowledgement can be to oneself or to others. Of all the costs cited by women in this study, acknowledging intercourse to oneself was named most frequently. (For an overview of exactly how often each theme in this chapter was cited, see Table 2.) Technically, of course, all acknowledging of costs calls for some degree of acknowledging to oneself, privately, that intercourse is occurring. The cost of this acknowledgement, however, was evidenced by women who said that contraception is "unnatural." This implies a belief that sex is "natural" but that rational planning for it in terms of contraception is not. Also, it is traditionally the woman who has held the decision-making power over whether or not intercourse should occur. Thus it is possible for a woman to acknowledge only minimally that she is having intercourse, because without artificial contraception lovemaking is more "pure" and has only a nominal connection with sex. To reverse this statement in terms of costs, the use of contraception would compel the acknowledgement that intercourse is occurring to this person, *just as it does to everyone else.* The degree of planning and foresight that contraception demands can make a desirably warm and intimate emotional experience appear impersonally "cold-blooded" and hence costly:

I: How did he feel about using rhythm?
R: We were being puritanical because we didn't want to use artificial things.
I: Artificial?
R: Just a chemical effect on your body or having something inserted in you.

TABLE 2

Costs of Contraception: Frequency of Four Cost Themes
Cited by Women Clients of The Abortion Clinic
(Reliability coded at 94 percent)

Social and cultural costs		*Maintaining costs*	
Acknowledging costs	46	Costs of "Carry-through"	24
Planning costs	30	Male attitudes	36[b]
Continuing costs	21	Ignorance	9
Spontaneity costs	10	Collusion	24
		Resistance	4
Structural problems and prices		*Biological and medical costs*	
Costs of obtaining, "clinical"	28	Side effects, concrete	56[c]
Costs of obtaining, "drugstore"	26[a]	Side effects, general	14[d]
		Iatrogenic effects, direct	26[e]
		Iatrogenic effects, indirect	21[f]

[a] Includes "aesthetic side-effects" of drugstore methods.
[b] Range defined in text.
[c] Concrete side effects were coded when the woman mentioned a specific side effect: "it gave me headaches to use the pill"; "I've had a vaginal infection for two years and I've finally cured it and apparently the pill makes it return"; "the foam gave me a rash."
[d] General side effects were coded when the woman mentioned vague (non-somatic) symptoms, e.g., "it drove me out of my mind"; and/or when a global fear of the method was mentioned, e.g., "I've heard the pill isn't good for you," "I had my loop taken out because I was afraid of having a mechanical thing inside of me."
[e] Direct iatrogenic costs are when the medical person involved *directly* and *actively* interferes with the contraceptive process, as when the pill is stopped "to see if you're ovulating."
[f] Indirect iatrogenic costs occur when the medical person involved indirectly and passively creates fears of infertility on the part of the woman which subsequently lead to the discontinuing of contraception as a result of the double barreled process noted in the text. Note that in *direct* iatrogenic costs, the doctor assumes the burden of the decision to stop contraception, and in *indirect* iatrogenic effects, the woman assumes that burden as a result of a medical interaction, e.g., "I think he created in my mind the doubt that I could get pregnant after using the pill." "I didn't think I would need them (pills)," "I never thought my system was working properly."

The collusion of the male partner in this strategy is also evident. As one male respondent said:

> R: It seems kind of phoney to use contraception. It doesn't seem natural or the right way.

More significant for most women, the decision to obtain contraception acknowledges to others whose opinions count that sex is occurring, and the cost of this can be very high. Whether the "significant other" is the sex partner, parents, or some abstract moral judge (as, for example, the Catholic Church), the woman is reluctant to take steps which might notify them that she is participating in sexual behavior which she has reason to suppose they will disapprove. This splitting off of the action from the acknowledgement of the action—the belief that it is one thing to have intercourse and another to admit such intercourse openly—is not unique to people breaking sexual taboos. Since by their standards they are deviant, in order to be contraceptively protected they would have to be openly deviant. Few deviants, or pseudo-deviants such as these women (premarital intercourse is far from statistically deviant), are willing to risk the costs of *public* deviance, no matter what the benefits. This is particularly true in the case of contraception, when the benefits are ambiguous. In avoiding contraception, the woman is protecting herself from a present cost (the censure of significant others) at the expense of a future cost (the possible occurrence of a pregnancy):

> I: You said that you had used the pill previously and had run out. Where did you get the pills the first time?
> R: A family planning clinic in Southwest City.
> I: Why didn't you get the prescription refilled?
> R: Because of my father. . . . We live in a small town, and the medical and dental people are very close, and I couldn't go to another doctor without his finding out and I think it would hurt him.

The focus on the present to the exclusion of the possible future also acts as a leveler between the heavier but future costs of an unwanted pregnancy, should it occur, and the lesser but more immediate costs surrounding the acknowledging. (This process of discounting longer-term costs in favor of immediate costs will be examined in detail in Chapter Five.) As one male respondent said:

I: Why did you not use the pill?

R: (Male) We were worried about the financial hassles involved in getting the pill.

I: But isn't an abortion more expensive than using the pills?

R: (Male) Yeah, but it took us six and a half months to need an abortion. And we didn't think we were going to need an abortion, anyway.

The fact that this couple was a married couple, and hence not risking an illegitimate pregnancy, brings to light another important aspect of the acknowledging process, the role of internalized norms. Perhaps the most frequently cited "significant other" in this study was the Catholic Church. (Catholics made up approximately one-third of the clientele of the Abortion Clinic, and they represent about one-third of the total population of the greater Northern California metropolitan area where the study was made.)[8] Church dogma presents the normative standard that the only acceptable intercourse is for procreation and not for personal pleasure. By this standard, both married and unmarried Catholics can have "deviant" sexual intercourse. There was a noticeable tendency in this population for Catholic respondents to conform to and reject the Church's teachings at the same time, in a "zero sum" game fashion: to engage in deviant intercourse but not to compound that "sin" by using contraception, which is both a deviant act by Church standards and an acknowledgement that premeditation precedes the sin:

I: Did you think you might get pregnant not using contraception?

R: I thought so, I mean, I knew there was a possibility. But there was this problem of my religious background. If you are familiar with the Catholic Church it is against the Church to use contraception or to have premarital sex, and I was always brought up in a strict Catholic home. It was always "do this, don't do that." Just using a contraceptive seems like you're planning.

Thus the individual has to answer for only one deviance at a time: deviant intercourse, but not deviant intercourse plus prohibited contraception. That a later, costlier deviance—an induced abortion—was the outcome for all the risk-takers in this study, Catholic and non-Catholic alike, only demonstrates once again the tendency to focus on present and obvious costs rather than on future and ambiguous costs.

The concurrent accepting and rejecting of normative standards (speci-

fically those of the Catholic Church) tends to produce either erratic
behavior patterns or erratic belief systems in the same individual. What
this appears to represent is a desire to conform to an ideology when
feasible, but in a context where feasibility is constantly being redefined
over time. Incompatible goals and beliefs are exhibited in the following interview statement, where one "significant other," the mother,
supports the ideological position of a second "significant other," the
Church, and the respondent rejects both as unreasonable but refrains
from using contraception herself:

I: Why didn't you use more effective contraception?
R: I always thought about it, but never did anything about it. I used
       to think about the pill, but my sister used it, she's married now
       and stuff, and my mother used to tell me she'd die. That it
       would wreck you up. She's really Catholic. But it seems as if
       most of my friends are on it.

The conflicting pressures faced by this respondent include her perception that her sister has "gotten away with" contraception with no side
effects, her perception that predictions of death are unreasonable, an
implied normative demand on the part of the mother, and a competing
normative structure presented by her peers, most of whom are perceived
as taking the pill. When buffeted by such conflicting demands and
pressures, it is not surprising that respondents often postpone any action
whatsoever, or engage in erratic contraceptive behavior.

Costs of planning contraception. Structurally, as first discussed, this
means that contraception forces a woman to define herself as a person
who is sexually active. Planning specifically suggests not only that a
woman has been sexually active once, but that she intends to be so
again. A woman who plans is actively anticipating intercourse; in the
terminology of the women interviewed, she is "looking to have sex."
A woman who is "looking to have sex," then, is a woman who must
take initiative, view herself as sexually aggressive, and abandon the
traditional role of female passivity. Thus the costs of planning can be
very high. As an example, one woman who was interviewed had a hard
time saying openly that she had had intercourse, much less planned to
have it again, despite a relationship of fairly long duration with one
man:

I: Did you ever think about getting pregnant?

R: Sometimes I thought about it, but I didn't really pay too much attention, because we weren't really into . . . we were goofing around . . . in an intimate . . .

I: Could you clarify that?

R: We started in on one thing and then we would go on to another thing and finally we would have intercourse. We never said, "Well, we're going to do it today." It just happened.

The pretense that it always "just happened" (in this case almost every night for over a year) is one way of escaping the social definition of being a person who is sexually active by choice.

A woman who plans intercourse is also socially defined as an experienced woman: virgins and "innocents" do not use contraceptives. A woman may refuse to plan contraception to avoid a social (and male) definition of being a "woman who's been around."

I: How did you decide not to contracept this time?

R: Actually sex for me wasn't steady and it was really with only one or two people I knew. It's been a year leading up to when I got pregnant that I slept with anyone.

A woman who is "too active" sexually loses status. One woman in the study, for example, said that women who are too active are contemptuously referred to by both men and women in her circle as "rabbits." One way to avoid this definition is to have each and every sexual encounter be unanticipated, and hence free from the stigma of being continuous:

I: Did you think about what might happen if you didn't use contraception?

R: Yeah, I thought about it to a certain extent, but I thought it could never happen to me. It wasn't something I'd planned for. If I'd planned to have intercourse every night—you know what I'm trying to say.

Costs of continuing contraception. Just as a woman beginning her sexual career may find it costly to acknowledge herself as a fully sexual person who expects to have sexual intercourse and plans for it, the woman who has been successfully contracepting within a relationship must acknowledge to herself that she intends to remain sexually available if she continues contraception after the end of that relationship. This appears to be the reason why so many women have "relationship-specific" contraceptive patterns. They use contraception effectively with one male friend (or husband) but discontinue contraception when the relationship ends. The following pattern is typical of women who experience this group of costs:

I: According to the information on the fact sheet, you said you used pills with your first boy friend, and stopped when you broke up with him. Why didn't you use contraception with this boy friend?

R: In this first place, this guy I was going out with, I thought I wouldn't need to . . . I had already decided to go away. If I had gotten pills I would have had to wait.

I: Did you think of using any other contraception that you wouldn't have to wait for?

R: Not at the time.

I: Did you think you could get away without using contraception?

R: Yes.

Again the pattern of not expecting intercourse is displayed, but unlike women who have never had regular intercourse (and thus have some grounds for not expecting sex), women in this group typically had extensive contraceptive experience in one or more long-term relationships, and gave reasons like this:

I: What made you go off the pills?

R: About the time I started the pills we started not getting along and I came up here to live and they didn't agree with my body so I gave them up.

Or this:

I: What made you choose rhythm after you went off the pill?

R: I didn't have regularized sex.

Two things make it costly to continue contraception after a relationship ends. First, to continue contraception implies that one expects intercourse with a new partner, and this flies in the face of a strong taboo; sex is to be expected only within a relationship of some duration and commitment:

I: Why did you go off the pill?

R: At the time I broke up, I had no reason to continue and then, well, my first guy, I was engaged with, Larry, when we broke up, there was no logical reason to continue, so I didn't. I have nothing against sex, but I feel that there has to be a mutual feeling, that you have to be very much in love. It's my way of giving everything I have to someone.

This statement exposes a second belief that makes continued contraception costly. If sex is defined as "giving everything I have to someone," to continue contraception would be to acknowledge an expectation of readily meeting another person to whom one could "give everything," which would cheapen both oneself and the gift. Experiencing this conflict between romantic values and pragmatism is a heavy cost for many women. Continuing contraception beyond the confines of one relationship forces a woman to acknowledge that she is always sexually available—a "sexual service station" as one woman bitterly expressed it. Both men and women share in this assumption, so that a woman who continues to take the pill or who keeps her IUD in place is by social definition frankly admitting that she is available. Not only is this an unpleasant acknowledgement for a woman to make about herself, but it loses her an important bargaining position. If she is frankly expecting sex, as evidenced by her continued use of contraception, she need not be courted on the same terms as a woman whose sexual availability is more ambiguous. For many women, the loss of this bargaining position outweighs all the benefits of contraception.

Costs to spontaneity. Finally, the use of contraception can kill feelings of spontaneity. One part of the sexual ideology surrounding intercourse is that it must be romantic, an act of impulse infused with passion and noble feelings. Introducing contraceptives (except the pill and the IUD) into this act can seem dishearteningly "mechanical":

I: Did you consider using foam or condoms?

R: I did, I bought some, and I didn't even open it. It just seems like a hassle. I don't know, it's just my damn carelessness. But I bought the foam and never used it. It's hard to jump out of bed, it just ruins the whole mood.

The mechanics of any type of contraception remind people that while engaging in a romantic act, or looking forward to it, they are also engaged in the down-to-earth process of preventing a pregnancy. In addition, the particular methods of contraception used by the Clinic population (and many other women) have undesirable effects on pleasure or aesthetics:

I: What did you think about using contraceptive foam?
R: Well, the foam is such a bitch to use. Especially for him because it just gets all over the place.

I: How did you decide not to use your diaphragm?
R: God, I used to get so turned off putting it inside me, so I tried to get him to help do it, like they say in those marriage manuals and it just turned us *both* off.

The use of contraception obviously demands that women feel at ease with themselves, their bodies, and their lovers, and also be able to accept some of the less romantic aspects of bodily functions. A great deal of motivation sustained over time is needed to continue accepting and carrying through the contraceptive act under these conditions.

Sometimes, the costs to romantic spontaneity alone are enough to make women skip the use of contraception "just this once," even though in the long run "just this once" tends to end in pregnancy. A powerful demonstration of exactly how high these costs can be, and how important the corresponding benefits can seem, may be found in the following statement (by a woman in her middle thirties with two children, which reminds us that costs to spontaneity are not restricted to the young and unmarried):

I: How did you get pregnant this time?
R: The children had left for the weekend with their grandparents, so we could be alone together. We'd gone out to dinner and we'd enjoyed ourselves very much. Our backyard ends and all we have is National Park. We're very isolated. My husband was feeling very amorous, and when we pulled up in our driveway he went to the trunk of the car and pulled out an Army blanket, and proceeded to take me by the hand, over the fence into the National Park. And to the edge of the bluffs overlooking the river, a forty-foot drop into the West River. It was beautiful, the moon was just reflecting off the water and he spread out the Army blanket and what came next was that I was pregnant. He was so cool. I'm so in love with that guy. Here I am mar-

I: ried to him for six years and I'm more in love with him than
ever.

I: So you used nothing?

R: No Delfin cream, no nothing. One night. But it was worth it.
It cost us three hundred dollars, but it was worth it.

In summary, the larger social and cultural meanings that society
assigns to sexuality can often make the use of contraception seem costly
in the short run. When using a contraceptive socially proclaims the user
to be a sexually active woman, a "cold-blooded" planner, a hard-eyed
realist with no romance in her soul, and a woman who is perhaps too
sexually active to be a "lady," it is not surprising that women often
prefer to avoid contraception rather than run the risk of having to deal
with these unpleasant "social halos."

COSTS OF OBTAINING ACCESS TO CONTRACEPTIVES

A woman must also pay various costs simply to obtain contraceptives;
whether she goes to a doctor or to a drugstore, the procedure can be
embarrassing or complicated.

Costs of clinical methods. The prospect of a visit to the doctor, which
is a matter of course to an older woman or one who feels at ease with her
sexuality, can be a deterrent to some women:

I: Do you have any idea why you didn't get contraception?

R: I'm sure this is a silly reason. For some reason it's because of
the way I was brought up. I don't consciously have anything
against birth control—aside from being afraid of the pill at one
time last year—but the reason I can think of is that I didn't want
to go to a doctor's office and give them my history in order to
get contraceptive devices or pills and I didn't know about
family planning clinics, or how they worked at any rate, and I
simply put it off.

Alternately:

R: I really didn't know how to go about it, getting pills, seeing
the doctor, and I didn't have the money to pay for it myself,
and I just didn't.

Furthermore, despite the obvious commitment of many doctors to the
idea of birth control and the proliferation of family planning clinics,

these doctors and organizations have policies determined by their own needs—and more importantly by their belief that women must take some responsibility for protecting themselves against pregnancy. Inevitably, they are less than responsive to the woman who has conflicts around the use of contraception. A desperate last-minute attempt by a woman to see a doctor, for example, often conflicts with the organized routine of the typical doctor's office or family planning clinic. The following response is typical:

I: You stopped the pills right before you got pregnant?
R: Yeah.
I: How did that happen?
R: I had a rash and my doctor said it was a drug reaction. I was supposed to get an IUD so when I had my next period I called and they said they couldn't possibly fit me in so I didn't go back and I got pregnant.

Epitomized here are the very different "definitions of the situation" made by medical practitioners and agencies on the one hand, and by women who are contemplating contraceptive risk-taking on the other. This difference makes it impossible for either group to respond to the needs of the other. The contraceptive clinics and doctors' offices tend to work on the assumption that an unwanted pregnancy is of negative value and that any rational woman will undergo some degree of inconvenience to avoid it. If women are unwilling or unable to plan their contraceptive appointments properly, or unwilling to postpone intercourse for some period of time, then they are "ambivalent" or "self-destructive" and beyond the reach of the agency. This attitude was well expressed in an incident noted by a participant observer. A woman called on a contraceptive clinic to ask for an immediate appointment because she was just beginning her menstrual cycle. (Both the intrauterine device and the birth control pill demand close timing: the IUD can be inserted only during the menstrual period because the cervix is not sufficiently soft at other times, and birth-control pills may not be effective unless a woman begins taking them within five days after the onset of menstruation.) The appointments clerk could not find an appropriate appointment, and dismissed the woman. Turning to the observer, she said that if the woman had *really* wanted contraception, she would have made arrangements for an appointment at an earlier time.

Once again, the demand is put upon the potential risk-taking woman to be unconflicted and highly motivated in order to get highly effective contraception. Many women, of course, are just that. When faced with problems in obtaining medical help concerning contraception, they will abstain from intercourse until they get their contraception.

For the more ambivalent woman, however, the situation is not so simple. If she has been experiencing one or more of the "cost themes" outlined in this chapter, it will be less likely that she will have the motivation to carry on her search for effective contraception or postpone intercourse until structural and procedural barriers can be overcome. Thus, ironically, the women who need contraception most, because they are momentarily running a high risk of becoming contraceptive risk-takers, are the very women for whom the institutional structure for delivering contraceptive services is most dysfunctional. Highly motivated women, who are least in need of contraceptive services because their motivation gives them other strategies to fall back on, find it easy to get what they want from contraceptive clinics. Risk-takers, on the contrary, are forced by the structure of medical services to pattern themselves after the highly motivated women. When they do not, or cannot, they are defined as personal failures, not as women whom the structure is inadequate to serve.

Costs of drugstore methods. The structural problems of getting contraception are not automatically avoided by choosing one of the methods of contraception that does not require a visit to a clinic—the so-called "drugstore methods," for example. As we shall demonstrate in Chapter Six, the current ideology about birth control makes it unlikely that women will choose the "drugstore methods" in the first place, because these are generally thought to be so much less effective. An unconflicted woman might feel that a less effective method is more effective than no method at all, but many of the women interviewed seemed to feel that choosing a "drugstore method" would amount to defining themselves in advance as risk-takers.

Even if a woman does choose a drugstore method (condoms, spermicidal foams, and jellies) these methods still evoke all the cost-acknowledging mentioned earlier; in this case, one must acknowledge to the general public (or at least to the general public in the drugstore) that one is planning to engage in sexual intercourse later in the evening. For people who are less than totally comfortable with themselves as sexually active people, this can be too high a price to pay.

Even if one partner or the other does manage to evade or transcend the "acknowledging costs" inherent in the public purchase of a "non-medical" contraceptive, bringing it home and using it evokes still other costs. "Drugstore" contraceptives are often intrinsically unpleasant to use because they dampen the romantic spirit. Of more direct concern here is that they demand that one or both of the partners consciously and with full attention, touch, explore, or probe their own genitals. At first, it would appear that this is hardly a cost: after all, sexual intercourse demands contact with the genitals. But whereas sexual intercourse typically consists of romantic genital contact with the partner, the use of foam, condoms, jellies, and suppositories call for contact with one's own genitals in a less than romantic way. In particular, both men and women reported uneasiness about applying the contraceptive in front of the partner. (Parenthetically, the situation is only a little better with medical methods: the diaphragm must be inserted and checked before intercourse, and proper use of the IUD calls for a woman to manipulate her cervix at regular intervals to ascertain that the threads of the device are still in their proper place. Only the pill is free from these costs, and as we shall see in Chapter Five, it has other costs of its own.)

Thus the demand that a woman (or a man, for that matter) use effective contraception is a demand that she be able to plan and carry through a difficult and time-consuming series of transactions with a medical clinic, or alternately, that she be comfortable enough with her own body and sexuality to be able to purchase and use a chemical or mechanical method. In both cases, the status of the risk-taker becomes "value added": the more ambivalent and less motivated she is, the harder it will be for her to make use of the institutional structure for obtaining contraception.[9]

COSTS OF MAINTAINING CONTRACEPTION

We have outlined above how changes in the larger social life of contra-ceptive users—the breakup of a relationship, the changing of sexual partners, or, as we shall see later, the conviction that one is "too old" to bear more children—all bring about changes in contraceptive patterns. Here, however, we are interested in another kind of contraceptive change, where the woman and her partner begin to take contraceptive risks after a considerable period of effective contraception with one another, and in the absence of any of the larger social "events" noted above.

The costs specific to maintaining contraception over a period of time, which are more common than one would expect, seem to arrive from two sources. First, the ongoing practice of contraception calls for a high level of carry-through all the time. Second, the attitudes of the men involved may change dramatically as time goes on or become more salient as a relationship grows.

Costs of "carry-through." Relationships, like people, change. As a relationship progresses, one or both partners may feel a greater need to assert spontaneity and romance in the relationship or to demonstrate very clearly the extent to which they are committed or not committed to each other. Because of the constant nature of contraception, contraceptive practices become increasingly vulnerable to these pressures over time.

One woman expressed very clearly in her interview the conflicting pulls in each direction: to maintain contraception, and to skip it "just this once":

I: Did you ever think you might get pregnant?

R: Sure, yeah, I thought I might get pregnant because it's there all the time, no matter what. There's such a discrepancy in what people do and say. I don't really think I want to be pregnant. I was miserable at the time. But at that moment I didn't make the decision to protect myself. This time I got pregnant on my diaphragm. As I look back, my husband had gone to the National Guard. He was gone for two weeks. I went to see my mother. I just packed everything, but I didn't take my diaphragm, I didn't think I would be able to see my husband. He had said there was a chance but a small one. Four days later I found out I was going to be able to see him. I tried to get a diaphragm. A doctor I knew ordered me one. So I went to pick it up, but they said I should have come sooner, it was too late. The next day I went to see my husband and for two days we didn't use anything. When I'm pregnant, I don't like it. But

> my husband's been married before and he has a child. His ex-
> wife has a lot of hold over him because of that and maybe I
> wanted to get knocked up for that.

Maintaining contraception over time has costs of its own and the temptation to take risks must be met and dealt with over and over again. This woman had already experienced one unwanted pregnancy, and had been using a diaphragm for over two years, but she went to visit her mother without her diaphragm, even though she knew there was a slight chance of seeing her husband. She then made earnest efforts to get another medical appointment and another diaphragm, but arrived too late to pick it up. She then gave up her efforts and did not turn to drug-store methods such as foam or condoms. Her case illustrates how the cost of maintaining motivation and action all the time can often make risk-taking the "line of least resistance." Parenthetically, it also illustrates an idea we shall develop in greater detail in Chapter Five—that costs are a function of benefits, and work in a complementary fashion, so that just as costs can change over time, so can benefits. It is unlikely that this woman—or any of the others of her age, marital status, and contraceptive experience—would find taking the diaphragm along so costly were it not for the built-in benefit attached to the pregnancy: "My husband's been married before and he has a child. His ex-wife has a lot of hold over him because of that and maybe I wanted to get knocked up for that."

Costs of male attitudes. Since all intercourse requires a partner, what-ever feelings the man has about the use of contraceptives can have an impact on the woman's decision to take a risk. In both the reports of the women in this study and the responses of the men who were inter-viewed, men's attitudes about risk-taking ranged from passive approval of risk-taking to active opposition to contraception. The most passive position on this continuum was represented by those men who were unaware of what contraception the woman was using, and who failed to ask if she was contraceptively protected. Although more typical of the "one-night stand," this attitude was also found in what appeared to be relationships of some duration, as in this one:

I: How did the pregnancy happen?

R: I got really drunk one night and this guy took advantage of me
     more than anything else.
I: Was this Jack?
R: Yeah, the guy I was going with at the time.

Or in this one:

I: What was this guy like?
R: He was really strong and bullheaded. I told him I didn't want to
     [have intercourse]. He said "either you give it to me or I'll
     take it." And I was shocked at his reaction. I said, "If you're
     gonna take it you'd better try really hard." And he did. He was
     taking me home. I don't think it was really rape, but I think it
     was force.

More common, in the middle-range position, where men who were
aware of the contraceptive risk-taking, but did not take any steps to end
it, or passively participated:

R: Like John said, he should have pressured me and he didn't.

Alternately:

R: (Male) When we first started I used contraception for a while.
     It was a hassle and we just went along a month at a time.

Or again:

I: Did he know you were off the pill?
R: Yes. Well, I told him about the IUD and I told him I couldn't
     get it, and when I told him about the abortion he said it was his
     fault because he should have pushed me.

The least common position, but one taken frequently enough to be
striking, was represented by the man who actively opposes the use of
contraception:

I: Tell me about the guy by whom you were pregnant the first
     time.
R: He was a guy just back from Vietnam. He'd been forced to kill
     a lot of women and children. He was stationed out here. He
     ended up getting two girls pregnant and unfortunately I was
     one of them. He told me he had a vasectomy and since he was
     younger I questioned him and he came up with some pretty
     good answers. I have a theory why he did that. He wanted to
     bring some children into the world because he's had to kill
     them. I didn't love him, and when I told him that, he married

the other girl and walked out on her a year later. He was furious
at the abortion, just furious.

Although this illustration is somewhat unusual in its details, male opposition to all contraception and trickery by men concerning their own
fertility was infrequently but consistently reported in this study.

The weight that male attitudes have in the joint decision-making
process appears to depend in part on how active a role the male takes in
sexual matters and in part on the strength of the woman's decision to use
contraceptive measures. A woman firmly committed to contraception,
one for whom the benefits of contraception are high and the costs low,
will risk male disapproval to carry out her decision to protect herself
contraceptively:

> R: Before, I was always paranoid about getting pregnant. I'd
>   always make sure the person was wearing a rubber or some
>   kind of protection. I was so careful before I went overboard.
>   Guys used to think, "You're so weird, you're so careful."

When the weighing process that results in contraceptive risk-taking is
more precarious, however, male attitudes can become costly to the
women in a variety of ways. Many women fear alienating the male by
asking for his cooperation in the contraceptive act, even if that cooperation is limited to postponing intercourse or using an interim method
until one of the more exclusively female-oriented methods can be
started:

> I: Did you think you might get pregnant?
> R: Yeah, I thought of it a lot. I thought without some kind of con-
>   traception I was bound to get pregnant. I knew I was going to,
>   but I didn't know when or how. I still don't know when. . . .
>   I suppose I thought if I told him no, he would leave.
> I: And then what would happen?
> R: I would have felt bad. I was really depressed when my first boy
>   friend wanted to go out with other people. I guess I found this
>   guy because I didn't want to be alone. I didn't want to be hurt.

Another problem is that women have traditionally been expected to
be more passive than men in all aspects of sexual interaction. Thus if the
man does not initiate a discussion of birth control (and apparently many
men do not, believing that widespread use of the pill means that *all*

women are always protected), or if he actively opposes the use of contraception when it is suggested by the woman, it is often hard for the woman to insist:

I: Why did you use condoms with the first boy friend but not with the second?
R: Well, the second wouldn't wait until I got the pill, and he wouldn't use the rubber.

Or again:

I: You said that condoms were your main method of birth control. Were you using them all the time?
R: Not really. He used them in the beginning, but after a while he couldn't see them.

Both of these statements reflect the dominant role the male can play in the decision to take contraceptive risks. From the male point of view, such a decision has its own costs and benefits:

I: Whose decision was it not to use contraception?
R: (Male) I would've wanted her to and talked to her, but I didn't take a firm hand. Thinking of myself, I didn't want to use condoms, I couldn't ask her. We just went from one time to the other without thinking of the whole thing.

Implied in this statement is some confusion about who has the ultimate decision-making responsibility for contraception. As we shall elaborate in Chapter Five, recent changes in the technology of contraception and in the ideology of the sexual revolution have left some people at a loss as to who has what obligations in a sexual relationship. When people have a tenuous relationship with one another, or when they fear the feeling of "couplehood" that joint decision making implies, there appears to be a tendency for both of them to postpone action because each expects the other to take the dominant role. Parallel with this, of course, is the feeling expressed here that the man "should have taken a firm hand"—that is, when the consequences become real, he senses that he has evaded his masculine responsibilities.

BIOLOGICAL AND MEDICAL COSTS

The fourth and last category of potential costs that women perceived in contraceptive use was that of biological and medical side-effects.

Although these costs were mentioned more frequently than any others in this study, it is important to remember that ex-pill users were the single largest group within the Abortion Clinic's clientele, and that side-effects of the pill, both real and potential, have received more publicity than adverse effects of any other form of contraception—which is to be expected, since the pill, like any systemic drug, could pose immediate threats to health. (After the study was completed, similar life- and health-threatening side-effects were reported in congressional hearings on the IUD.)

It is also important to repeat here that the costs in this category are both potential and relative, as they are in any other. When women or doctors report that they have stopped using or prescribing pills because of "side-effects," it is easily assumed that side-effects are a clearly defined phenomenon with unambiguous costs. This is rarely the case. The costs of side-effects, like all the costs described in this chapter, are determined by personal "cost accounting," by a weighing of what one person perceived as the risks of use against the risks of non-use.

Unfortunately, both women and doctors often think of side-effects as being medical in nature, and therefore absolute and not relative. But many other medical examples could be used to clarify the relative value of drugs. Both patients and doctors, for instance, tolerate a higher level of side-effects from cortisone used after a kidney transplant than they do for aspirin used to reduce the fever of a cold.

Similarly, the risks associated with pill use are defined in the context of their intended benefits, but they vary according to what women and their doctors define as the benefits and the alternatives. If, for example, both parties assume that another method of effective contraception is readily available and will be used successfully, then their tolerance of side-effects will be low. If, on the other hand, they assume that the alternative is an unwanted pregnancy, an abortion, or other problemati-cal outcomes of pregnancy, then relatively serious side-effects will be tolerated. It is therefore easy to see how various women (and various doctors) will have very different opinions of exactly how costly side-effects are. For women, the question echoes that of the doctors: how safe is pill use? And in both cases the answer is the same: safer than what?

Women in this study mentioned many potential side-effects of the pill. Some are specific; others reflect generalized concern about the safety of all pills and drugs.

R: I was afraid of taking the pill, because in my work I meet many young girls who have very serious side-effects. At any rate, I became scared of birth control pills, and because I'm so regular, I figured I could rely on that.

The most frequently mentioned side-effect was the possibility of weight gain:

I: Did you ever consider getting more effective contraception?
R: Yeah, I wanted to go on the pill, but because of my job [modeling] I was hesitant, I was concerned about weight gain. When I first started at my job, I gained over my maximum and they took me off the payroll for thirty days and I had always heard that pills could make you gain weight and I was always very paranoid about that. And I was also very regular so I thought it would be safe enough, which was very stupid.

Both of these women had concrete evidence to support their fears—in the one case, actual observation of side-effects, and in the other the fairly well documented evidence that women may gain weight with pill use. Additionally, in both cases the contextual nature of the risk is neatly outlined:

R: I was always very regular, so I thought it would be safe [to use a rhythm method].

The second most frequently named side-effect was more ambiguous: women said that it caused psychological changes in them: "It drove me out of my mind," or "It made me depressed and irritable." It is hard to tell how well-founded a concern this is. Certainly a hormone ingested systematically might have effects on the emotional state of the user.[10] On the other hand, the mere fact of using contraception, or the other costs which it might create in the user's life, could also cause emotional changes. Here again the contextual nature of the issue was evident: all the women who said they had emotional problems with the pill expected to use some other method.

Last, women mentioned a catch-all of side-effects: "I've had monilia [a vaginal infection characterized by itching, discharge, and pain] for two years and finally cured it, and the pill encouraged it to return." Or: "I had a rash and my doctor said it was a drug reaction." In most of these cases the women themselves pointed to the relative nature of the side-effects: "I got Ovulen [a popular pill brand], took one, and was nauseated. I decided I didn't want to take the pill, probably because of my Catholic high school background."

Apart from these medical side-effects of contraception, there are "iatrogenic" or doctor-produced effects. As a notable example, doctors are often concerned with whether women are ovulating, or whether the pill has suppressed ovulation beyond the time covered by actual pill use. This concern, at least in our Clinic population, led women to find out the hard way that they were in fact ovulating:

> R: I was on the pills for eight months. I came out to California and
>   I ran out of pills and I went to a gynecologist I knew out here
>   and I didn't tell him I had a previous abortion, and I was just
>   embarrassed. I told him I was out of pills and I needed a pre-
>   scription and he said, "If you're having a relatively inactive
>   sex life, I'd like to take you off the pills for three months to see
>   if you ovulate." I didn't like the idea, but I said to myself, he's
>   the doctor. He told me to use foam.

Although it is true that this woman withheld important information from the doctor (that she had a previous abortion and therefore had been a risk-taker in the past), it was risk-taking behavior on the part of a doctor to withhold pills from a single, 21-year-old woman with no expressed desire to have children at the time, in order to see whether she was ovulating—no matter how "inactive her sex life."

This concern of gynecologists with potential fertility was a recurring theme throughout the interviews. In every case, this concern led directly or indirectly to risk-taking on the part of women, and hence (in this population) to pregnancy. We would suggest that this is because gynecologists are also obstetricians, and thus tend to value potential fertility in the future more highly than actual (and problematic) fertility in the present. In the case of pill use, there are some grounds for their concern; there have been reports of a "post pill syndrome" in which women fail to ovulate after pill use.[11] How many of these women had failed to ovulate *prior* to pill use of course cannot be known. Since gynecologists are professionally committed to protecting a woman's ability to bear children (because of their role definition and values) they are likely in cases of doubt to try to resolve the issue once and for all, even if the circumstances of a woman's life make it highly inappropriate to do so. In short, doctors are once again doing their own "cost accounting": better to risk an unwanted pregnancy now (a risk which is discounted by most doctors) than to risk discovering impaired fertility at a later date, when a woman has fewer fertile years in which to conceive (a risk taken seriously by people committed to the bearing of children).

This professional commitment to the ability to bear children produces a second variation of the "iatrogenic" theme. Just as doctors concerned about the "post pill syndrome" often try to verify ovulation, doctors will often tell women whose reproductive organs vary from the norm that they may have trouble conceiving. In fact, what the gynecologist usually means is that if, at the appropriate time, women find they have trouble conceiving, they should investigate medically the possibility that their physical idiosyncracies are the cause. Women, however, tend to hear this pronouncement as meaning that they are sterile or at best infertile. Thus an incredible two-thirds of the women interviewed said that they had been told by a doctor that they couldn't get pregnant, or would have trouble doing so. Further probing in the interviews and consultation with at least some of the doctors who examined these women suggested that it was their careless statement of a gynecological generality that led to this assumption, and rarely, if ever, a specific condition which would complicate or prevent pregnancy.

Such a statement ("you may have problems getting pregnant") sets the stage for risk-taking in two ways. First, it exerts a pressure on women to take risks to prove that they are in fact fertile.

I: What do you mean the "doctor set the stage"?
R: To some degree he made me wonder if I was ovulating or not.

Second, by creating a doubt in women's minds that they are fertile, it makes it harder for them to maintain continuous contraception, since the purpose could be irrelevant:

I: Did you ever consider using anything else?
R: Well, no. I think it was because I never figured my system was working properly.

In conclusion, then, women take risks because they make a cost

accounting of utilities and risks. They weigh the disadvantages and
benefits of contraception against the disadvantages and benefits of an
unwanted pregnancy. The costs of contraception are the personal and
social costs of acknowledging sexuality, planning, and engaging in
continual sexual activity; the structure-related costs (obtaining contraception); the costs to a personal relationship; and the costs related to
contraceptive technology. The other part of a theory of risk-taking—and
a highly significant one—is the assignment of costs and benefits to pregnancy, even when that pregnancy is later defined as unwanted. This will
be the focus of Chapter Four.

4

The Benefits
of Pregnancy

Just as the use of contraception has potential costs attached to it, which can be activated under certain social conditions, so a pregnancy has certain potential benefits attached to it, even if it ultimately ends in a therapeutic abortion. In this chapter we will demonstrate how women weigh these potential costs and benefits in deciding whether or not to engage in contraceptive risk-taking. It is important to note here that there is a vital difference between the two: the woman must perceive contraception as costly before risk-taking can occur; but the benefits of pregnancy never become actual until at least a month after the decision to take a risk has been made. In other words, the decision to take a contraceptive risk is typically based on the *immediate* costs of contraception and the *anticipated* benefits of pregnancy.

This difference is important, because for the women in this study the potential benefits of pregnancy seldom became real: they vanished with the verdict of a positive pregnancy test or were later outweighed by the actual costs of the pregnancy, hence the decision to seek a therapeutic abortion. Therefore what we are examining are not the actual but the *potential* benefits to pregnancy—the benefits anticipated at the time of the decision to take a contraceptive risk.

In order to understand the potential benefits assigned to pregnancy by risk-taking women, it is important to realize that pregnancy is more than a biological occurrence; it is an event of immense social significance. It connotes fertility, femininity, adulthood, independence, and a wide variety of other meanings. Thus the potential payoffs of a pregnancy include being able to take on the attributes and privileges which society assigns to pregnant women.

PREGNANCY AND THE WOMANLY ROLE

Nowhere is the social significance of pregnancy more dramatically illustrated than in a frequent benefit of pregnancy cited by the risk-taking women in this study: being pregnant proves that you are a woman. (Overall frequencies of the themes discussed in this chapter are given in Table 3.) "Proving" womanhood is desirable in part because society is experiencing a massive redefinition of what constitutes appropriate male and female behavior. The reconsideration of "the feminine mystique," the emergence of women's liberation, and the cultural phenomenon of "unisex" all create a certain degree of sex-role confusion. In particular, the challenging of gender stereotypes makes this a difficult period of transition for many women. Although it is sometimes hard for feminists to realize, the traditional female role, with all its limitations, is nonetheless a comfortable one for many women. In the long run, it is undoubtedly for the best that people be allowed to do what they want with their lives whatever their gender, but in the short run, many women find the loss of traditional female prerogatives (such as passivity and the right to be protected) frightening. Becoming pregnant is one way of resolving conflict around the changing definitions of what it is to be female. To be pregnant is to be at the core of the traditional definition of the female role, and it is one way of dealing with the new and sometimes frightening roles that society is demanding of women. For women who have been raised in all the traditional female virtues—compliance, nurturance, dependence, self-effacement—the demand to be an assertive, independent adult is sometimes difficult.[1] Thus one potential benefit of becoming pregnant is that it defines a woman as irrevocably female in the most traditional sense of the word, and permits one to claim traditional prerogatives:

I: Are you involved in Women's Liberation?
R: No. I think you should have equal opportunity and things like that, but I don't think marriage should be abolished or anything like that. I definitely think that there are things men should do and things women should do.
I: For example?
R: I like the idea of men taking care of you. I don't like the idea of women having to pay for dates. I think men should do things for women.

TABLE 3

Benefits of Pregnancy: Frequency of Benefit Themes Cited
by Women Clients of The Abortion Clinic
(Reliability coded at 89 percent)

Pregnancy and woman's role	17	Pregnancy and significant	
having a child to love	5	others	53
Pregnancy and self worth	12	husband	8
		lover	22
Pregnancy as a proof of		parents	7
fertility	15	"punish" parents	4
		mobilize parents to help	3
Pregnancy and relationships	44	surrogate parents	4
testing the man's		Pregnancy as a plea for help, as	
commitment	15	a psychiatric organizing	
bargaining for		technique	8
marriage	23		
shoring up an existing		"Pure" risk taking for the fun	3
marriage	6	or erotic thrill of it	

Discussion:

The totals add up to more than the sixty women interviewed, because women typically presented more than one expected benefit. Subheadings in this table ("having a child to love") indicate a discernible subcategory within the larger analytical category.

The two themes of "pregnancy and relationships" and "pregnancy and significant others" are somewhat overlapping when it comes to the role of the male partner qua partner and of the perception of the relationship as a whole. The coding rule was that when a significant other was mentioned (as in the case noted in the text where a woman bargained via pregnancy for marriage and lost twice with the same man), the "benefit theme" was coded as having some anticipated positive effect on the significant other. However, the theme was only coded for a "relationship effect" (e.g., "I wanted to see if he would support me," "I wanted to get married," "I wanted to save our marriage") when an *explicit* effect on the relationship was anticipated. Thus an *implicit* effect on the relationship via an effect on the significant other was coded only as an effect on the significant other, not on the relationship. When both were mentioned ("I wanted to see how he felt about me and if he would marry me"), the item was coded in both categories.

I: How about marriage?

R: In a marriage the woman takes care of the kids and the man works.

It is important to stress here that role conflicts probably trouble a great many women, and that pregnancy is by no means the only way of dealing with them. But as we shall note in Chapter Six, women as a group do not have many productive and satisfying alternatives to the traditional role as yet, so they are definitely limited in the kinds of ways they can deal with these conflicts. Finally, it appears as if the female role benefits of pregnancy are ones which are particularly likely to be evoked at times of role stress: upon graduation from college or high school, when dissatisfied with a job, or when feeling that it is time to get married. Thus it is quite possible that any woman will begin to view pregnancy as a potential benefit in her attempts to define herself as really female if the social stresses around her are high enough.

PREGNANCY AND SELF WORTH

A variation on the theme that pregnancy proves one is female is the theme that a potential mother is a valuable person. Anthropologically, this is a time-honored idea: in some societies, a pregnant woman is considered more desirable as a marriage partner because her fertility is already proven.[2] In many other societies, a barren woman is considered without value.

Not surprisingly, this idea was far more frequently expressed by the women who chose to maintain their pregnancies (interviews not quoted here), because only those women came to experience the actual benefits of motherhood. Nonetheless, this attitude was mentioned several times by the abortion-seeking women:

I: You said that you had a strong maternal urge. So you think that could have been a factor in getting pregnant?

R: I think so, yeah. I don't know how exactly, but taking a wild stab, I think it would be that getting pregnant means having someone who will take my love and care, 'cause lots of times I think no one else wants it.

This is another comment on women's roles: when the society makes some women feel that only a child would want their love and attention (and their interest and commitment), the benefits of getting pregnant are obvious.

PREGNANCY AND FERTILITY

Besides defining a woman as clearly female and valuable, pregnancy proves conclusively that one is fertile. In the abstract, this would not appear to be a significant benefit, particularly when we remember that statistically, in a year's time one hundred non-contracepting women will produce approximately eighty pregnancies.[3] When a woman does not want a child at a given time, it seems irrelevant for her to want to prove that she can become pregnant.

In real life, however, women have many reasons for wanting to test their fertility. As we noted in Chapter Three, fully two-thirds of the women interviewed reported that their gynecologists had told them that they would have trouble getting pregnant. In addition, as we shall demonstrate in Chapter Five, after women have been taking contraceptive risks for some period of time, they begin to think they are sterile because they have not already gotten pregnant. Finally, the stigma of infertility is so strong that any woman who has reason to suspect that she may be infertile has a powerful reason for wanting to find out. Fertility is like money in the bank: it is nice to know it is there, even if there are no immediate plans to use it. As one woman put it:

I: What do you mean when you say that you felt "Freaky but far out" when you found you were pregnant?

R: Just, wow, me, I'm gonna have a baby, one of those things that are so cute and you think of having someday, but I'm having it now.

I: Didn't you always think you could get pregnant?

R: Yeah, but I never really realized it until someone told me I was pregnant. It was never real to me that I could until I did. That I could really do it made me feel far out. All my freaky feelings were about the responsibility stuff.

Another stated it more explicitly:

I: Was the pregnancy reassuring from the point of view of your concern about not being able to get pregnant?

R: Oh yeah, it solved that quick enough. As a matter of fact, when the doctor said that the test was positive, I just grinned. He said, "Well, you're taking this *very* well." But I was just plain relieved.

I: Do you think that that might have had to do with getting pregnant?

R: I think so, I think I was daring it to happen. I think a subconscious thing was working saying, "Go ahead, try it."

Another potential benefit of pregnancy is that it provides a situation in which the woman's sexual partner must define his relationship and commitment to the woman. Empirically in this study, these benefits were expressed in a number of ways. In the most general example, a pregnancy is a way of testing the man's general emotional attitude:

R: You always wonder how well a fiancé or a boy friend will react to what society says is a responsibility of his. Will he freak out, say "get away," or will he be loving? He became more loving, and so I think for us a pregnancy makes you work out a lot of things with each other.

More specifically, pregnancy has a potential benefit of sometimes leading to a commitment to marriage. Although it rarely happened in this study, many women expected that their men would be pleased (or dutiful) and would suggest marriage as a resolution to the problem of pregnancy. Three examples:

R: I didn't bother to use contraception because I thought I knew where I stood.
I: Where did you stand?
R: Well, because when we were going together, what he said his feelings were. . . . Well, you know, when you're going with someone, you just talk about the future, and marriage and everything.

I: How did you feel about getting pregnant?
R: I thought I would probably get married, that he would want to. I never, ever thought I'd go through an abortion. That never entered my mind at all.

I: Did you ever consider contraception?
R: No, I never thought about it. I guess by then I thought we'd be married, or getting married or something.

Thus the connection of pregnancy and marriage acts in two ways to promote risk-taking. When women assume that marriage—and children, a home, a place in life—is imminent, contraception becomes irrelevant. When it is assumed that pregnancy will (or might) lead to marriage, then the functional value attached to risk-taking increases.

A third way in which a pregnancy can be beneficial is that it can force a man to think through his conflicting obligations and declare his intentions, as we can see from this statement:

I: What's your boy friend like?

R: He's older, he's twenty-one, usually the people I hang around with are older. He's quite different. He was married, that kind of blew me away. He's been married for three years. His relationship with his wife is lousy, as far as I can see. The only reason I can come up with [for his] not getting a divorce is that he has a little girl that he doesn't want to leave.

Or this one:

R: I kidded him when I first found out I was pregnant. I asked him if he wanted to live with a pregnant lady, no strings attached. He said no, he couldn't handle that. And I know that he couldn't. But I think there's always the underlying thought that if you go through getting pregnant together, you'll end up together. I wouldn't mind marrying him. I care about him a lot.

Another potential benefit of pregnancy in this category, one which will be examined in more detail in Chapter Five, is that it can shore up or redefine a marriage; there is a considerable body of folk wisdom on the theme of "having a child to save the marriage." Thus the social meaning of pregnancy can act, at least potentially, to influence, test, or change the man's relationship to the pregnant woman, and it is the assessing of these potential benefits which often leads to risk-taking. For the women in this study, however, few of these benefits proved valid once the pregnancy occurred: the man refused to get married, said he couldn't "handle it," or continued in his relationship with another woman. The potential benefits were not actualized, and abortion was the end result.

PREGNANCY AND SIGNIFICANT OTHERS

A pregnancy forces others besides the male sex partner to deal with the pregnant woman, and this, too, can be seen as a potential benefit. In this sample of primarily younger women (the mean age was 22), the others who most often fell into this category were parents. The pregnancy of a daughter forces parents to pay attention to her, to react to her, and to some extent to deal with her as an independent person. It also forces them to deal with her as a person who can become pregnant—that is, as an adult.

The women in this study presented pregnancy to their parents in a variety of styles, each of which brought with it its own benefits. As one example, getting pregnant can be an act of rebellion aimed at defying the parents and their values, and at proving dramatically that the woman is a separate entity from her parents:

> R: My dad is real strict. He drinks a lot and when he gets mad he hits me. But nothing, not even him, can ever take away the experience of being pregnant.

Although this particular theme is extensively explored in the literature on illegitimacy (some authors going so far as to suggest that it is the major contributing factor),[4] it appears that it also occurs among women who have the option of terminating their pregnancies with an abortion. Thus it is the act of getting pregnant, and not the birth of a child, which is important for women with this option. (Chapter Five will argue, however, that several kinds of benefits must occur to a woman before she decides to take contraceptive risks, and that no one factor is the "major" or "only" contributing factor.)

Another way of presenting a pregnancy to parents, and of getting a different set of payoffs, is to use the pregnancy to punish parents for their inattention or lack of warmth. One woman, for example, successively got pregnant with two non-Caucasians in order to upset her father, whom she defined as an "upfront racist." As is true of most of the elements in risk-taking, this gambit probably expressed a desire for at least two benefits: first, that the parents would mobilize their forces and come to their daughter's aid, showering her with love and affection; and second, that they would feel responsible for her problems and resolve to change their ways. Still another woman reported that her parents were "not too understanding or close—I could never really go to them." She then described the problem pregnancy of her older sister:

> R: My older sister had an abortion a couple of years ago without my parents' consent and it was an awful mess. It was a legal one, but at that time my parents had to sign and they wouldn't 'cause they're Catholic. So she got one at [a hospital] through the help of friends. She must have been 19, she's 22 now.

I: What were your feelings about your sister's abortion?

R: What bothered me most was that it created a big family feeling and . . . my mother, it bothered her almost to the point where she had a nervous breakdown. It was really sad to see what happened between my sister and my parents, it was worse than the abortion itself, seeing the coldness and the distance.

This woman had undergone not one but *two* therapeutic abortions within the previous two years, the effects of her sister's abortion notwithstanding. Indeed, it seems plausible that it was precisely the parental suffering caused by her sister's abortion that she sought to gain from her own two abortions.

Another style of presenting the pregnancy to parents involves asking them for help, rather than directly punishing them. In some ways, the motive can be similar—to notify the parents that they have not been properly attentive or loving—but the aim is not so much to punish them as to force them to make changes in their attitudes and behavior. It is my impression that this is one of the few benefits that were actually achieved with some frequency. Just as families will mobilize their psychic forces to help a family member who attempts suicide,[5] so in several cases in this study, by the time of the two-week follow-up interview, the family had gratifyingly closed ranks around the formerly pregnant daughter. How long this psychic support tends to last is only conjecture: in some cases it may become a permanent change, whereas in others it may be a temporary change brought on by crisis, to be replaced later with recrimination or benign neglect. Nonetheless, at least in the short run, the benefit was concrete, as here:

I: How did your parents react?

R: They took it really good. They were really helpful. Anything they could do, they did. I think they realized that it wasn't the end of the world.

And here:

R: My mother was the distant type and you could never talk to her, but after the pregnancy I told her, and she was kind of shocked but she didn't want me to be hurt—my welfare to be ruined and she was really nice. The abortion really brought us closer together.

In some cases, the parents took on the burden of resolving the pregnancy, and went to extraordinary lengths to do so. The parents of the following young woman arranged for, paid for, and provided a cover story for the abortion, even though it required the three of them to leave their home in the Southwest and fly to California:

> R: I came home and the doctor had called my parents and they just told me I was pregnant, and momma asked me what I wanted to do about it, and I said an abortion and that was about it. They called the doctor and she told them about this center, and they came here with me. They told my school they were taking me with them on a business trip.

Sometimes a surrogate parent plays the same role as the parent, with the same results. In the following case, the woman was closer to her partner's mother than to her own mother, who had deserted both husband and daughter to live with another man in a nearby town. Although the daughter's risk-taking may have been aimed at her absent mother, it was her partner's mother who provided the moral and actual support:

> R: I missed my period and then I missed the second one . . . so I went to my boy friend's mother and told her that I didn't have my period. I wasn't sure, but she was sure that I was pregnant, so she made me go have a lab test, and I was pregnant, so she called me down here and arranged the abortion for me. At first we were going to have it in Northern City, but we had to go through a hassle and they weren't sure they could do it, so she called down here and arranged it and drove me down.

PREGNANCY AND THE PLEA FOR HELP

Related to the specific benefit of obtaining parental support and loving is a more general series of benefits to be anticipated when the pregnancy becomes a generalized plea for help. The problem pregnancy has typically been defined as a situation appropriate for social intervention: the illegal abortion, the legal abortion, and the illegitimate pregnancy are all assumed by the "helping professions" to be evidence of psychic stress. As we noted in Chapter Two, the women who came to this Clinic got pregnant for many reasons, and simple psychic stress is not an adequate explanation. But just as Cicourel found that a social definition of delinquents as children coming from broken homes made social agencies more likely to define children from broken homes as delinquent,[a] so the social definition of a problem pregnancy as evidence of the need for counseling sometimes makes women who need counseling feel that getting pregnant is one way to get it:

R: I had no one to talk to, and so coming here was a real help. Like some people slit their wrists. Well, this is my version. And I'm sure that's the way a lot of girls do, if they realize it or not.

R: I think I realized I needed help with professional people. So I went this drastic way to get it. I got myself into real trouble so I would have to go for help.

A variation on this theme of pregnancy as a plea for help is the benefit of pregnancy (particularly the problem pregnancy) as a psychological organizing technique. When women feel vaguely under stress, one of the benefits of pregnancy is that it focuses the stress in one place:

R: I was vaguely depressed. This way I was concretely depressed, and it was like I had a reason to be depressed and I could work on that one reason and it helps to get out of the depression, the overall depression.

Additionally, when a woman is under stress, sometimes the pregnancy can act as the "last straw" which will tip the situation in the direction of intervention by someone else, or create a crisis where energies can be mobilized:

R: If you're down low, it really doesn't matter if you get pregnant, I mean, it can't upset the equilibrium. In my case I was almost glad of it in one respect. I needed to go lower into that low to get out, and that pregnancy did it.

Other research has shown that a significant number of women use the abortion as a psychological organizing technique, whether or not they planned it that way. Wallerstein has shown that on a six-month and

a. See Aaron Cicourel, *The Social Organization of Juvenile Justice* (New York: John Wiley and Sons, 1968). Subsequent research (by Barbara K. Moran, forthcoming) on child abuse suggests that the self-definition of being a child abuser may act the same way. A social milieu which is reluctant to provide psychiatric services to women under stress will often react swiftly and effectively to women who say that they fear they will abuse their children.

one-year follow-up study, most women have used the experience as a creative one, and one which builds ego strength.[6] Thus the potential benefit of pregnancy as an organizing technique and a plea for help is relatively likely to be actualized, even for women whose pregnancies end in abortion.

PREGNANCY AND PURE RISK-TAKING

The least frequently mentioned benefit to pregnancy, but one which does occur, was the idea that the risk of pregnancy brings an excitement of its own to the sexual act or enlivens an otherwise dull existence:

> R: I think for me it's a subconscious desire to get pregnant. I sense it but I don't understand it. Maybe it's a subconscious self-destructive thing. I was aware of other methods of contraception. Marvin would pound them into my head, but I still went my own way. I *dared* fate. I just dared it. When I think about it I just draw a blank, so I think about other things. Maybe I just wanted to see if I could. I don't know why people do things that aren't good for them. It's like being a maniac driver on the freeway, it's asking for trouble. You know, I think we control our fate, but some of us will have to go the limit, just to see what will happen. I don't know what *makes* me do it, personality make-up I guess.

Although pure risk-taking as a cause of unwanted pregnancy has been given heavy emphasis in at least one other article,[7] this quote demonstrates that "pure" risk-taking is a complicated phenomenon. This woman mentions several other benefits to pregnancy—testing her partner's commitment, testing her fertility, asking for help by engaging in a clearly self-destructive act—and she also underlines two other parts of the risk-taking phenomenon: she notes indirectly that people other than women take risks ("it's like being a maniac driver on the freeway"); and she suggests, by her comment "it's personality make-up," that there are a variety of risk-taking styles, which have already been noted in Chapter Two.

Some women mentioned (in follow-up interviews six months later, not reproduced here) that sexuality had lost its pleasure for them without the element of risk, although again this was a relatively rare comment. It is interesting to speculate exactly what this means in terms of risk-taking. We are inclined to suspect that just as "pure" risk-taking is usually preceded by the perception of a configuration of benefits to pregnancy, so the loss of pleasure associated with the lost risk in fact represents a multitude of social "costs": a feeling of being burdened by contraception; a feeling of unfairly having had to pay the cost of risk-taking which involved two people; a feeling of a loss of bargaining power with the man involved; and perhaps a belief that continued contraception is not without the costs outlined in Chapter Three. It is also possible that the feeling of loss when the element of risk is eliminated may represent the internalization of norms that women have to pay for their sexuality: without the prospect of being punished for a pregnancy, the enjoyment of sexuality is burdened with guilt. But whatever the origin, "pure" risk-taking appears to be a relatively rare but interesting benefit connected to anticipated pregnancy.

In conclusion, then, there are many positive values attached to getting pregnant. Pregnancy can be proof of femaleness, self worth, and fertility, and it can provide opportunities for different interactions with the sexual partner and with others such as parents. It is my contention, however, that rarely is one of these potential benefits alone sufficient to create contraceptive risk-taking: the benefits of pregnancy are usually interwoven with the costs of contraception. It is this interweaving or working together of costs and benefits which will be the focus of the next chapter.

5

Toward a Theory of Contraceptive Risk-Taking

The process of living is a series of calculated risks. In order to decide whether or not to cross the street, or take a flyer on the stock market, or get married, people typically weigh the alternatives, assign values to various choices, calculate the "foregone opportunities" involved in each choice (an investment in the stock market, for example, means that the same money cannot be spent on a vacation), and then ultimately decide which of the options open to them they will choose. These choices are not always explicit or clearly articulated: in perhaps the majority of life situations, this calculation of the "risks of life" is a subtle, intuitive, continuing process. The intuitive nature of most of the decision making that goes on in everyday life is sustained by the fact that the social milieu dictates exactly how explicit such decision making can be. It is one thing, for example, to study stock prospectuses, or the performance rating of different brands of cars. It is an entirely different thing to evaluate explicitly the health, education, and future earning power of a potential mate, although there is ample sociological evidence that most people weigh those factors implicitly.

The model we will use in this chapter—that of classical decision-making theory—assumes that individuals perceive options, assign values to these various options, choose one option as preferable to another, and then act to implement that choice in behavioral terms. We shall use this model to argue that women who do not use previously demonstrated contraceptive skills in order to protect themselves from pregnancy are nevertheless women who in fact have engaged in a "rational" decision-making process (in a goal-directed sense of the word).[1] This process consists of a series of decision junctures at which women must assign values to certain variables and plan their behavior on the basis of these assigned values. When we compare each risk-taking woman's history with her prior history of non-risk-taking (by definition, each risk-taker in this study had more contraceptive skills available to her than she used), we shall demonstrate that each decision juncture must be negotiated in a particular way in order for the "career" of risk-taking to continue. When alternate values are assigned to the variables at each decision juncture, risk-taking does not occur.

The use of the word "rational" to describe the decision-making processes of risk-taking women, even when used in the strict sense defined by this study (the use of appropriate means to achieve goals), should not be construed to mean that these decisions are necessarily explicit and articulate. Rather, we shall use the model to open up for analysis what are typically inarticulate and less-than-fully conscious decisions. To date, the use of this kind of model to examine the decisions made by contraceptively risk-taking women has been hindered by the fact that women almost always decide to take a contraceptive risk *before* they become pregnant, and while they think that it is unlikely that they will become pregnant. In fact, as we shall demonstrate below, assigning a low likelihood to the occurrence of pregnancy is one of the vital decisions which must occur before contraceptive risk-taking can happen. Once women actually become pregnant, however, the decision process which led to their pregnancy is reevaluated both by themselves and by the outsiders with whom they come in contact (doctors, nurses, social workers) in the light of the new event. Once one part of the process—the evaluation of the likelihood of pregnancy—is shown to be invalid, the whole process is defined as an irrational one. However, this definition assumes that women should have at the beginning of the decision process information which in fact only becomes available to them as a consequence of the risk-taking, which is the end product of the process. When the decision processes which precede the pregnancy are reconstructed and the alternatives and information available to the women themselves are examined, the decision to take a contraceptive risk begins to appear a reasonable one under the circumstances. Our task in this chapter will be to demonstrate these circumstances and to account for the risk-taking behavior of women.

This theory of contraceptive risk taking—that it is a product of a series of decisions which appear rational to the decision makers themselves—asserts that the behavior of people can be predicted if the range of alternatives open to them is known and if the assigning of value to the various alternatives can be defined. In this particular study, the postulation of a decision-making model to account for observed contraceptive risk-taking is analogous to the postulating of a transformational grammar to account for a speaker-hearer's ability to produce and recognize grammatical sentences. Analytically, each apparatus is theoretically capable of generating the observed output. Empirically, the subject's ability to make discriminations and talk about the phenomena of interest is used to guide the construction of the models. Finally, each model serves as a metaphorical representation of an observed set of skills, rather than a description of behavior in specific situations. Thus the model used here is an analytical one, and only by extension, a causal one. It accounts for behavior, and we would tentatively suggest that it also predicts behavior (although we have not tried to make predictions in this study).

To the women themselves, this whole process of decision making appears to parallel Thomas C. Schelling's concept of "tacit bargaining," which defines tacit bargaining as "[that] kind in which adversaries watch and interpret each other's behavior, each aware that his own actions are being interpreted and anticipated, each acting with a view to the expectations he creates."[2] In a special case of tacit bargaining, which Schelling calls "tacit coordination," people bargain with themselves in order to figure out what is the most reasonable course of action, given the expectations of what the most reasonable course of action is to others. He argues, for example, that if a person tries to meet someone in New York when no prior meeting place had been set up, it is likely that both would end up under the clock in Grand Central Station. The tacit bargaining, that which leads to such a meeting place, stems from thinking "what would the other person do if he were wondering what I would do, wondering what he would do?" Thus mutual expectations are set up and tacit coordination occurs.

Schelling's concept deals with coordinating behaviors between two parties in ambiguous situations. We suggest that it is clearly possible to have an analogous but purely individual "tacit coordination," often not explicitly articulated, where the actions and expected actions of others are but one of many inputs. Thus, for example, risk-taking women try to evaluate simultaneously inputs from both the costs of contraception and the benefits of pregnancy. The line of thinking they use parallels Schelling's concept: "If I do take a contraceptive risk, a pregnancy might result, but a pregnancy might not be such a bad thing, and it probably wouldn't happen anyway." Of course, once a pregnancy does occur, the cost accounting is radically reassessed in light of the new event. What we are presenting here, then, is the initial pre-pregnancy, pre-abortion cost accounting.

THE COST-BENEFIT "SET" TOWARD RISK-TAKING

As the first step in the tacit decision-making process of whether or not to take a contraceptive risk, women must come to a general, global stance toward risk-taking, a stance we have called the cost-benefit "set." This "set" is the product of a weighing process which considers the costs of contraception and the benefits of pregnancy outlined in Chapters Three and Four. Obviously, as in any decision process, the alternatives—in this case the benefits of contraception and the costs of pregnancy—are considered as well. As Figure 4 demonstrates, the costs and benefits of both contraception and pregnancy (we have used the term "utilities" to cover the range of both costs and benefits) act independently to create a "set" which makes risk-taking either more or less likely. Empirically, however, we suggest that since women are engaged in a constant assessment of the utilities of both contraception and pregnancy, each of these factors is constantly being reexamined in the light of the other so that they have an additive effect. A woman may have a chronic disaffection with her contraceptive method (expressed here as "low utilities of contraception") which is not of itself sufficient to create a favorable "set" toward risk-taking. When something changes in her life so that pregnancy becomes more desirable (expressed here as a "high utility of pregnancy"), the addition of this factor to the chronic disaffection can change the "set" to a position favorable to risk-taking.

It is this process that we earlier called the "contextual" nature of costs and benefits underlining how they add up to work in tandem. The reader will recall, for example, the woman in Chapter Three, who first outlined the costs involved in getting a diaphragm to visit her husband in the National Guard, and then quickly volunteered that he has had a

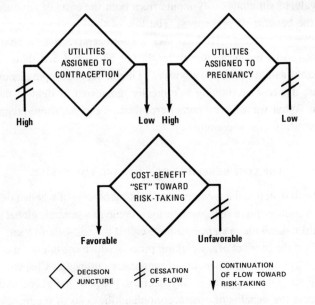

FIGURE 4. Arriving at a cost-benefit "set."

1. The utilities of contraception and pregnancy are assessed in the light of each other, until a cost-benefit "set" toward risk-taking emerges.

2. The lower the utilities assigned to contraception, the more likely a "set" favorable to risk-taking will emerge.

3. The higher the utilities assigned to pregnancy the more likely a "set" favorable to risk-taking will emerge.

4. Since the risk-taking "set" is a product of both the utilities assigned to contraception and the utilities assigned to pregnancy, a low utility assigned to contraception will be more likely to produce a favorable "set" when combined with a high utility assigned to pregnancy and vice versa.

Notation in Figures 4-9 is adapted from Gear, *Introduction to Computer Science,* and Raiffa, *Introductory Lectures on Choices under Uncertainty.*

child by a previous marriage which afforded his former wife considerable power over him; hence she herself suggested in the interview that she might have wanted to get pregnant in order to replace the other woman's power with hers. Virtually every woman in this study presented similarly interwoven patterns of costs to contraception and benefits to pregnancy which led to contraceptive risk-taking. Frequently these women did not identify these factors explicitly. One woman, for example, described why she couldn't go on the pill because she might gain weight, and then went on to say:

R: Ever since I met John, we've gone through an experience with his parents. They're very, very backward and prejudiced people. They're straight over from England. From the first time they ever met me, they've never accepted me because of my religion and nationality. . . . [At] first the biggest hangup was sneaking around and having to worry about that. Now it's the same thing. Before, they threatened not to help him get started in college or car insurance and things like that if he saw me. Now they've told him they'd completely disinherit him. . . . But in the long run, it's them who's going to be hurt more. When we get married and have grandchildren, they'll never see their grandchildren, nor their son either for that matter.

Thus the benefits accruing to pregnancy (it could make John admit openly his relationship with her, possibly force a marriage, and defy the discriminatory parents), when added to the costs attached to using contraception (gaining weight), make her cost accounting overwhelmingly favorable in the direction of not using contraception. As another example:

I: What contraception were you using when you got pregnant the first time?
R: Withdrawal and rhythm.
I: What was going on in your life when you got pregnant?
R: It was a very difficult time because my fellow was separated, not divorced. That summer his mother was discovered to have cancer and it was inoperable. So a divorce would have been very difficult at that time. So I told Frank I was pregnant and we decided to get an abortion.

After recounting the details of the particularly costly and traumatic

saline injection abortion which ended her first pregnancy, this woman
went on to say:

I: What contraception were you using this time?
R: Rhythm.
I: How did you decide on an abortion this time?
R: We felt monetarily that we couldn't get married right now. His
      father is elderly and my father isn't well, and Frank felt it would
      have been difficult. Not as difficult as last year, but difficult.

Both these abortions occurred within the space of a single year, and
serve once again to demonstrate the power of costs and benefits working
together. This woman has very powerful reasons for getting pregnant:
each time she does, marriage is discussed, although Frank seems to
have an endless supply of reasons as to why it is not a good solution to
the problem of the pregnancy. This woman was Catholic and had said
that her upbringing made it difficult for her to acknowledge herself as a
pill user and hence a sexually active woman; this cost of contraception,
when combined with the potent potential benefits of pregnancy, made
risk-taking more likely.

As a counterpoint to the cost-benefit "set" that favored further steps
toward risk-taking, women often gave examples from earlier in their
lives of how assigning low utilities to getting pregnant and high utilities
to using contraception can lead to a cost-benefit "set" that discourages
risk-taking:

R: Before, I didn't want a child at all, ever. It sounds weird. . . .
      I was *so* careful before—I went overboard. Guys used to think
      "you're so weird, you're so careful."

R: Before, I was always paranoid about getting pregnant. I'd
      always make sure the person was wearing a rubber or *some*
      kind of precaution. I used to think, "Sure, he'll marry me, but
      who will take my exams?"

R: I had a reluctance about using pills for the rest of my child-
      bearing, and then when my father died, it just became too
      much trouble to do it.

R: I never had any trouble with the pills before, but about the time
      we started not getting along, they started to not agree with me.

As these examples demonstrate, the most typical pattern in this study
is represented by women who have a relatively stable evaluation of their

contraception, who are not entirely happy with it, but who are unwilling to stop using it. When some event happens in their lives which makes the values of a pregnancy seem higher, this chronic dissatisfaction with the contraception, coupled with the new evaluation of pregnancy, shifts the cost-benefit "set" in the direction of risk-taking.

It is our contention, then, that what risk-taking women are constantly in the process of doing is tacitly bargaining with themselves (or to use Schelling's term more strictly, "tacitly coordinating" with themselves) to determine the costs and benefits of contraception, the costs and benefits of pregnancy, and the likelihood that pregnancy will occur. Thus a hypothetical tacit argument carried on intrapsychically could run: "Well, it's really a bother to get out of bed and put more jelly in the diaphragm and it's right before my period, so I probably won't get pregnant and if I do get pregnant maybe we can get married." Or alternately, "If I go on the pill, I might get blood clotting and who knows how serious this relationship is anyway, and chances are I won't get pregnant." (The implicit assumption here being that if she does, it is one way to test the commitment of the man involved.) Tacit coordination from a non-risk-taking stage might be: "I'm worried about the effects of the pill, but I really can't afford to get pregnant right now, so I'll have to live with my concerns."

Once women have reached a cost-benefit "set" favorable to risk-taking, at least two other decision junctures must be negotiated in order for risk-taking to occur (see Figure 5). At each of these junctures, women must assign values to the variable involved in that decision, much as they assigned utilities to contraception and pregnancy. Additionally, each juncture contains the possibility that a woman can evaluate the variable in such a way that she will make a decision bringing risk-taking to an end, at least for this particular exposure. To reiterate the obvious, we must note that women have literally thousands of exposures to intercourse over their lifetimes, all of which call for the renegotiation of the course diagrammed in the flow chart in Figure 5.

SUBJECTIVE PROBABILITIES OF PREGNANCY

The next decision juncture that potential risk-takers must face (once they have arrived at a cost-benefit "set" conducive to risk-taking) is

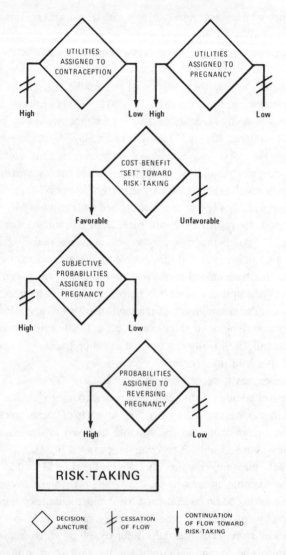

FIGURE 5. *Decision steps in the process of risk-taking.*

In order for risk-taking to occur, the decision maker must assign values at each of the decision junctures. Depending on which value she assigns at a given decision juncture, she either stops the flow toward risk-taking or continues it. For convenience, values are dichotomized, although empirically a wide range of values are observed. Each individual is assumed to have a threshold point where values are judged to be "too high" or "too low," thus the dichotomization.

deciding exactly how likely it is that they will actually become pregnant. (In the Figures we call this juncture "subjective probabilities assigned to pregnancy.") If women think it is relatively likely that they will become pregnant, they are less likely to continue moving through the decision process toward risk-taking than women who think that getting pregnant is a relatively unlikely event. Women risk-takers, then, "discount" the possibility that they will become pregnant, and assign low probabilities to the act of getting pregnant. They know it can happen, but for a variety of reasons, many of which are realistic, they think pregnancy is unlikely to happen to them: they "discount" the possibility.

"Discounting" as a social process explains why people in general engage in obviously bad risks. Smokers, for example, run a significant chance of one *very* high-cost risk—lung cancer—and a wide variety of other high-cost risks, such as heart disease and emphysema. It would seem, then, that this runs contrary to the argument that the higher the cost of "losing" the risk, the smaller the pool of risk-takers; after all, there are a significant number of smokers. But few if any smokers think that it will happen to them. Either they think they will be among those people who smoke and never suffer any of the consequences, or they dispute the evidence that smoking leads to negative consequences.

Similarly, women in this study thought "it could never happen to me."

I: Did you think you would get pregnant?
R: At first I just couldn't believe I was pregnant. It just doesn't happen to me.

I: Did you ever think about getting pregnant before this happened?
R: You never think it will happen to you. We didn't do anything to prevent it.

I: Did you or he think you might get pregnant?
R: He worried about it terribly, but I would just shrug and say, "It can't happen to us." I did say to him all this time, "We've lived on luck and I don't think one of us is fertile," and he said, "Don't take your chances." But I did.

Although other writers have concluded that this kind of thinking is "magical thinking" and hence immature,[3] there are several social factors that make it more reasonable. First, there is a time-related aspect to risk-taking, which we will explore below: the longer a risk-taker ''gets away with it'' the more likely risk-taking is to continue. Second, as previously noted, the chances of getting pregnant are not known to the women themselves: they know that the likelihood is somewhere between zero and one, but they have no way of assessing the likelihood in any one exposure or over the long run. Third and last, immediate costs are always more costly than long-term costs, especially when no one knows how likely it is that the long-term costs will in fact become due. Thus for risk-taking women, the immediate costs of contraception are more costly than the long-term costs of abortion, particularly when there is no certainty that an abortion will in fact become necessary.

As proof that so-called ''magical thinking'' is not restricted to contraceptive risk-takers, nor to women, there is a study which shows that over two-thirds of the cars on the road in America have a safety-related defect that could cause an accident.[4] People put off repairing these defects for financial reasons, the study reports, even though an accident caused by these defects will almost invariably be more expensive than the preventive costs. The drivers of these cars, then, are engaged in exactly the same kind of tacit bargaining as are risk-taking women. The costs attached to immediate repair of a car are known and expensive, whereas the costs attached to leaving the part unrepaired and having an accident are long-term and unknown, and there is always the chance that the driver can ''get away with'' not fixing the car.

What discounting represents, then, is an assessment of how likely pregnancy, or other accidents, are. Discounting means that the assessment is consciously lowered, because it is considered unlikely. When pregnancy occurs, however, it makes it clear to women that their particular assessment of likelihood was wrong:

I: Did you think it was likely you would get pregnant?
R: Yeah, but not as likely as it turned out to be.

When prior non-risk-taking contraceptive histories are examined, it becomes clear that risk-taking, for some women, hinges on the assigning of subjective probabilities to pregnancy. Even with a cost-benefit ''set'' favorable to risk-taking, their assumption that pregnancy was a likely occurrence was enough to stop the risk-taking decision making:

R: I took a health ed. class and they said you could only get pregnant during three or four days. I thought it was easier to get pregnant, and I was way more careful, until I took that health ed. class.

When women were asked to account for their previous patterns of effective contraception, they sometimes gave accounts like this one:

R: Well, mostly, I really thought it was easy to get pregnant. You know, if you kiss a boy you'll get pregnant. Then I didn't use the foam a couple of times and nothing happened, and I thought that I was too paranoid.

In other words, until the probabilities of pregnancy are assumed to be low, or are revised downward as a result of tentative risk-taking, risk-taking is less likely to occur.

Risk-taking over time. The process of becoming an unsuccessful risk-taker (that is, one who becomes pregnant) is even more complicated than we have suggested so far. Time, for example, has an effect on contraceptive risk-taking in two ways. First, it is important to remember that contraceptive risk-taking as diagrammed above is in fact a dynamic process, the end product of a decision chain that is constantly being reassessed in the light of new information. We cannot agree with writers who suggest that there are "successful contraceptors" and "unsuccessful contraceptors," and that these two types of people are differentiated by "future time perspectives," "emotional maturity," or psychological differences such as those which show up on standardized tests like the MMPI.[5] We would suggest instead that contraceptive risk-taking is a decision-making *process,* and one in which *all* women are engaged, although many women do not follow the process all the way to a risk-taking conclusion.

Eighty percent of the women who came to the Abortion Clinic were "successful contraceptors" at some point in their lives. Although we lack a control group of prospective risk-takers, it seems likely that women who are now "successful contraceptors" may well be women who have escaped the consequences of earlier risk-taking, or have not yet taken risks. Over the whole of a woman's sexual and reproductive career, the elements that work together to create contraceptive risk-taking are both so powerful and so prevalent in everyday life that we suspect few women will have reached the menopause without at least one incident of contraceptive risk-taking. In short, we suggest that all sexually active women are potential risk-takers.

What, then, separates those women who have taken a sufficient number of risks to become pregnant from those who have not? It appears that many factors are at work. First, classical decision-making theory has suggested that there are risk-taking "styles" among people: some people prefer the long chance, and others prefer the conservative approach of "little ventured, little lost."[6] This is probably as true of risk-taking women as of any other group of risk-takers. Second, there are biological differences in fertility among women: some women simply get pregnant more easily than others. It may, for example, be that women whose risk-taking ends in pregnancy are women who as a group are more fertile than those whose risk-taking does not. Third, the different social situations in which women find themselves produce different cost accountings, some of which make risk-taking far more likely and consistent than do others. Fourth and last, there is an element of randomness: in order to become pregnant during the time in which she is risk-taking, a woman must have sufficient exposures to a fertile male while she herself is biologically able to become pregnant.

Therefore we cannot accept the simplistic assumption that risk-takers are categorically different from non-risk-takers; becoming a risk-taker, and furthermore a risk-taker who becomes pregnant, is a complicated social process. Whereas the social situation sets up the background for who will and will not become a risk-taker, by providing the elements to be interwoven into a cost accounting, both time and random chance play a role in determining those women whose risk-taking ends in pregnancy. Some women have taken contraceptive risks for years without pregnancy, and some women become pregnant the first time they take a risk.

This leads to the second way in which time has an effect on contraceptive risk-taking. Although women discount the likelihood of pregnancy, they are not denying that it exists.

I: Did you ever think you might get pregnant?
R: Yeah.
I: How come?
R: Well, people usually do when they have intercourse. Most people usually do.

I: Did you think using the rhythm might fail?

R: I thought about it. You might say it was in the back of my mind all the time, but I never came to any final conclusion about what to do.

I: Were you surprised to get pregnant?

R: Not really, I wasn't really surprised.

I: Why is that?

R: Because we've just been having intercourse for so long I just expected to sooner or later. We never took any precautions.

As these statements show, some women anticipated pregnancy fatalistically. They also reflect the fact that pregnancy is a "risk" of unknown magnitude. It is always in the offing, but when and where it will happen and whether it will happen at all, is not known.

The unknown nature of the risk involved in using inconsistent or non-existent contraception therefore makes time a very salient factor. Although it is possible for a woman to "get caught" by the first risk she takes, so many factors are involved (her fertility, the fertility of the man, the timing of the intercourse, whether any contraception at all was used) that getting pregnant on the first attempt at risk-taking is a relatively rare happening: most women get pregnant after some extended period of taking risks.

Also, because of the biology of pregnancy, the consequences of risk-taking are rarely immediate. A woman can easily engage in two weeks of risk-taking before the consequences of the first attempt can be measured, assuming that the fertile period falls approximately in the middle of a 28-day cycle. Thus the risk of pregnancy is not only an uncertain one, it is to some extent a delayed one.

This creates a situation in which time, specifically the length of time involved in "getting away with it," becomes a condition for further risk-taking (see Figure 6). Many women originally assume that it is fairly easy to get pregnant, and thus undertake their first attempt at risk-taking cautiously. They either hedge their bets with some inconsistent contraception at what they consider their "unsafe" times, or they wait to see if they menstruate, thereby proving they are not pregnant. As risk-taking continues over time, however, women are increasingly likely to revise downward their assessment of the likelihood of pregnancy. They assume that "if it hasn't happened yet, it won't happen." They further assume, as a quote noted earlier demonstrates, that if they

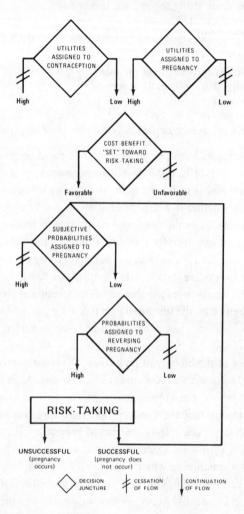

FIGURE 6 *The effects of time on risk-taking.*

Once successful risk-taking occurs, women reassess their subjective probabilities assigned to the occurrence of pregnancy. Note that this model demonstrates that such reassessing can occur in either direction: it can promote the risk-taking, if a woman decides on the basis of her experience to revise downward her expectations of the likelihood of pregnancy (discounting), or it can act to discontinue risk-taking if she uses her experience to decide that pregnancy is *more* likely than she had thought, and that only luck accounts for her escape this time.

have not gotten pregnant immediately, perhaps they or their partner are sterile.

I: Did you think it might be possible that you might get pregnant?
R: Yeah, but time went on . . . in the beginning I was kind of paranoid about it, but as time went on, I figured that proved it was O.K.

Two things happen as women take risks over time without immediate consequences. First, they tend to abandon the caution which marked their earlier attempts at risk-taking: they undertake multiple risks over a short period of time or they omit the contraception they were using during what they guessed (very unscientifically) to be their fertile period. Second, when women "get away with" risk-taking over time they do not assume that they simply have not hit upon the right time, place, and partner to get pregnant, but that not getting pregnant is something intrinsic to them. We have noted one aspect of this, which is that women begin to assume they are sterile. (The reader is reminded that over two-thirds of the women in this study reported some outside evidence from gynecological examinations to sustain this idea.) A second notion, less frequently cited, is that you have to want to get pregnant in order to do so—a psychological "mind over matter" (or mater) theory of pregnancy. Although there is some evidence in the literature that psychological states may affect fertility, it is unlikely that they do so to the extent which women sometimes think:

I: Did you think you might get pregnant?
R: I don't know. It was like it couldn't happen to me. It was like a psychological contraceptive I built up for myself. And I didn't get pregnant.
I: Could you tell me more about a "psychological contraceptive?"
R: It was like I couldn't handle it, I was still in high school, I wasn't sure I was in love with him, and so I built it up like there's no way I can get pregnant with all these reasons why I shouldn't.

Once women have defined not getting pregnant as something intrinsic to themselves rather than a product of the situation, the situation can change radically and women will continue to take risks:

I: Did you think you might get pregnant?
R: No, because I went for six months without taking pills and I didn't get pregnant.

I: Were you making love frequently?
R: During the first six months, no. During the last two months, yes, 'cause I moved in with my boy friend.
I: Did you think living with him might make it more likely you'd get pregnant?
R: Well, I didn't think about it. . . . Afterwards I did.

Another woman who had been prescribed female hormones to treat a non-reproductive condition continued to use the rhythm method even though a doctor told her husband the drug would probably make her more fertile.

I: Did you think about the effect it [the drug] might have on the timing of your cycle?
R: I didn't somehow take that into consideration, I was obviously in left field.

For women who are unable to see that the likelihood of getting pregnant is intrinsic to the situation and not necessarily intrinsic to them, continued risk-taking creates a "feedback loop" for further risk-taking. Each "successful" risk substantiates the idea that one can continue to "get away with it" indefinitely.

REVERSING A WRONG COST ACCOUNTING

The next decision juncture which potential risk-taking women are forced to negotiate is assessing the reversibility of a wrong decision: in other words, what the chances are that the decision flow can be reversed if it turns out that wrong assessments have been made at earlier points in the decision process (Figure 7). In this study, reversing the decision process empirically meant reversing the consequences of the process— in other words, "undoing" the pregnancy. For women in this study, then, the variable "probability of reversing the pregnancy" means how extensive a woman's knowledge is about the abortion situation. A woman who knows that abortions are available, that they are not terribly dangerous, and that medical plans or Medi-Cal (welfare) will pay for abortions is more likely to take a contraceptive risk than a woman who thinks that the consequences of risk-taking are either a dangerous illegal abortion, a shotgun wedding with an unwilling partner, or an out-of-wedlock pregnancy.

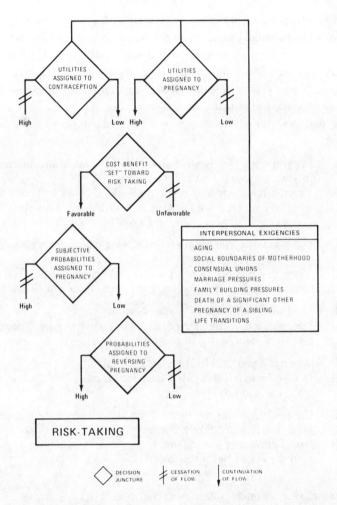

FIGURE 7. *The effect of social contingencies on the decision to take risks.*

Certain social and psychological events in a woman's life may act to make risk-taking more likely by bringing the cost-benefit "cost accounting" into more salience. Although the data in this study are not extensive enough to specify exactly how this "salience effect" occurs, we suggest that empirically it can occur in two ways. First, it can act directly by altering the utilities assigned to either contraception or pregnancy. Second, (although not diagrammed in this flow chart), certain of these interpersonal exigencies, particularly the time-related ones, can act to bring a latent cost-benefit "set" to prominence, and thus set the decision process into action. This second effect was relatively uncommon, but was reported.

The advent of readily available abortion in California has increased the pool of potential risk-takers, we would argue, by lowering the ante attached to making a wrong decision. Every woman interviewed in the study was well aware that abortion was legally and readily available (although many were ignorant of the real financial and social costs attached to it), and virtually all of them said or implied that they knew that the most serious consequence of risk-taking would be a legal abortion.

I: Do you think having an abortion available made any difference in your not using contraception?

R: Yeah, I think so. You don't really think about it. Like "Oh, wow, if I get pregnant I can get an abortion." But my sister had one a couple of years ago, so I knew.

I: Did you know you could get an abortion if anything went wrong (with the rhythm method)?

R: Yeah, that was one factor. I wasn't really thinking about it at the time, but it was a factor I knew I could draw out to solve it.

I: How did you decide to get an abortion?

R: I decided long before I ever found out I was pregnant. I decided that if I ever did get pregnant, I would get an abortion.

I: When did you decide to get an abortion?

R: It was funny. I knew if it ever happened to me I knew just what I would do.

I: Do you think having abortion available made a difference in your deciding to "take a chance"?

R: Um, I guess in a way maybe, but not that I would want to make a hobby out of having an abortion.

Almost every woman interviewed reported having a friend or an acquaintance who had had an abortion. (And 8 percent of our study population had personally undergone one abortion already.) The availability of abortion is not only an element in the larger social sphere of risk-taking women, but also a part of their immediate social experience. But since explicitly planning on abortion if anything goes wrong is considered both heartless and callous, the availability of abortion becomes another tacit part of the risk-taking equation: "If I use such and such a contraception, certain costs will result, but I probably won't get pregnant, and if I do, certain benefits might emerge; and if they don't, I can always get an abortion.'' Tacit coordination is therefore occurring at every point in the decision chain.

As a contrast to the patterns presented here for risk-takers, women who don't know whether or not they can reverse a pregnancy tend to be non-risk takers, at least as evidenced by the prior contraceptive histories of women in this study. In part, this is because the consequences of risk-taking (or rather the projected consequences) are taken into account in the decision-making process. In everyday life, people consider risks with possibly fatal outcomes more seriously than risks with relatively trivial outcomes. For women in this study, a lack of knowledge about the ability to reverse a pregnancy (knowledge about the availability of abortion) at an earlier point in a woman's history usually led her to avoid risk-taking:

R: I was really careful before, I guess because I thought I would end up in a home for unwed mothers.
I: Did anything change your mind about that?
R: Well, my sister had an abortion.

Probably because this particular decision juncture occurs at a relatively late point in the overall process, few women in this study presented a prior contraceptive history suggesting that this was the critical juncture for moving into or out of risk-taking. On the other hand, it is interesting to note that no less than nine young women interviewed in the course of this study reported getting pregnant immediately after completing a research paper on abortion for a school project. (This information was usually volunteered in the interview, in response to the question of how they came to be referred to this particular clinic.) The staff at the Abortion Clinic tended to see this as a psychodynamic factor, a preliminary ''acting out'' of conflicts which were later to find themselves expressed in a pregnancy. While this may well be true, it is equally possible that writing a term paper or report on abortion would supply a potential risk-taker at this juncture with more information for making a decision conducive to risk-taking.

In passing, we should note that an important social issue is raised by our contention that liberal abortion laws and practices give rise to more abortions. It would be easy as a result of this contention for critics of the current abortion situation to argue that the way to cut down on the incidence of abortion in California would be to restrict the availability of abortions. This would act to discourage women from taking risks with their contraception by raising the costs attached to such risk-taking. But it would also once again force individual women to pay the costs for a social decision. Since there will always be risk-takers, for reasons outlined in this study, it seems more rational for a society to tolerate a slightly greater number of potential risk-takers in order not to penalize women who have no workable alternatives to risk-taking, women whose interlocking networks of costs and benefits make risk-taking virtually inevitable. This is analogous to a social assumption made in jurisprudence. As pointed out by Thomas Scheff, the thinking behind the dictum "innocent until proven guilty" is that the social system, with its larger resources, can better tolerate an occasional wrong cost accounting that lets a guilty person go free, in contrast to the limited ability of individuals to tolerate a wrong cost accounting that detains them when they are innocent.[7]

RISK-TAKING AND THE SOCIAL MILIEU

Along with all the decision junctures outlined so far which a potential risk-taker must negotiate, there are many events in a woman's immediate social life which tend to make the decision process more salient and risk-taking more likely. In some cases, these events are added to the variables under consideration at each decision juncture; in other cases, they act to "draw out" a latent conflict and make it part of an overt decision. In this study, such events seem to fall into two categories: demographic and social.

Demographic events are those that concern a woman's ability to get pregnant and her movement into and out of categories socially defined as appropriate to pregnancy. As women move from one demographic category to another, the transitions themselves tend to evoke cost accounting: the imminent departure from a situation defined as appropriate for pregnancy is as likely to bring about risk-taking as is the imminent entry into such a category.

One of the most frequently cited demographic events that acted in this study to evoke risk-taking was the factor of aging: as women grow older, different pressures emerged to make contraceptive cost accounting more salient. In part, growing reproductively older is a biologically based phenomenon. While men can father children until late in life, the biological ability to become pregnant is time-bounded for women. In addition, women feel (and there is some scientific evidence to back them up) that fertility declines as they get older. Also, the medical risks to both mother and child are widely supposed to make child-bearing undesirably dangerous after the early thirties.

However, as is usually the case, these biological realities are used to build a social "definition of the situation" which is a step removed from the biology of reproduction. Until recently, the social norm in this country has been early marriage, early child-bearing and closely spaced children, and the ending of significant child-bearing before the age of 35.[8] Thus a woman approaching her late twenties who has not yet borne children faces both socially and medically oriented pressure to become pregnant. As noted, there is a biological base for the argument that women should have their children relatively early in life. In particular, certain syndromes, such as Down's syndrome (mongolism) have been classically demonstrated to be far more prevalent among the children of older mothers.[9] But the risk of late child-bearing has been emphasized chiefly because it is not in conformity to average American child-bearing patterns. For example, most of the data on the risks of late child-bearing have been collected in a time when few women engaged in late child-bearing, and hence those who did were a self-selected sample. Further, some of these data do not even distinguish between birth orders. A thirty-five year old woman delivering her tenth child is clearly a different epidemiological risk (and is most probably in a different social category) than a thirty-five year old woman delivering her first child. Finally, at the present time techniques do exist to minimize the risks attached to late child-bearing; amniocentisis (the drawing off of a sample of amniotic fluid) is possible (and recommended for older women) in order to determine whether or not gross chromosomal abnormalities exist.[10] If they do, a therapeutic abortion can be arranged and another pregnancy attempted.

Biological factors have therefore been used as support for the social assumption that earlier child-bearing is both desirable and appropriate. The same women who will not take contraceptive risks at twenty-two may begin to take them at twenty-nine. The benefits of pregnancy may be the same at the later age, but they are made more salient in her mind because of the assumption that if she doesn't get pregnant soon, she may never be able to do so. Again, this category of demographic events underlines the interactive nature of our theory of contraceptive risk-taking: if the combined effect of costs and benefits is powerful enough, even a twenty-two-year-old (or a sixteen-year-old) will take risks. Older women may well maintain an ambiguous but stable cost accounting over an extended period of time, until the demographic definition of themselves as "elderly" (gynecologists refer to any first-time mother over thirty, and sometimes over twenty-five, as an "elderly primipara") leads them to make a new cost accounting favorable to risk-taking.

A variation on the demographic theme of aging is the situation, reported several times in the interviews, in which a woman is aging past the social boundaries of motherhood. At least two women were prompted to take contraceptive risks by the departure of their youngest child to school. In other research, Blake has argued that the social role of motherhood is in practice so mutually exclusive of other roles that it is difficult for women to minimize their only effective social role by limiting child-bearing.[11] The number of women over thirty-five in both the study population and the interviews was too small to explore this idea extensively, but the data from the two interviews already noted make it clear that the imminent termination of the full-time mother role can act to bring cost accounting to the point where it becomes a causal factor in contraceptive risk-taking.

A second theme in demographic events that acts to present a cost accounting favorable to risk-taking is the changing nature of a woman's social relationship to her partner. In the next chapter we shall explore the more general nature of a woman's social relationship to her sexual partner, but here we are interested in the specific structures of that relationship: marriage, divorce, and consensual unions.

Recent Census data have suggested that an increasing number of people are living (or are willing to admit that they are living) with a member of the opposite sex.[12] Although little is known about the status and growth of consensual unions ("living together") it is clear that this is a current American phenomenon, and one well represented in the study population. (As we will see this is in part an artifact of the study population, because married women are far more likely to have a personal obstetrician to go to for an abortion.) Although stable monogamous unions without joint living arrangements were the most frequent sexual style reported in the study, consensual unions were the second most frequent: of the approximately 320 single women in the study, slightly less than a quarter (79) were living in consensual unions.

The frequency of consensual unions in this population is important, because these unions create their own pressures and conditions for contraceptive risk-taking. They act, for example, to create many of the same pressures for risk-taking as marriages do: much of the material below on marriage and risk-taking is equally applicable to consensual unions. In addition, women living in consensual unions have approximately the same rates of sexual exposure as do married women: when compared to women who are "dating," women in consensual unions have many more chances to take contraceptive risks. The conflict arises because while consensual unions resemble marriages in the risk-taking pressures they generate, they add special pressures of their own. As a beginning, it is important to note that consensual unions lack formal social support; thus there is a tendency to enter into them as if they were "trial marriages," according to the women interviewed. The ease with which consensual unions can be established and broken is one of their more attractive features to participants, but one which is a double-edged sword.

As we will argue in Chapter Six, women are at a disadvantage in the marriage market, and it is to their advantage to strike a marital bargain as early as possible. For a man, the later he makes his marital choice, the more likely he is to have greater bargaining power in his choice of mates. Thus the goals of the two sexes are diametrically opposed. At least for the women in this study, the consensual union, with its ease of creation and dissolution, can often begin to feel like a bad investment as time goes on. Particularly when there is joint ownership of furniture, cars, and checking accounts, women in the study began to feel after some period of time spent in consensual unions that they were not only being taken advantage of, but that they would be wasting the best years of their lives should the relationship not end in marriage. The pressure to test commitment and to force a declaration of intentions is an ideal precondition for contraceptive risk-taking.

Marriage, on the other hand, creates a separate group of pressures toward contraceptive risk-taking. In this era of widespread contraception, it is sometimes difficult to realize that for all practical purposes this generation is the first generation of families who have had to make a conscious decision to have children. Until quite recently, child-bearing, and especially the beginning of child-bearing, has been something over which little control has been exercised. It is true that Americans have long had a history of attempting to limit the ultimate size of their families, and more recently the timing and the spacing of births of their children. But it is only with the advent of widely distributed, effective contraception in the form of the pill that couples have had to consciously decide to stop contraception and engage in child-bearing. For the women in this study, and we suspect for women more generally, such a conscious, thought-out decision is an abrupt and sometimes difficult one to make. Tacit decisions, which do not require a critical examination of assumptions, are more easily made; a conscious, planned cost-benefit analysis of having a baby demands a more conscious and unambivalent commitment on the part of both husband and wife. In an earlier era, the tacit agreement not to use the diaphragm from time to time probably took less effort than is now needed to discontinue pill use. Contraceptive risk-taking within marriage may be a way of sidestepping the greater commitment needed to "cold-bloodedly" plan the stopping of contraception and the beginning of child-bearing. In particular, it is a way of testing the commitment of a husband who will not overtly agree to begin child-bearing, but who, it is hoped, will not suggest that the pregnancy be terminated once it occurs.

In many ways, then, the risk-taking of married women resembles that of unmarried women who are testing for the commitment of marriage. For married women, though, the commitment is to start building a family. Although control groups are lacking, we would suspect that just as some women successfully parlay contraceptive risk-taking into a marriage, other women successfully take contraceptive risks in order to begin building a family. In other words, for some women the contraceptive risk succeeds. Since the norms about the timing of a first child are flexible (as long as it is born more than nine months after the wedding), theoretically one would suspect that many more women successfully take risks in order to begin family building than in order to get married.

Of course, for all the married women in this study (and the unmarried women as well, of course) the risk-taking did not succeed. Once pregnant, the cost accounting of continuing the pregnancy became too high. Just as the unmarried woman often sought abortion because of what she considered to be the grudging and coerced nature of the offers of marriage from her partner, so married women in this study were deterred by the unenthusiastic response of the husband to the fact of the pregnancy.

I: How did you decide on an abortion?

R: Materially, financially, I should say. I don't think we're in a good situation right now. And my husband is of the old-fashioned cult that women should take care of the house and children, but he's not so old-fashioned that he thinks I shouldn't work. So I didn't want to be faced with the responsibility of taking care of all that just yet.

I: You thought it was your province to decide what to do?

R: Yes, I do, because the ultimate situation is that the woman—at least in our family—is responsible for the child. I guess in any family, ultimately, the woman is the closest. If the marriage dosn't work out, she has to take the children, that sort of thing. . . . My husband is more financially in tune than I am, and he was concerned about the financial aspect in respect to his job.

When the husband actively opposes or passively does not want a child, risk-taking is a way to determine whether the attitude is abstract, or whether it will be redefined in the presence of an actual pregnancy.

As another example of the social milieu leading to risk-taking, the impending prospect of a divorce (or of the breakup of a consensual union) is one of the more classic situations for contraceptive risk-taking, and one which has been noted, at least briefly, in popular literature. In many of the same ways that women take risks to gamble for marriage or the right to begin family building, risk-taking around divorce is a way of attempting to sustain the relationship. The gamble appears to be that with a pregnancy as an accomplished fact, a man will perhaps reassess his decision to leave. To a lesser extent, the pregnancy can act to sustain the relationship symbolically. This woman, whose partner had left for a year's study abroad, said:

R: I thought, if I'm pregnant and something happened to Jack, would I keep the child? I love him so much it would be nice to have his child, to have part of him with me always.

(When the man discovered the pregnancy in this case, he immediately flew home to rejoin his woman, and thus reassured, she reconsidered her decision to continue the pregnancy.)

For divorcing women there appears to be a pattern whereby a separation is effected, contraception is stopped (because "I won't need it anymore"), and a brief reconciliation with sexual involvement occurs, with pregnancy as the result. Like so much of risk-taking, this pattern appears to be a product of both costs and benefits working together: it is rational, as we have noted in Chapter Three, for a woman to discontinue contraception after the breakup of her marriage in order to demonstrate that she is not "looking for sex." In addition, the added benefit of testing how firmly committed the man is to a separation, by presenting him with a pregnancy, makes contraceptive risk-taking even more likely.

In addition to demographic events that predispose toward risk-taking, there exists a diverse group of social or "life events" which do not appear to be immediately connected with contraceptive risk-taking. Yet the women interviewed volunteered that these events were part of the overall gestalt of factors which helped make them become pregnant. Moreover, the same events were reported over and over again by different women. It is impossible here to state precisely how these events lead to risk-taking without some comparison of how frequently these events occur to other women, and whether they led to risk-taking in those cases. It could be that the "life events" which fall into this category are more directly concerned with the psychology of pregnancy than the sociology of it, and are hence beyond the scope of this study. Nevertheless, it may be useful here to present the dominant themes suggested by the respondents and make some guesses about their meaning.

The first theme in this group is the death of a significant other, in particular a parent. Occurring largely to older women (primarily because older women are more likely to have an elderly parent), the death of a significant other seemed to precipitate contraceptive risk-taking in every case in which it occurred. There is some suggestion in the psychoanalytic literature that a pregnancy in these circumstances is an attempt to replace the loss of a loved one. We would suggest in addition, however, that death in the family is a very disorganizing event, socially as well as psychologically. It may well be that the social turmoil of dealing with the death of a loved one makes life too complicated for some women to sustain their motivation to use contraception. Thus social factors may precipitate the risk-taking.

A second theme is the pregnancy, usually the problem pregnancy, involving a sibling, either brother or sister. Again, in every case where the woman reported the pregnancy of a sister or brother, contraceptive risk-taking followed within six months. What process this represents is not clear, however. One woman quoted in Chapter Four suggested that a pregnancy can be a plea for help and attention, analogous to a suicide attempt. It may be that in the family dynamic, the attention and concern that is focused on one pregnancy, particularly when it is a problem pregnancy, leads other siblings to try the same gambit for the same ends.

A third theme concerns life crises and times of transition. In this study, the most frequent transition reported as a prelude to risk-taking was graduation from either high school or college. This is probably due in part to the average age of the study population (which was twenty-two); these women were too young to have experienced many other transitions. Although it is only conjecture, it sems plausible to suggest that graduation implies an uncertainty about future role prospects, and thus a traditional role prospect such as marriage and a family may become more inviting at these times, making risk-taking more likely.

For much the same reasons, we suspect that the fourth theme mentioned in this category, that of vague dissatisfaction with a job or career, also leads to risk-taking. We will note in Chapter Six that as a group, women have relatively few alternate roles open to them. Thus when a chosen role or job turns out to be less satisfying than expected, it creates the same situation as an imminent role change, such as graduation from school. Again, motherhood and marriage begin to appear more inviting and more rewarding than the reality of a less than perfect job or career choice. Because contraceptive risk-taking is one way, at least in theory, to achieve both marriage and motherhood, it becomes more likely in the presence of an unsatisfying life situation.

RISK-TAKING AS A DYNAMIC PROCESS

We have already shown (Figure 6) how "successful" risk-taking (that which does not end in pregnancy) is fed back into the decision-making process as a way of reevaluating the probability of getting pregnant. Similarly, once a woman "gets away with" successful risk-taking, she must once again begin to evaluate her contraception, evaluate what a pregnancy would mean, evaluate how likely pregnancy is, and evaluate how reversible a pregnancy would be should it occur, all in the light of her previous experience. As Figure 8 demonstrates, successful risk-taking puts the risk-taker back at the beginning of the decision process, armed only with the information which has become available to her as a product of successful risk-taking. In this study, successful risk-taking only provided women with information that was ultimately faulty, by convincing them that all of their prior decisions were accurate. Only unsuccessful risk-taking (risk-taking ending in pregnancy) eventually provided them with accurate subjective information on the likelihood of pregnancy, and on the real costs of reversing a wrong cost accounting.

Thus an interesting problem is to account for the behavior of the women who were unsuccessful risk-takers at some earlier point in their lives, but who continued to take risks even after the first pregnancy— women like the one quoted earlier in this chapter,who, after a particularly traumatic and painful saline abortion, became pregnant a second time within the year with the same man and with the same dubious contraceptive method, the rhythm method.

Lest this one woman seem particularly "self-destructive," 10 percent of the five-hundred women in the study population had had a prior "problem pregnancy" (8 percent were abortions and 2 percent were out-of-wedlock pregnancies; for more details, see Appendix Two). And it is not unlikely that many of the women in the study who were having their first "problem pregnancy" will have subsequent problem pregnancies: Rovinsky and Margolis in a six- and twelve-month follow-up of abortion patients reported a 10 percent and 5 percent repeat abortion rate respectively.[13] In addition, fully a fifth of the women we studied left the Abortion Clinic without adequate contraceptive protection. Some did so because they came only for the abortion and skipped the follow-up appointment; but a significant number came to the follow-up

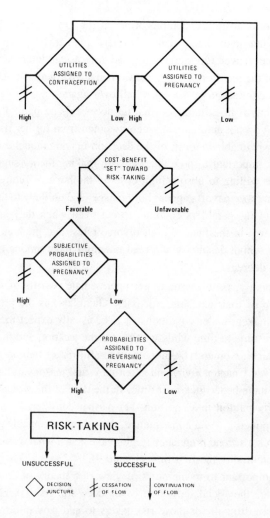

FIGURE 8. *Successful risk-taking and its effects on future decisions to take risks.*
Risk-taking is a dynamic process because women must constantly renegotiate the
decision whether or not to contracept. This flow chart diagrams the fact that women
who have taken a successful risk must face the decision process all over again armed
only with the fact that they have not gotten pregnant. This fact makes a decision
process favorable to risk-taking more likely to occur, since little new information is
available to challenge the previous decision process. In earlier parts of their contraceptive histories, however, women reported that risk-taking made them reconsider
more closely the utilities of contraception and pregnancy, and thus led to an un-
favorable "set" toward risk-taking.

meeting, only to refuse contraception on the grounds that they were never having intercourse again. Further, another 10 percent of the women interviewed reported having had unprotected intercourse within ten days of the abortion. Thus these women are particularly "at risk" of becoming contraceptive risk-takers all over again.

Surprising as this finding is, that unsuccessful and painful results of risk-taking do not automatically deter women from further risk-taking, it is still explainable in terms of the decision-making model used so far. First, it is important to note that decision-making theory suggests that people are willing to absorb high costs in the hope of future payoffs, even when those payoffs appear both meager and unlikely to the outside observer. Thus gamblers continue to bet even when they are losing, people marry in the face of high divorce rates, and graduate students remain in school despite widespread unemployment among holders of advanced degrees.

Additionally, people usually get intermediate payoffs of some kind as a result of their decision processes. Gamblers, as the prototype of decision makers under conditions of risk, usually expect to win small sums from time to time while waiting for the jackpot, and they usually do. Similarly, women who take unsuccessful risks often do gain some benefits (see Chapter Four) and often they find reasons to believe that they will have better luck next time. In the case of the woman with the particularly painful first abortion, her partner considered marriage but then postponed it. As a consequence, there were reasonable grounds to believe that a second pregnancy might make actual what was considered only a potentiality the first time (Figure 9).

Most important from the point of view of a theory of contraceptive risk-taking, the social definition of unsuccessful risk-takers makes it particularly difficult for those risk-takers to add new information into the decision process which would make risk-taking less likely. As noted early in this chapter, the general expectation is that women should have known at the beginning of the process information which in fact only becomes available at the end of the process. By definition, women who become pregnant as a result of risk-taking are women whom the society defines as having taken a "poor risk." There is a great deal of pressure, in consequence, for women to admit that their risk-taking was irrational in the light of the subsequent pregnancy.

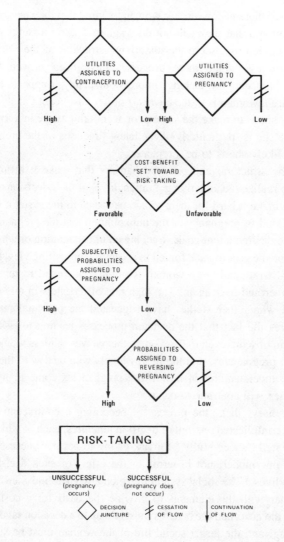

FIGURE 9. *Unsuccessful risk-taking and its effect on future decisions to take risks.*
Taking an unsuccessful risk does not necessarily end risk-taking: it merely provides
women with more information to negotiate the decision process. The fact of becoming
pregnant may well act to verify women's ideas about the utilities of pregnancy (even
though the pregnancy is ultimately terminated) and may serve to impress them with
the idea that a pregnancy is readily reversible. When either of these two ideas occur,
the model demonstrates that risk-taking is likely to continue.

Likewise, there is pressure for women to admit that they have learned their lesson and that they will not do it again. These pressures make it hard for women to discern the underlying structure of their decision-making process, since these processes have been proved wrong. Although hard data are lacking, impressionistically it appears that the more aware a woman is of the *elements* of her cost-benefit analysis, the less likely she is to make the same poor accounting twice in a row. The less aware she is, particularly of the latent functions of the pregnancy, the more likely she is to be a repeater.

Both the structural and personal barriers that make it difficult for women to realize the underlying "rationality" of their decisions to take risks also make it hard for them to add new data to the system, such as the likelihood of pregnancy or the unlikelihood that the pregnancy will lead to the desired latent goals. Lacking an understanding of why she is doing what she is doing and forced to accept the prevailing view that she is acting "irrationally," a woman is often condemned to repeat that process over and over again. The high rate of repeaters in this population, and what other studies have suggested are potential repeaters, underscores the fact that the decision processes leading to risk-taking can remain obscure even to the women themselves. Unless women with unwanted pregnancies, and the professionals who deal with them, can reach an understanding of how those pregnancies come about, such pregnancies will continue to occur.

In summary, then, the process of becoming a contraceptive risk-taker is a complicated one full of decision junctures, each of which must be negotiated "successfully" for risk-taking to occur. (Successfully in terms of our model, not in terms of the effect of such decisions on women's lives.) The social system in which a woman finds herself must present her with the elements to provide the basis for a cost-benefit analysis; the costs and the benefits must add up to a decision favorable to risk-taking; and the larger social life of the woman must be such that these elements are made significant and thrust into a dynamic decision process. Further, she must assume that the chances are unlikely that she will get pregnant, and likely that she can "undo" a pregnancy should it occur. In order for a woman to become a risk-taker whose risk-taking ends in pregnancy, the conditions are still more complicated, but as a rule she must take risks over a sufficient period of time; she must be fertile herself and must take risks with a man capable of impregnating her; and all these conditions must be present during the very short time of her ovulation.

If it were not for the fact that women are exposed to opportunities to take contraceptive risks literally thousands of times over their sexual careers, unwanted pregnancy would be a rare thing indeed. But the opportunities to become pregnant are many, and the conditions for risk-taking during those opportunities are both powerful and prevalent. Deciding whether to take a risk, then, is a significant part of the sexual life of women, and the chances for negative consequences are many. Until contraceptive risk-taking is more fully understood, particularly by risk-taking women themselves, unwanted pregnancies will continue to occur.

6

The Politics
of Pregnancy:
The Social and Cultural
Context of Contraceptive
Risk-Taking

Up to this point, the argument that contraceptive risk-taking has its origins in social factors—although it admittedly has important psychological and physiological components as well—has been explored by examining the immediate social world of the risk-takers in this study, all of whom found themselves with pregnancies that they eventually terminated. In this argument so far, the social pressures toward pregnancy and against contraception have been examined in some detail, and we have shown how the constellation of social pressures for any individual woman could make contraceptive risk-taking a "rational" decision, at least in the strictly technical sense of the word "rational" as used in Chapter Two.

Now, however, it is important to consider the broader social context of contraceptive risk-taking—the political, economic, and macro-social milieu in which risk-taking occurs. Since we have argued that individual women find themselves caught between the costs of contraception and the benefits of pregnancy, it is important to remember that there have been important changes in the social meanings of both these phenomena in the past few years. At this time, effective contraception is significantly available to major portions of the female population; the option of therapeutic abortion is legally, although not always consistently, available as a result of recent Supreme Court decisions; women are beginning to postpone the birth of their first child; and there is evidence that the total number of children they intend to bear is decreasing.[1] These social changes surrounding pregnancy and contraception, however, have been so rapid and so pervasive that they are rarely thought of as problematic—they are just "the way things are." In this chapter we shall argue, on the contrary, that this is not "the way things are" but rather the way things have become, and that this process of becoming has been so sudden and so total that customs are still in transition and important areas of culture lag exist. These areas of culture lag represent places where normative values do not reflect current technological reality, where modern technology has outdated social patterns developed in congruence with an older technology, and where ideologies have anticipated social and cultural change. They are all important parts of the macro-social world in which risk-taking occurs.

As an anticipation of the argument that will be more fully developed in this chapter, it must be noted that recent years have seen significant changes not only in the technology of contraception and the availability of abortion, but in the ideology surrounding sexual intercourse and the "exchange system" of courtship, as well as in the status of women. All of these social and technological changes, it will be argued, have an impact on contraceptive risk-taking. When these changes are rapid and multiple, as they have been, they tend to increase risk-taking by creating "problems of transition" as people try to assimilate these changes into their personal and social lives.

The model of argument used here is one which sociologists would consider neither narrowly Marxian nor narrowly Weberian. Although we shall argue that changes in the technological aspects of American life have had real and as yet undealt with effects on norms and values, we shall also argue that changes in norms and values have consequences for technology as well. Thus this line of argument is closer to what Walter Buckley has called a "cybernetic" argument, in that there are independent sources of causality in both the "infrastructure" and the "suprastructure" that work in feedback loops to sustain and advance social change in both spheres.[a] Thus a change in technology can have an impact on ideology, which can then have a reciprocal impact on technological development, and so on ad infinitum. It is precisely because these changes are neither predictable nor exact that problems of transition occur, and we shall argue that it is the unanticipated spinoffs of interactive technological and social change that lead women—at least at the macro-level—to take contraceptive risks. In other words, contra-

a. Walter Buckley, *Sociology and Modern Systems Theory* (Englewood Cliffs, New Jersey: Prentice-Hall, 1967). Note that the present model does *not* presuppose a return to the status quo ante. In this sense, it is a dialectical model.

ceptive risk-taking is not only "rational" at the level of the individual woman, but can also be explained as a product of changes in the larger social context in which women are operating.

These changes in the larger social structure that affect contraceptive risk-taking occur most prominently in three major areas—changes in the role of courtship in the United States, changes in contraceptive technology over the last two decades, and changes in male and female definitions of accountability and responsibility in the sexual and reproductive spheres.

THE ROLE OF COURTSHIP

With respect to the first area, there is reason to believe that changes in the American pattern of courtship over the last decade have been extraordinarily pervasive and dramatic.

Traditional literature in the field of marriage and the family has frequently viewed courtship as a paradigm of exchange theory.[2] This view focuses on the bargaining efforts of the two parties as they endeavor to make the best "deal" for themselves vis-à-vis a mate. Potential earning power, physical attractiveness, prestige, and status are all variables which in combination make individuals better or worse "catches" in the marriage market.[3] Depending on the sex of the bargainer and the society in which the courtship is occurring, these variables will have greater or lesser weight in determining the "worth" of the potential mate. Physical attractiveness, for example, has traditionally been more highly valued in women than in men in this country.

However, whatever the "worth" of the eventual marital partner, both parties in a traditional exchange paradigm of courtship stand to gain. A successful courtship (one ending in marriage) brings with it more than a "good" partner; it also brings, for example, the right to have sanctioned sexual intercourse, to enjoy a more efficient division of labor, and to bear and raise children. These are powerful inducements to engage in courtship, and most people do.

Recent social change, however, has altered the balance of payoffs that marriage makes available to men and women. Most important to contraceptive risk-taking, it has altered them in different directions for the two sexes. The three general rewards that both men and women could expect from marriage—sanctioned sexuality, a more efficient division of labor, and the right to bear and raise children—are becoming relatively less valuable inducements to marriage, but in different ways for men and women. For example, the more efficient division of labor that a marriage can provide has been made largely irrelevant by the increasing specialization of the American economy. Whereas in a less developed society it makes more economic sense for the male to provide primary support for the family (either by hunting, agriculture, or income earnings) and a wife to specialize in the multitude of tasks necessary to support the family as an on-going unit (family maintenance), in developed economies such role specialization becomes increasingly superfluous.

In the United States, as in most developed societies, virtually all of the traditional roles of the wife in family maintenance can be "boarded out" to specialized sectors of the economy, such as laundries, super-markets, clothing stores, and even cleaning agencies.[4] Although it is true that the "boarding out" of these functions has been paralleled by expanded demands on the *quality* of wifely roles (although few women grow and can their own vegetables, they are increasingly expected to be gourmet cooks),[5] these expanded demands have less to do with survival than with the quality of life, and hence are more expendable.

As we shall see below, current disparities in earned income make "boarding out" more functional for men; men can afford to "board out" cooking and cleaning to specialized agencies, but women cannot board out the higher income-earning power that husbands have.

Concurrently, there is at present a devaluation of child-bearing and child-rearing as a necessary inducement to marriage. Whereas there was a remarkable consensus on desirability of the three-child family in the years just after the Second World War, there is today a significant trend in opinion toward preferring a smaller family, perhaps in response to the widely popularized problems of overpopulation.[b] Although opinions are only one part of the variety of social and personal pressures that go

---

b. "The proportion of Americans who favor large families has declined dramatically and is now at the lowest point in the 37 years that regular surveys on the subject have been conducted." Roper Public Opinion Research Center, *Current Opinion*, Vol. 1, Issue 4 (April 1973), p. 38 (data from The Gallup Poll, January 1973).

into child-bearing, such a dramatic change in opinions represents a significant lessening of the culture-wide pressures to become parents. As Alice Rossi has said recently, "the cultural lid is off."[6] This lessening of pressure, as reflected in public opinion polls, also lessens the value of marriage as a vehicle for child-bearing. Once again, women and men experience this devaluation differently. Women have fewer socially approved roles open to them as an alternative to child-bearing when compared to men; also, should a woman decide to have a child without the benefit of marriage, she is likely to be faced with normative pressure to raise the child herself. The social, legal, and normative pressures to make a man maintain the father role are remarkably less powerful than those that force a woman to maintain the role of mother.[c]

It is in the area of sanctioned sexuality that women suffer the most dramatic loss of bargaining power in courtship. Under the traditional taboos surrounding intercourse for the first half of this century, sanctioned sexual expression was a scarce commodity and one which was a powerful inducement to marriage. In general, we would argue, the stricter the norms against premarital intercourse, the more valuable sex becomes as a currency of bargaining in the marriage market. In a system like that of Western Europe and America, where men traditionally initiated sexual approaches and women had the responsibility of controlling those approaches, the ability to grant sexual favors has been a powerful bargaining item for women.

In recent years there is increasing evidence of the fact that premarital intercourse for women is becoming both more frequent and more normatively acceptable.[7] These two changes, which have led observers to speak of a "sexual revolution," make it less possible for women to bargain for marriage sexually. First, withholding the promise of sexual fulfillment as an inducement to marriage has been devalued ideologically, since such an act would be both old-fashioned and unliberated. Second, withholding sexual favors is pragmatically less feasible, owing to the changes in the frequency of premarital intercourse in the society as

---

c. Weitzman has found, for example, that only a small percentage of fathers continue to make child-support payments after the divorce. See Weitzman, L., "Legal Regulation of the Marital Contract, Tradition and Change: A Proposal for Contracts in Lieu of Marriage," *California Law Review* (June 1974).

a whole. If almost half of the 19-year-olds in the United States have already engaged in premarital intercourse (as a recent study suggests), the ability of any one woman to bargain sexually is compromised by the general availability of non-marital sex in the market: bargaining flourishes only when the commodity is scarce.

Parenthetically, it is of minor importance whether or not the "sexual revolution" is primarily one of norms or of behavior; the net effect on female bargaining power is still the same. Even if sexual behavior has not changed markedly since 1920, as James McCary asserts,[8] a culture that normatively taboos premarital intercourse creates deviants who are unlikely to compare notes because of normative pressures. Thus they are likely to live in a condition of pluralistic ignorance, where each couple knows itself to be deviant but assumes it is the only one. The net result is to maintain the ideology that sanctioned sexuality is available only in marriage and thus maintain the bargaining power of withholding sex until marriage or until the commitment to marriage (engagement) is made. (Note in this context that almost half of the women with premarital sexual experience in the 1953 Kinsey studies subsequently married the man with whom they had had intercourse, and three quarters of these women did so within a year after beginning their sexual relationship.)[9]

This threefold loss of bargaining power for women in each of the functional inducements to marriage is of consequence in a study of contraceptive risk-taking because marriage has different values, both economically and non-economically, for women than it does for men. In folklore and joking behavior, for example, it is popularly assumed that the male is trapped, fooled, or seduced into marriage, thus suggesting that marriage is an institution primarily benefiting women. This popular view is not unknown in traditional anthropological thinking, which has tended to see marriage as a social institution which by either positive or negative sanctions induces the male to involve himself in the biological unit of mother and helpless child.[10]

That the view of marriage as a primary benefit to women is not entirely accurate in its reflection of social reality is suggested by the fact that married men do better than unmarried men on almost every index, be it demographic, psychological, or social.[11] They have better health, they live longer, their mental health is better, and they are less likely by half to commit suicide. Equally important, married men do better in several ways than married women: men report more marital satisfaction than women do, fewer men than women have considered divorces, married men have fewer psychological problems than married women, and should mental illness occur, married men are more likely to recover than women.[12] That these differences are the product of the differential effects of marriage, and not merely of gender, is demonstrated by the fact that single women not only do better than married women on these measurements, they also do better than married men.[13] Thus statistically at least, marriage is an institution which, to reverse Disraeli's famous dictum, every man should engage in and no woman.

Perhaps the contradiction between the evidence that marriage is statistically more functional for men than for women, and the common assumption that women are more eager to marry than men are, is explained by the fact that women are more dependent upon marriage in a variety of ways than men, at least during this transitional period in our history.

As one example of women's relatively larger dependence on marriage, full-time women workers in 1968 earned 58 percent of the income of full-time male workers.[14] Moreover, the income differential actually increased between 1958 and 1968.[15] When education is held constant, women still earn less than men: a woman with one year of graduate education earns just slightly above the national average income (106 percent of the 1968 average income) whereas a man with a year of graduate education earns almost twice that figure (188 percent of the national average).[16] (All figures are for full-time, year-round workers.) In the field of academic sociology in 1968, full-time women sociologists could expect a $3,000 a year differential between their incomes and those of their male peers.[17] As a result, marriage for women represents a significant upgrading of the standard of living available to them. Because of these income discrepancies, it makes more sense economically for women to marry than to work. If a woman can both marry and work, she stands to gain even more. Generally speaking, however, men stand to gain far less economically by marrying, since even a working wife has a great disadvantage in the income market. (There are exceptions, of course: the current Census suggests that it is precisely by marrying working wives that younger black males can enter the middle class.)[18]

Related to this is the fact that women are severely underrepresented in all of the major professions: they comprise 6 percent of the doctors in the United States, 3 percent of the lawyers, 22 percent of the academics, and 6.3 percent of upper-echelon business executives.[19] And even these women tend to be disproportionately clustered in the less well paying and prestigeful ranks of their chosen professions.[20] As a group, women are likely to be found exclusively in "female typed" jobs (jobs where over 70 percent of the occupants are female) that are perhaps not coincidentally of lesser status and lower pay than "male typed" jobs.[21] Edward Gross constructed an index of sex segregation in jobs (borrowing from the Blau and Duncan measures of racial segregation) and found not only that two-thirds of the employed women (or men) would have to change jobs in order to achieve a sexual balance in job distribution, but that this level of job segregation had not changed significantly since 1900. When this measure was controlled for changes in the occupational structure since 1900, the measure of segregation dipped slightly, but almost all of the drop was accounted for by men going into female typed jobs, as for example, men becoming nurses.[22]

This occupational discrimination has two consequences. First, it contributes to the income differential noted above, which makes marriage more functional for women than for men. Equally important, however, it restricts women to the less challenging and less interesting jobs, and to those which have the fewest chances for advancement. Thus the socially rewarded alternatives to marriage are limited for women. In terms of role gratifications, the most socially available avenue to a rewarding career still appears to be marriage—particularly when marriage can be combined with a job (as opposed to a career).

As a result of both these factors (income discrimination and limited role alternatives) women place a great deal of emphasis on marriage and family as an important component of self-identity. As part of the interview schedule, women in the study population were asked an open-ended question: "When you were a little girl what were your fantasies about what it would be like to be a grown-up?" It is striking to note how often their answers focused almost *exclusively* on fantasies about marriage and family. The argument we have developed to this point suggests that this focusing is not, as psychological literature would have it, a focusing on marriage and family as a result of inadequate ego structure, but rather the psychological reflection of a social reality. Women in this study, like women in the larger society, narrow their "fantasized realities" to marriage and family because there are few effective and visible alternatives open to them.[23]

I: What were your fantasies when you were a little girl about what being grown up would be like?

R: I suppose like any other kid—be married and have a family and be happy—I guess all little girls have that.

R: To grow up, get married, and have children . . . find a handsome guy and stuff like that.

R: I used to have fantasies about when I get married I'd have a big church wedding and live happily ever after.

R: I really didn't see myself as married with kids and neither could anyone who knew me—they always said they could never see me with a bunch of kids—but I could see myself with *some* kids. I've never seen myself as very career-minded. I've always seen myself as married, with a station in life, and the "good life." I've kind of seen myself as being married to an executive type person in a lovely home, entertaining a lot and one or two children and money enough to travel, like to Switzerland to ski. I mean, who wouldn't like a life like that?

These themes were repeated throughout the interviews. Few women saw themselves as "very career-minded," and even those who did were not able to actualize that reality in a fulfilling way. The following young woman, whose father was a surgeon, typifies the downgrading of expectations and the consequent depreciation of social roles that often occur to women and that seem to emphasize marriage as the only acceptable role for achievement:

I: One question I've been asking people is what they thought being grown up would be like when they were little . . . what your fantasies were.

R: I guess I wasn't the typical little girl. I wasn't interested in Girl Scouts or things like that. I was pointed toward the medical profession because of my father. You know little girls and fathers— they think fathers are the greatest thing in the world. Other than playing doctor and nurse, I didn't have any fantasies.

I: You said you were going back to school. Are you going into
      pre-med?
R: Laboratory technician.
I: You've decided against being a doctor?
R: Yes, I guess the schooling—the years and years of it. That's
      mainly it. My father's convinced me that laboratory technician is
      the thing to do.

Thus this woman (who was preparing to marry within the year, by the
way) illustrated pointedly the situation that women face: laboratory tech-
nicians are more likely to feel the need for additional sources of prestige
and income than surgeons are, and marriage is a viable way to achieve
them. However, this creates a dilemma. Women are dependent upon
marriage as a source of the "good life" and "a station in life," as well as
for income and role satisfactions, but they have fewer resources with
which to bargain for it because of the social changes noted earlier in this
chapter—the decline in the value of child-bearing, the increased availability of "wifely" goods and services in more specialized sectors of the
service economy, and the increased availability of sexual intercourse outside of marriage. In the open market of contemporary courtship, therefore, women as a class are bargaining with a deflated currency.

A further complication is that for women, unlike men, there is an
advantage to striking a bargain as soon as possible, because they largely
bargain with ascribed characteristics (beauty, youthfulness, "sexiness")
while men bargain with achieved characteristics (power, income, prestige). Thus women's potential depreciates over time; they get older, less
beautiful, and less sexually attractive with the passage of years. Men, on
the other hand, get richer, more powerful, and have more status with the
passage of time—or it is assumed that they might. As a consequence, the
time variables structuring the bargaining of the two sexes run in opposite
directions.

The "option squeeze" that women currently face, as marriage
becomes a less viable option (8 percent fewer women aged twenty to
twenty-four are married now than were married a decade ago)[24] and other
alternatives are only slowly becoming open to them, creates a pressure to
take contraceptive risks. This "option squeeze" has a built-in time lag,
owing to the amount of time needed to prepare for the prestigious and

well-paying jobs (even if medical schools began to admit a 50 percent female class this year, for example, it would still be an average of eight years before there was a significant change in the number of women doctors); and this time lag creates a transitional period in which women are likely to feel the loss of traditional options before the real availability of new options becomes an accomplished fact. One way to deal with this transition period is to find new ways of achieving the traditional options, ways such as contraceptive risk-taking. This is not to suggest that because women are at a competitive disadvantage in the marriage market they then go out and become pregnant in order to get married; few women are that calculating or that naive. On the contrary, it suggests that when women are at a competitive disadvantage, contraceptive risk-taking has a socially induced halo of functionality surrounding it, a halo of which women are often only subliminally aware.

It might be asked how contraceptive risk-taking in a depressed marriage market differs from the traditional folklore notion that women routinely get pregnant in order to bargain for marriage. We propose that the current situation is different in two ways. First, although it may well be true that the individual woman in the past who felt herself to be at a particular disadvantage in the "dating and rating" market[25] may have turned to pregnancy as a technique for achieving marriage (there is no hard empirical evidence to support this, of course), we are now arguing that women as a group suffer from competitive disadvantages, whatever their personal "mate value," and thus the pool of potential risk-takers has increased astronomically. Second, as we have pointed out in Chapter Four, risk-taking as a marriage gambit is no longer a zero-sum game: whereas in the past women were faced with the options of either marriage or an illegitimate pregnancy should the gambit fail, today the easy availability of therapeutic abortion means that risk-taking which ends in pregnancy can be fairly easily reversed, should the hoped-for marriage not occur. In brief, contraceptive risk-taking as a gamble for marriage is not a high-risk gamble. Should it fail, the costs are relatively low.

(In describing the structural pressures on women to take risks, we run the risk of making the reaction to these pressures appear overrationalized and thought out. Once again it must be emphasized that these are complex and interwoven pressures in the social sphere that may be necessary but not sufficient causes for risk-taking. What typically happens is that a woman finds herself in one of the situations conducive to risk-taking outlined in Chapter Four, and then feels more vulnerable to the social effects of the macro-pressures that we have been describing.)

That all of the women in this study decided to terminate a pregnancy with an induced abortion rather than opting for marriage reflects the work of three factors. First, almost all the unmarried risk-takers in this study had the option of marriage: only three men deserted the woman upon learning of the pregnancy, thus repudiating their responsibility. But since the women were tacitly bargaining (in Schelling's sense of the word) for real commitment,[26] the half-hearted and coerced commitment that they were usually offered led them to choose abortion. They preferred to bargain for a genuine commitment from a man in the future, rather than a technical commitment in the present. As one woman said, "I didn't want to spend the rest of my life with a man who would tell me every time he got mad, 'I only married you 'cause I had to'." Second, the fantasies that many women had of marriage—of beautiful church weddings, romantic bridegrooms, and happily everafters—were usually either informally or structurally denied the premaritally pregnant women, only in part because of the coerced nature of the masculine commitment. Much of the ritual surrounding weddings is considered inappropriate for pregnant brides, for example, and all of the women in the study realized, once they were pregnant, that a woman who "has to get married" generally loses status. The implication is that she could not attract a marriage offer on her own merit but rather had to force a commitment. She is, to use the market analogy implied in the exchange theory of courtship, "distressed merchandise" and her value as a wife is in serious question.

Lastly, and this brings us to what we have argued is the second macro-social influence on contraceptive risk-taking, the technology of current forms of contraception has so radically changed the accepted definitions of male and female accountability that women lack social support to compel a man to take responsibility for a pregnancy that he has helped to cause. We shall argue that in direct contrast to the past, when social custom pressured men to "make honest women" out of the women they had impregnated, our present contraceptive technology has increasingly created an ideology that says an unwanted pregnancy is the woman's fault.

CHANGES IN CONTRACEPTIVE TECHNOLOGY

It is startling to realize that only slightly over a decade ago the most common contraceptive in the United States was the condom.[27] The overwhelming reliance on the pill (and to a far lesser extent on the IUD) is a product of only the last few years.[28] What is striking about the rapidity of this change in contraceptive patterns is not only its pervasiveness, but its totality: the erstwhile preeminence of the condom is largely a forgotten fact in the popular culture.

Reliance upon the pill as the most effective contraceptive ever used also shows up in the study population: 20 percent of the 15- to 19-year-olds, 60 percent of the 20- to 24-year-olds, 80 percent of the 25- to 29-year-olds, 65 percent of the 30- to 35-year-olds, and 60 percent of the over 35's used the pill as their most effective method of contraception. Presuming a strict cross-sectional analysis, the curve of the trend is surprising: why should women over thirty be less likely to use the pill than women twenty-five and older? In the cohorts prior to the over 30's, pill use increases dramatically with age. Older women, it is clear, represent a departure from the pattern, which underscores the fact that heavy reliance on the pill is a practice of comparatively recent origin. Older women show lower rates of pill use because as a group they have chosen, and stayed with, another method of contraception.

The massive shift in contraceptive practice from a variety of methods to a heavy concentration on the pill has unexpected social consequences for contraceptive risk-taking. It is important to remember that the condom, the most common American contraceptive until recently, is a male contraceptive. (Parenthetically, the demand that someone should invent a male contraceptive shows how total the attitudinal and technological changes have been.) In fact, all of the common methods of contraception in pre-pill days were to some extent "male" contraceptives (although technically it would perhaps be wiser to call them "couple contraceptives" that call for varying degrees of male participation). This is primarily because virtually all contraceptives prior to the pill were intercourse-related. Admittedly, some methods, such as the diaphragm, call for relatively lesser degrees of male participation and some call for relatively more, as for example withdrawal. But since all are used within the context of sexual intercourse, there is an invariant threshold at which the male must acknowledge their presence and involve himself more or less directly in the decision to contracept.

With the advent of the pill (and again to a lesser extent with the IUD), this situation changed dramatically. Not only are both these methods used outside the context of intercourse (the pill is typically taken either first thing in the morning or last thing at night, and the IUD is inserted by a physician once and presumably for all), but they are both exclusively female-oriented methods, and male participation is reduced to a minimum. There is some indication that this was a deliberate decision at the technological level: early references in the scientific literature on contraceptive research present the unchallenged research decision that the bulk of research should go toward female contraceptives which were not intercourse-related.[29] The reasoning behind this decision was that only women are motivated to contracept because only women get pregnant, and that women's motivation tends to be higher and more committed outside of the emotionally charged context of intercourse.

Such reasoning is a classic example of what we have argued earlier is a "cybernetic" social system in microcosm. To assume that only women are motivated to use contraception because only women get pregnant is to confuse value judgement with scientific fact. Biologically both men and women become pregnant—immaculate conceptions are virtually unknown in the literature. More importantly, the definition as to who gets pregnant—that is, who bears the responsibility of a pregnancy—is a social product: when examined cross-culturally there is a wide variation in the assessment of the responsibilities for pregnancy. In some cultures, for example, the male parent is involved in the pregnancy to the extent of having sympathetic labor pains. (Anthropologically inclined readers will recognize this as an institutionalized custom of the "couvade.")[30] In other societies, members of the community remark upon a man's youthfulness, if he is the father of many children.[31] Lest one think that variations in male responsibility are only a product of primitive and pre-literate societies, consider the recent French Supreme Court decision which holds that *any* man who has intercourse with a woman during her probable time of conception is legally the father (and if there are several men who fit this definition, they are assigned to share social and financial responsibility for the child).[32] Thus who gets pregnant is a social and not a biological question, and it is the most unsophisticated form of biological determinism for scientific researchers to implement social custom as if it were scientific fact.

The contraceptive products that came out of these research assumptions about female responsibility and motivation then began to make those very assumptions come alive. Hence the cybernetic effect: value judgements about the nature of social reality influence research, which creates a specific technology, which then institutionalizes and furthers the value judgements. In the present case, the development of highly effective contraception which was uniquely female and non-intercourse-related had a variety of effects. First, since the statistical effectiveness of the new methods was higher than the older "couple" or "male" methods, there developed a pressure for women to use the newer methods lest they be thought of as old-fashioned or deliberately foolhardy. Second, also because of this improved statistical effectiveness, doctors were reluctant to prescribe or approve of the methods that subsequently began to be known as the "less effective" methods. Effectiveness, however, as we have noted in Chapter Two, is not a one-dimensional problem. There are statistical problems with it: Judith Blake has pointed out that the "use effectiveness" statistics of the older methods were typically collected in family planning clinics, thus selecting for a population more likely to have had problems—notably an unwanted pregnancy—with their chosen method of contraception.[33] And there are problems of definition with the concept of "effectiveness" as well: a high proportion of women "drop out" of pill use within the first year of use.[34] Thus effectiveness in the laboratory cannot be confused with effectiveness in real life; clearly, a method that large numbers of people fail to use in real life cannot be very "effective" no matter what its laboratory effectiveness is.

CHANGES IN THE SOCIAL DEFINITION OF
CONTRACEPTIVE ACCOUNTABILITY AND RESPONSIBILITY

The value judgements surrounding the invention and popularization of the pill and the IUD are of interest because their unexpected "spinoffs" have had an effect on contraceptive risk-taking; the popular and medical rush to the pill as a contraceptive method has solidified certain notions about the social context of contraception. Since the female methods represented by the pill and the IUD are statistically (and in the popular mind actually) more effective than the older methods, it follows that contraception by people who seriously wish to avoid a pregnancy is increasingly defined as female. Few couples will premeditatedly risk the use of a male method such as the condom, or couple methods such as foam, because they perceive these methods to be radically inferior for preventing pregnancy. Since real effectiveness is perceived both medically and popularly as a property of exclusively female methods only, contraceptive responsibility is accordingly viewed as exclusively female.

Of equal importance, however, is the fact that contraceptive *accountability* has become exclusively female as well. In other words, it is not only the women's task to take care of contraception in any given relationship or encounter, it is also her fault when anything goes wrong, such as a pregnancy. Once again, the cybernetic effect: the development of the pill and the IUD rested on the assumption that men were too irresponsible and too unmotivated to use contraceptives, and the development of the pill and the IUD and its subsequent social impact make that assumption true, whether or not it had been so before.

Changing social definitions of contraceptive accountability and responsibility also have consequences for contraceptive risk-taking: women resent the socially induced burden of unshared responsibility for an act that is of obvious benefit to both parties. The structural situation, as we have noted, "sets up" a man to be detached and noncommitted to this vital part of the sexual relationship, and women often feel not that they have "control over their own bodies" but that they are being used. When asked why she did not use contraception, this young woman stated forcefully what many of the women in the study said in one way or another:

R: All the other times when I did care [about contraception], when I was so afraid, I didn't get any satisfaction out of it at all, even during the whole intercourse. It seemed so one-way. Here I'm so wrapped up in being scared and he's getting the good end of it. He's not really worrying about what's going to happen to you. He's only worrying about himself. This time I think what I really thought was if you don't think about it, maybe you'll get something out of it. So I guessed it wouldn't be a hassle, I wouldn't worry about it. And I did get a lot more out of it, not worrying about it. I had thought about getting birth control pills with the boy friend before, but that worked to where it was a one-way street for his benefit, not for mine. It would be mine because I wouldn't get pregnant, but safe for him, too, because I wouldn't put him on the spot. So I get sick of being used. I'm tired of this same old crap, forget it. I'm not getting pills for his benefit. So I never got them and I never thought I would have to 'cause I wasn't looking for anyone since I was tired of being used. Sex was a one-way street. He gets all the feelings, girls have all the hassles. She gets more emotional and falls head over heels while he could give a damn. I'm sick of it, so I thought hang it all.

Not only does this comment demonstrate the lack of commitment that the contraceptive technology has engineered for the male, it also suggests the anger and frustration of women for whom contraception is a "one-way street." There are, of course, several ways out of this dilemma. To offer one example, women could demand that men join them in contraception by using either a male method or a couple method, with a therapeutic abortion available as a "back-up" method. As a second solution, women and men could equalize the contraceptive costs of the relationship in other terms: they could continue to use the so-called "more effective methods" but share the "costs" of the relationship in more equal terms so as to compensate the woman for exclusive contraceptive responsibility. As one example, men could share (or take over) the financial costs of contraception, which can often be considerable: with two visits to a physician and a year's prescription of pills, contraceptive costs can run over a hundred dollars a year. (With public clinics, of course, the financial costs can be less but they are still considerable; this calculation, for example, does not include any indirect costs of pill use, such as more frequent vaginal infections and hence a higher probability of more frequent medical visits.)

Both these solutions, however, are based on the assumption that contraceptive responsibility is a consequence of intercourse and not of gender: that both parties who engage in sexual intercourse should share the burdens attached to it. A decade or so ago this would not have seemed a radical assumption. With condoms being the most popular contraceptive, men were normatively expected to take on a significant, if not a major, part of the contraceptive tasks. Currently, however, the technological and social change concomitant with widespread pill use has produced a generation of men and women socialized into the notion that only women have contraceptive responsibility. So pervasive and total are the normative changes surrounding contraception that neither men nor women can effectively conceptualize, much less carry through, alternate patterns of contraceptive responsibilities.

Just as important, women have now internalized the idea that getting pregnant is their fault, even when it occurs in the context of male collusion with the risk-taking. (Male patterns of collusion will be discussed shortly.) Thus the women in the study were unable (and unwilling) to ask the male partner to share accountability even to the minimal extent of paying for half the abortion. Less than ten percent of the women interviewed said that the man was paying for the abortion, or for some part of it. More frequently they reported that the man offered to pay but that they were unwilling to accept the offer. Ironically, for example, even the woman quoted above who spoke out so strongly against the consequences of exclusive female responsibility found herself suffering exclusively female accountability:

R: I had a hard time getting money. He wanted to pay. I wouldn't let him. I didn't want him to help me in any way. In fact, I didn't want to talk to him. I didn't want him to pay 'cause I thought it would ruin it if he thought he'd *have* to pay.

The only significant variable that influenced the sharing of accountability and responsibility was marriage. In all but a very few instances, married couples perceived an unwanted pregnancy to be a joint responsibility, or at least a joint problem.[d] In part this finding seems self-evident: marriage brings with it a great deal of shared responsibility in many spheres of life, and pregnancy is one of the most salient. However, what this differential proves is that the assigning of both contraceptive responsibility and accountability are not, as popular thought assumes, a biological *fait accompli* brought about by the fact that women most visibly bear the effects of pregnancy. Rather, it proves that the assigning of responsibility is primarily a social product, and that men routinely share contraceptive burdens and consequences when they are in the "right" social category—that is, married.

But for all the currently unmarried women in the study (unmarried women represent about three quarters of the women seeking abortions in the state as a whole, see Appendix Three),[35] the social definitions of who gets pregnant and who bears the costs of pregnancy put women into an

---

d. It is striking to note, however, that even among married couples, all but three reported that the husbands had left the bulk of the decision up to the wives.

"ideological triple bind." First, it is self-defeating for women to demand that men share contraception by using a male method or a couple method if any resulting pregnancies are still going to be defined as the woman's fault and her responsibility. Simple self-interest would dictate that a woman use the most effective contraceptive available, even if that means accepting exclusive responsibility.

Second, women have been so socialized into the norm of exclusive responsibility that they feel they do not have the "right" to ask men to join them in contraception. This becomes most evident when women in the study who had failed to make any provisions for contraception were asked why they did not suggest the use of a condom, which is inexpensive, readily available, and infinitely more "effective" than unprotected intercourse. A few women reported that they had raised the issue:

R: I tried, but he just wouldn't use a condom, he wouldn't hear of it.

More typically, however, the women interviewed were shocked by the question: condoms are considered to be so inconvenient and unpleasant for men to use that women would prefer to run the risk of pregnancy rather than suggest them or insist upon them.* Practically speaking, the alternative to male methods or couple methods is pregnancy for these women, and still they are unable to take initiative when it involves asking for male participation.

Third, women feel that exclusive control over contraception is essential to "control over your own body," and that women must control contraception in the interests of liberation and self-determination. But this "right" is an illusory one: rights are only possible in the context of choice. As we have shown, women have the "right" to control their own bodies because neither the social structure nor the normative climate permit them any other options—it is a right that society is only too willing to accord them. Thus although the right to control one's own body is an important one, and one which should not be taken away from women, it is critically important to develop alternatives—for example, norms that encourage men to share some of the burdens of continuous contraception.

This ideological "triple bind" in which women find themselves would

---

*In this, these women are speaking more from a social myth than from personal experience. By and large, these women and their partners have *never* used condoms.

remain peripheral to a study of contraceptive risk-taking were it not for the fact that the situation is basically unstable and hence a causal factor, at least macrosocially, in the decision to take risks. As we have seen, social and structural factors make it virtually impossible for women to undertake any of the alternatives outlined above—sharing contraceptive tasks, sharing other relationship costs—in order to relieve the pressures of exclusive female responsibility and accountability. Hence the instability: the women in this study feel trapped by the burden of changing social definitions around contraception, but they perceive no attractive alternatives. Since effective contraception takes foresight, a high level of motivation, and a great deal of "carry through," when women feel trapped and resentful they are less likely to be able to mobilize the energies needed. Thus a principle of inertia occurs as an overlay to the situations outlined in Chapter Three: a woman feels that the costs of contraception are high, but that the benefits of a pregnancy are moderately high as well, and experiences a latent but readily activated sense of conflict about the social meanings of contraception. Together, these factors guarantee the fact that the motivation to carry through with the repetitive act of contraception will not occur, or will occur only sporadically at best, and that repeated "acts of inertia" will lead to pregnancy.

The complex and rapid social and technological change surrounding contraception is equally important in explaining the behavior of the men in this study as well. These explanations must be tentative, since only 10 percent of the interviews included the male partner as an informant; but when these conjoint interviews are examined alongside female reports of male behavior, a striking pattern emerges. Although virtually every man in the study was reported either by himself or by a woman to be aware of the contraceptive risk-taking that was going on, no man in this study was able to effectively take action to stop the risk-taking. In part this is a definitional problem—after all, any man who did take effective action to stop risk-taking behavior by definition eliminated his partner from a study of women seeking abortions (barring those pregnancies which were a result of "method failure"). But the important question to ask is why so many men were not able to put a stop to the risk-taking, and colluded with the women in behavior that ended in pregnancy.

It is clear that any man who does not want to be a participant in an unwanted pregnancy and who knows the woman to be contraceptively unprotected has the option of refusing to have intercourse with her until

she is adequately protected. But few men in this study were able to
engage in this kind of decision making. Several of them reported, or were
reported by women, to have made tentative attempts to change the
situation:

> R: He would say, "don't you think you should go on the pill?" and
>   I would say that it would make me gain weight, and so we would
>   go on.

When these tentative attempts failed, however, the men perceived themselves as powerless to do anything further to prevent the inevitable. In at
least one case, a man is reported to have gone along with sporadic contraception which resulted in *two* subsequent unwanted pregnancies by the
same woman:

> I: What kind of contraception were you using?
> R: We were using rhythm, which was also ridiculous considering we
>   knew what could happen—what *did* happen. It's amazing that
>   two supposedly bright people could get into this twice.

Why the female half of "two supposedly bright people" found herself
in this situation (which was made even more traumatic by the fact that the
first abortion, which occurred less than a year prior to the current
abortion, was a "saline injection" abortion, a considerably more painful
and expensive operation than the evacuations done for women at the
Clinic) has been examined in detail in previous chapters of this study. At
this point, it is worthwhile to ask why the male half of "two supposedly
bright people" went along a second time with sporadic use of contraception when he was well aware of the effects of the first pregnancy and
abortion on his partner. Such disregard would appear to be callous exploi-
tation were it not for the fact that almost all of the men in the study had
similar, if less dramatic, patterns; it is hard to imagine that men as a group
are basically unconcerned with the comfort and welfare of the women
with whom they have sexual relations.

Although it is theoretically possible that this group of women represented a sample of women who had found themselves involved with particularly exploitative men, there are several reasons to believe that this is
not true. First, the large number of men involved makes it improbable (it
is hard to imagine that all five hundred women chose outstandingly

exploitative men); second, the sample includes many married men and their wives; and lastly, almost all (92 percent) of the unmarried women in the study were in stable monogamous relationships with the men involved and many (24.6 percent) were living together in consensual unions. All these factors indicate some degree of emotional involvement on the part of the men, thus making simple "careless love" arguments untenable. (It should be noted, of course, that since "promiscuity" is heavily stigmatized, particularly in a situation such as an abortion, where there are overtones of moral censure anyway, the findings that few of the women interviewed had had more than one partner in the month preceding the pregnancy should be taken with some caution. Internal consistencies in the interviews, however, which lasted on the average more than an hour, seem to suggest that "promiscuity" is indeed the exception and not the rule.)

Thus we come up against a paradox similar to the one presented in the first chapter, when we asked why women with considerable contraceptive skills chose not to use those skills even when that choice resulted in an unwanted pregnancy, which was then terminated in abortion. Although almost all other studies of unwanted pregnancies have focused exclusively on the female and demoted the male to the role of "biological tool," it is critical to ask in this study why these men, who were presumably aware of the facts of life and appeared to be consistently aware of the fact that their partners were not effectively contracepting, passively colluded with the decision not to contracept even when the risk was pregnancy.

Our answer, though admittedly speculative, is that men are socially cast into the role of passive spectators to contraceptive decision making by the same social and technological changes that structure the way in which women take risks. If, for example, the social definition is that only women get pregnant, men are socially excluded from a major part of being involved in the whole process of contraception and abortion. More important, if both responsibility and accountability are defined as exclusively female, men have neither the social means nor the personal motivation to take more active interest. We have already argued that most women are socialized into a "triple bind" which increases the probability that they will take exclusive contraceptive responsibility. What remains for us to demonstrate is that in conjunction with this same "triple bind" men are equally unable to change the "definition of the situation."

It is important to recall the extent to which accountability is considered female in nature. As we have already noted, few men involved themselves to the point of paying for half of the abortion, and this reluctance was not seen as directly problematic:

I: Who paid for the abortion?
R: I did. Well, he was going to, but he couldn't. He had the money for a while but something happened to it. He was going to for a while. . . . He paid for the trips down here [a fifty-mile trip] but I paid for the abortion. Well, he had a hundred dollars, but then we had a flat tire and we didn't get here the first time. Then he went to Los Angeles and he ended up spending it there.

This kind of ambivalent response to the problem of paying for the abortion was unfortunately typical in this set of interviews. What generally happened is that altruism was the only force motivating men to participate, and the ideology of accountability often made women refuse even those offers.

An even more dramatic demonstation of male disengagement from contraceptive responsibility and accountability may be found in an unpublished study by a local contraceptive clinic, which reports that fewer than one out of ten high-school and college age men asks a woman at first intercourse whether she is contraceptively protected. Although the clinic did not analyze this finding further, we would suggest that such a situation is possible only under two social conditions: first, when many women in the population are using effective contraception so that the chances are high that most women are contraceptively "safe"; and second, and most important, when the penalties attached to a wrong guess are negligible for the man. Although hard data is lacking, we would suggest that ten years ago, for example, the first condition would have been met, although certainly not to the extent that it is today; ten years ago a great many women were using effective contraception. It is the second condition which has shown the most obvious change. Ten years ago, if a woman became pregnant the "costs" to a man were high: chances were that he had to face a "shotgun" wedding, or help arrange for an illegal abortion, or prove by whatever means available that he was not the father of the forthcoming child.

Today, however, the advent of legalized abortion ironically makes it easier for men as well as women to escape the consequences of the decision not to use contraception. Like women, men are at least subliminally aware of the fact that the highest "cost" connected to neglecting contraception is an abortion, and that furthermore the ideology of female accountability means that it is unlikely that a man will be pressured either by social norms or by the woman herself into taking on the major part of the financial costs of the abortion. In addition, the current availability of abortion eliminates in practice the older social alternatives that were "costlier" to men, thus limiting even further their motivation for taking an active interest in the contraceptive process. With legalized abortion, for example, men can (and do) make half-hearted offers of marriage, but the existence of other options serves to make both parties feel as if the woman, rather than "fate" or "society," had manipulated the man into a situation against his will. As another example of changing "costs" for men, legalized abortion has made it harder, according to some lawyers, for women to initiate paternity suits. The informal thinking is that since a woman could have aborted the pregnancy, if she decides to continue it is her personal choice and there is no reason to ask a man to financially support what is her idiosyncratic preference. Thus, although the courts are (reluctantly) willing to support an already-born child, this informal thinking acts as a deterrent for women, causing them to reconsider the decision to continue the pregnancy.

Thus men, too, are caught in a social and ideological "triple bind," although one which is less immediately destructive to them than to women. It occurs for men because three circumstances make it hard for them to become more active in the contraceptive process. First, for reasons outlined above, it is difficult for women to conceptualize or accept alternate patterns of contraceptive responsibility because of the "triple bind" in which they find themselves. Second, the social definitions of responsibility and accountability are so pervasive that men find it hard to break out of the social mold. And third, the dramatic changes in accountability for pregnancy eliminate "enlightened self-interest" as a motivation for sharing the responsibilities of pregnancy. In other words, men, like women, find it hard to imagine alternative patterns of contraceptive responsibility, and women wouldn't accept those patterns even if men could conceptualize them—because of the effects of the

female "triple bind," and because men are not subjected to structural
pressures that make it imperative for them to conceptualize or insist. Thus
men as well as women face a principle of inertia that makes pregnancy
more likely.

The male "triple bind" has two consequences, one of direct interest to
a study of contraceptive risk-taking, and one of less direct interest. The
first consequence is that half of the people who could prevent an
unwanted pregnancy are structurally denied both the means and the motivation to do so. If men were able to take responsibility for their risk-
taking behavior (failing to ask a woman if she is contraceptively
protected, or colluding with her risk-taking if she is not) and were held
responsible for that behavior, the number of unwanted pregnancies
would decline, since biologically speaking it takes two risk-takers to
create an unwanted pregnancy. If men were as careful of their ability to
"become pregnant" as women are socially supposed to be, even women
who were under great pressure to take contraceptive risks would be
unlikely to become pregnant since their male partners would be using
contraception as well. The term "as well" is used advisedly: it is
assumed that both partners can and should use contraception, even if this
sometimes means that two people are independently using contraceptives
at the same time. When it comes to unwanted pregnancies, too much
contraception is preferable to too little.

The socially induced male passivity on issues of contraception and
abortion has another consequence, probably of less immediate significance in a study of risk-taking, but equally important in human terms.
When interviewed when their women were not present, many men
suggested that the structural passivity in which they found themselves
was as destructive and upsetting to them as to the women whom they had
made pregnant. One of these respondents expressed in poignant terms the
dilemma that men feel when society has demoted them to the role of
bystander:

R: (Male) It makes me feel like a creep or a heel or a slob or some-
     thing. She won't even talk to me, she makes me feel like it is all
     my fault but there's nothing I can do. She won't even let me pay
     for it. There isn't anything I can do to make things better.

How extensive feelings like this are must await further research;

obviously men who participate in the abortion procedure tend to be the more involved men. Nevertheless, one would tend to suspect that the psychological impact on men who have had abortions may be as significant in some respects, although far less visible, than the psychological trauma women face, particularly since women have social permission and a variety of institutions where they may discuss the effects of the abortion and ventilate psychic stress. The long-term effects on men of having had an abortion will be discovered only with time and further research.

Thus it is not men alone or women alone who irrationally decide to take contraceptive risks, but individuals of both sexes who find themselves caught in a web of individual pressures, idiosyncratic pressures, and technological and ideological pressures, a web from which risk-taking seems the most logical way out. Risk-taking, like most human behavior, can only be understood in the social context in which it occurs.

7

Options for
the Future:
Implications for
Policy Making

Any implementation of the findings of this study must rest on two assumptions, which have been stated in various ways throughout this book. The first assumption is that risk-taking behavior which ends in an unwanted pregnancy is the result of a "rational" decision-making chain produced by a person who is acting in what he or she perceives to be his or her best interests, although often in the presence of faulty data. The second assumption is that risk-taking behavior regarding contraception is only one of a variety of similar risk-taking behaviors that ordinary people regularly engage in. Each of these assumptions has its own implications for policy making.

There are three other assumptions behind our suggestions for policy change in the institutions whose specific aim is to serve women who take contraceptive risks. First, these institutions, like individuals, are constantly in the process of doing their own social "cost accounting," weighing costs against benefits in order to make decisions. Second, institutional cost accounting is rarely challenged in a fundamental way, as it is for a risk-taking woman who must face an unwanted pregnancy; for this reason, the institution's cost accounting tends to become reified into a "definition of the situation" that is considered to be the only valid assessment of reality. It is therefore usually assumed that "rational" people will act in the way that the institution expects, and that people who do not are by definition beyond the helping reach of the institution. Third, just as contraceptive risk-taking women are trying to do many things, only one of which is not to get pregnant, so these institutions are also trying to do many things, only one of which is serving their clientele in the most efficient and rational manner.

Ideally, this chapter would include a comprehensive survey of the two major kinds of institutions that serve women who take contraceptive risks: contraceptive clinics and abortion centers. Such a survey would outline the cost-accounting practices of each of these institutions, and a point-by-point analysis would be used to demonstrate how their own cost accounting often becomes an unhelpful or counterproductive part of the cost accounting made by risk-taking women. We would then show how institutional pursuit of a variety of implicit goals (including the classical goals suggested by organizational theory) often makes it hard for an institution to achieve its expressed goals of serving risk-taking and potentially risk-taking women. In other words, just as we outlined the competing goals that make it hard for women to maintain effective contraception, we would outline the competing goals that institutions face as they attempt to forestall contraceptive risk-taking or provide abortions for risk-takers who have become pregnant.

However, it has taken an entire study to demonstrate how this process works for risk-taking women alone. To extend the analysis to the institutions surrounding them would require still another study, one which is in fact planned for the future. In this section, then, we shall offer only some general comments about the social definitions of risk-taking that are made by institutions, and make some specific suggestions for institutional changes. Two kinds of institutions will be discussed: abortion centers, which deal with the consequences of contraceptive risk-taking, and contraceptive clinics, which seek to avert those consequences.

INSTITUTIONS AND RISK-TAKING

In general, the greater the difference between the cost-benefit analysis of a risk-taking subgroup and the analysis made by the social institution created to deal with the consequences of that risk-taking, the more irrational and censurable will appear the behavior of the risk-takers when viewed by the institution. In part, whether this kind of stigma is attached depends upon whether the consequences of risk-taking are defined as consciously self-induced (note that insurance policies often refuse to cover the medical consequences of attempted suicide or self-administered drugs). Thus alcoholics, for example, receive different treatment from social institutions than persons with liver damage caused by a drug sensitivity. In the first case, the medical consequences of liver damage from alcoholism are held to be self-induced; in the second, they are held to be "bad luck." Even more important, however, is the "social distance" between what the institution and what the risk-takers define as reasonable risks for reasonable gains. Skiers with broken legs, for example, are generally treated as "reasonable" people by insurance policies and medical institutions on the grounds that the pleasure of skiing (payoff) is worth the risk of bodily damage (cost), even though that risk is consciously courted. In short, many kinds of risk-taking are considered "reasonable risks" by social institutions because large or powerful segments of the population engage in these risks or agree in general with the cost-benefit analysis of them.

It is also possible that self-selection in the kinds of people who staff medical institutions may increase the "social distance" between contraceptive risk-takers and those who attempt to serve them. For instance, although hard data is lacking, it is possible that medical institutions tend to be run by people with a high tolerance for deferred gratification and people whose social and psychological "set" is on long-term goals. Contraceptive risk-takers, however, are by definition women to whom the immediate costs of contraception are higher than the distant costs of an abortion, and who are thus diametrically opposed in their social "set" to people who focus on long-term goals and costs.

THE DELIVERY OF ABORTION SERVICES: A CRITIQUE

The cost accounting made by the medical institutions delivering abortion is an example of this "social distance." Risk-taking women face, as we have demonstrated, a complex and intricate scheme of interwoven social pressures which make the decision to use contraception a difficult and at times impossible one. From the medical and institutional viewpoint, however, this intricate decision chain is presumed to be simple in the extreme: women should know that intercourse leads to pregnancy, so that any woman who is unwilling to pay what they view as the minor costs of contraception, when faced with the major costs of an abortion, is both self-destructive and irrational.

This viewpoint is built into social policy because the medical-institutional framework implements its own cost-benefit analysis as if it were the only one possible: since contraception is relatively less "costly" (or should be to rational women), abortion is a poor second choice, and one which should not be encouraged as a primary method of fertility control. The medical structure grudgingly permits abortions as the lesser of several evils (notably illegitimacy, illegal abortion, and unwanted children), but it is unable to perceive that contraception may *not* be à priori the least costly and most rational method of fertility control for all women at all times.

The abortion-delivery system in California at the time of this study was cumbersome and costly in almost every sense of the word. California law restricted abortions to hospitals accredited by the Joint Commission on Accreditation and further restricted their performance to licensed medical doctors. Furthermore, the price reflected the scarcity of these resources. These two facts effectively eliminated the possibility of having free-standing abortion clinics that could provide low-cost abortions (because they would not have to pay the overhead of fully staffed hospitals), or small specialized hospitals which could provide the same low-cost services for the same reasons. As a point of comparison, at the time of this study the price of abortions in Washington, D.C., where such provisions were not built into law, was only a third of the prevailing price of California abortions.

The medical policy makers and legislators who drew up California law (since superseded by Supreme Court decisions) undoubtedly felt that they were acting in the name of "good conservative medicine" by building in these protections for women's health. But what these provisions reflected was a low assessment of the potential benefits of abortion: because it was believed that abortions should serve only as a "back-up" to contraception, the risks to life and health inherent in a more available abortion-delivery service were not to be tolerated, since the benefits were viewed as not worth the risk.[a]

Ideally, all medical decisions would be made in the most conservative possible way, so that virtually no risk to life and health would be involved. In real life, however, this is impractical, and so a "tolerable level of risk" is defined against the backdrop of potential benefits. As we noted in our earlier discussion of side-effects (Chapter Three), the more

a. It is assumed in the family planning literature that abortion should not be a primary method of fertility control. See Hall (ed.), *Abortion in a Changing World*, Vol. 1 (New York and London: Columbia University Press, 1970).

serious side-effects of cortisone used after a kidney transplant have a higher "tolerable level of risk" than aspirin would have, because the benefits are held to be greater. In the present case, the "tolerable level of risk" of abortion is set at a very low level, and kept low by the legally required use of accredited hospitals and licensed medical doctors, because abortion is considered to have only the benefits of a "poor second choice" when compared to contraception.

It is important to emphasize that the level of risk we are discussing is very small indeed. For one thing, the low "tolerable level of risk" (risk of sickness or death) outlined by the cumbersome and expensive California law procedure is only a slight fraction of a percent lower than the "tolerable level" outlined in simpler and cheaper procedures in other states.[1] As another point of comparison, the overall risk of sickness and death associated with abortion in the United States is roughly that of birth-control pills.[2] The delivery of birth-control pills, however, is widely facilitated by medical structures and many agencies help subsidize the costs, even though the risk they present to the life and health of women is almost exactly the same as that of abortion. The delivery of abortion, on the other hand, is restricted, and few agencies act to subsidize the costs. Since the medical risks are virtually the same, the difference between the two delivery systems clearly illustrates how risk is defined in relation to perceived benefits, and how the perceived benefits of abortion are much lower than those of contraception.

This would be of mere academic interest but for the fact that women, and to some extent the larger society, have to pay for that lower "tolerable level of risk," Moreover, the cost accounting of medical institutions to the contrary, many women, as we have more than amply demonstrated, do *not* in fact have the alternative of contraception, and these women must pay a higher rate for their method of fertility control because the use of it does not agree with the "definition of the situation" accepted in the medical institutions.

This brings up the larger issue of socio-medical economics: who should pay what costs in order to assure what level of tolerable risk. A paradigm of this problem is that women in this study paid, as part of their $300 abortion fee, a $17 fee for a pathology test to determine the presence of choriocarcinoma, an extremely virulent cancer that attacks fewer than one out of every 100,000 pregnant women.[3] Proportionately, the women in the study were being assessed more than $1,700,000 in order to protect themselves from a disease that they had less than one chance in 100,000 of getting. Although there can be no price tag set on human life, we must ask if that kind of expenditure is reasonable for that level of risk, especially when the costs are being borne largely by young, non-earning women and only indirectly by the society as a whole. At a certain point, the "premiums" on insurance outweigh the potential benefits.

The structure for delivering abortion services in California is based on an assumption that women should pay the cost of a conservative "tolerable level of risk" because they should have used contraception as a primary method of fertility control.

The reality of the situation, however, is that the costs associated with contraception are often so high that abortion becomes de facto the only acceptable method of fertility control for many women. But because of the way abortion services are presently structured, these women have to pay for the fact that their cost accounting differs from that of the medical establishment. (We are inclined to suspect that this is no accident—that the nature of the medical cost accounting makes it reasonable to keep abortion costs high as a functional deterrent.) The cost accounting that medical institutions make on the issue of abortion is much like the cost accounting that women make, in that much of it is tacit.

We strongly urge that a conscious cost-benefit analysis be made by sociologists, demographers, and medical personnel in order to determine whether, from a social, medical, and demographic point of view, it is desirable to accept abortion as a primary method of fertility control and to make it as readily available and as socially subsidized as other methods, such as the pill and the IUD. Such an analysis would demand many forms of data as input: data on medical and biological risk; data on social costs, and data of the sort we have offered, which would enable us to predict the likelihood that women would use other alternatives; data on long-term social "spinoffs" of this kind of decision, and so on.

Until such a thoroughgoing analysis is completed, however, we would argue on strictly pragmatic grounds that since abortion accounts for almost a third of all the reported pregnancies in the state of California, it has become a de facto method of fertility control comparable to the pill, the IUD, and other methods, and that the delivery of it should therefore reflect this fact. It is not enough, as the President's Commission on Population Growth and the American Future has suggested (and the Supreme Court has accomplished), merely to remove restrictions from the practice of abortion.[4] (The Supreme Court decision, for example, has removed the restrictions limiting abortions in California to accredited hospitals, pointing again to the contextual nature of costs and benefits.)

We would argue that since abortion has become a primary method of fertility control, it should be offered and subsidized in exactly the same way that other contraceptive services are.

Concretely, this would mean several things. First, it would mean making abortions both inexpensive and readily available. Evidence from other countries suggests that the most efficient way to achieve this goal would be through free-standing clinics staffed by paramedics under the supervision of doctors. One would assume that there would be a system whereby high-risk women—those likely to have medical problems in conjunction with their abortions—could still be referred at a doctor's discretion to a fully equipped medical hospital. Experience from other countries also suggests that making abortion more available in this way would not significantly increase the medical risks of legal abortion.[5] Second, it would mean setting up a socially subsidized abortion service, so that all who need abortions could have them on a sliding fee scale. Although presently the state of California does subsidize a significant number of abortions through its welfare system, it does so at the inflated costs of a conservative medical delivery system. Opening up the abortion structure by the use of free-standing clinics and paramedics would lower the price of abortions to somewhere between $25 and $50, and many more could be subsidized by the larger society, just as it now subsidizes contraceptive services to the poor.

Of course, these two suggestions raise issues which are complicated and politically sensitive. Medicine, more than most other professions, has strenuously resisted the "boarding out" of specific professional services to less highly trained and thus less expensive paraprofessionals. The current abortion situation in California (and the rest of the United States as well) is a case in point. The two recent Supreme Court decisions have eliminated virtually all constraints on the performing of an abortion within the first trimester, except for the provision that such abortions must be performed by a doctor; but they have done very little toward creating the kind of socially subsidied abortion we described in the previous chapter. Although the price of abortions in California quickly dropped from an average of about three hundred dollars to about one hundred and fifty dollars after the court decisions were implemented, no further changes in either the price or the availability of abortion have occurred. Even the two feminist abortion centers in the state, which use paramedical personnel to perform all services except for the actual operation (counseling, pre-operative care, and most post-operative care), have not been able to lower the price of an abortion much below the state average, compelled as they are to pay medical personnel to perform the actual abortion.

Ideally, the changes we have suggested for the delivery of abortion would be part of a larger reform of the delivery of all medical services to women, and indeed to all people. The referral of only selected clients to doctors, the broad use of paramedics, and the social subsidization of medical care, which are a few of the demands made by critics of the larger medical care system, have generally been resisted by the medical community—*except* in the area of contraception, where the medical community, like the larger society, has tacitly accepted programs based on these very demands.

Not only are millions of dollars spent in attempts to provide contraception—the federal government spent 10 million dollars in fiscal 1972—but the medical profession has accepted within these programs procedures that in other circumstances it would regard as intolerable intrusions on professional prerogatives. Family planning clinics, for example, routinely "board out" medical tasks to paraprofessionals, nurse practitioners, and community workers, albeit under the supervision of physicians. Thus what is unthinkable to most of the medical profession in the larger field of health care is considered quite acceptable when the goal is fertility control.

We contend that abortion is subjected to rigid control not so much because the medical risks are higher (as noted, the mortality rates for abortion and birth-control pill use are about the same) as because the social payoffs of abortion are viewed through the dark glass of another definition. As further proof of this point, several medical researchers are now testing abortion techniques which can be performed by only minimally trained paramedics. Needless to say, these techniques are destined, at least at the present time, for use only in Third World countries, where the social advantages of readily available abortion are defined much more favorably.

There is one last aspect of abortion delivery systems which bears consideration and criticism, and that is the proliferation of abortion counseling services. These services were originally set up when the availability of abortion varied from state to state and from region to region, and they were designed to help women with unwanted pregnancies in deciding which of the available options to choose (abortion, "shotgun" marriage, giving the child up for adoption). An important side benefit of these services was their ability and willingness to refer women to abortion centers and to "coach" them on what to say during the psychiatric examination that was necessary for abortion approval.

As abortion became more available and psychiatric examinations before abortions went out of style, abortion counseling services tended to become integrated with referral agencies such as family planning clinics, or institutionalized as part of abortion clinics themselves. At the same time, more liberalized abortion meant that more of the women clients coming into these abortion counseling situations had already made up their minds about what to do with the unwanted pregnancy, especially when the counseling was part of the abortion process itself. As a result, the main thrust of abortion counseling changed, from a consideration of what to do with an unwanted pregnancy and how to do it, to a more subtle consideration of the factors underlying the unwanted pregnancy.

In the Abortion Clinic where we conducted the research for this study, abortion counseling had three tacit goals, which we suspect are given great importance in the majority of abortion counseling interviews across the country. First, the counselor attempted to ascertain whether the woman had any lingering reservations about her decision to seek an abortion, or whether she was being pressured to seek an abortion by someone else (such as her parents or her partner). Second, medical and technical aspects of the abortion were explained to her, in an effort to minimize her fears of the unknown. Finally, an attempt was made to help her "understand" her "self-destructive" behavior in becoming pregnant and then deciding upon an abortion. In most cases, the first two parts of the interview were conducted quickly and the rest of the time was spent on this third effort.

It is precisely this "understanding" of "self-destructive" behavior which acts most powerfully against women's best interests. At best, counseling which offers psychologistic explanations of why a woman got pregnant simply fails to help her to make a better and more rational decision next time. At worst, by presenting a woman's behavior to her as an irrational "acting out," it obscures the decision making that is part of becoming pregnant, and leaves her even less well prepared to think about taking risks next time. By analogy, we might imagine counseling a stockbroker who had taken a beating in the market. Explaining to him the irrational and emotional factors underlying his decision to invest in a given stock might make him a more insightful person, but it would be unlikely to make him richer; concrete data about the workings of the stock market would be more likely to do that. Similarly, if abortion counseling focuses on the elements of the decision-making process—on what we have called the costs of contraception and the benefits of pregnancy—it is more likely that women will be able to add information into their decision-making systems. If a woman became aware, for example, that she was bargaining for the right to be independent from her parents, she can focus on finding ways to achieve that goal which will be less costly to her. This is the kind of abortion counseling that could help women avoid the problems of repeated abortions.

This does not mean, however, that we are ready to argue that abortion should be popularized as one of several equally acceptable methods of fertility control, with the same techniques used to encourage women to get abortions as are now used to encourage them to use contraception. Although the actual delivery of abortion necessarily reflects its present status as a major method of fertility control, it is not clear that this necessarily means we should make an ideological commitment to it as a long-term method, or that we should abandon research into better contraceptives with lower social costs for both men and women. In Chapter Six, for example, we demonstrated the magnitude of the unexpected social "spinoff" brought about by widespread use of the pill. What the social and technological spinoffs of abortion as a socially preferred method of fertility control are, we can only speculate. On this note of caution, we turn to a critique of the delivery of contraceptive services.

THE DELIVERY OF CONTRACEPTIVE CARE: A CRITIQUE

We have shown earlier how the arrangement of contraceptive delivery systems makes it hard for the potential risk-taker to get contraception, and relatively easy for non-risk takers to do so. Ironically, non-risk takers have other strategies to fall back on, should they not get contraception from a contraceptive clinic, while risk-takers do not; those who need contraception the most are precisely the ones who have the most difficulty negotiating the institutional structure (Chapter Three). In this section we would like to offer some suggestions for making contraceptive-care delivery systems more responsive to a "high-risk" group in need of contraception. Since publicly and privately supported contraceptive clinics provided the bulk of contraceptive services to women in this study, we shall treat such clinics as the main component of any contraceptive delivery system.

The first suggestion for a more responsive delivery system calls for a more aggressive community "outreach" program, consisting of two parts. In the first part, contraceptive clinics should mobilize existing channels of communication (newspapers, radio, television) for public service announcements dealing with the risk of pregnancy. (As we have shown, most contraceptive risk-takers do not know how likely pregnancy actually is over the long run; they only know that it might happen.) At the same time, this community outreach should provide information about where to get and how to use non-clinic methods of contraception, notably spermicidal foam and condoms. Although these two methods are far from ideal, they may serve some risk-takers effectively for a long time, and they may serve other risk-takers until they decide to get more effective contraception.

Lest these suggestions seem unthinkable, it should be noted that steps have already been taken in this direction. Several public health agencies already present public service announcements on television, urging people to plan their families. Since most Americans have relatively few problems planning their *families,* only a slight change would be needed in these announcements to focus them on the real problem, that of planning *births*. In addition, more popular magazines and college newspapers should carry advertisements for spermicidal foam and mail-order delivery of condoms. Thus the outreach program we are suggesting would merely increase and refine already existing programs of public communication.

The second part of this community outreach program aimed at reaching risk-takers would give wide publicity to the hours, locations, and confidentiality of contraceptive clinics. As things stand now, the burden is on the risk-taker or potential risk-taker to have sufficient motivation to ferret out this information and act on it. A contraceptive clinic whose access paths were a matter of common public knowledge would reach a far larger number of risk-takers.

A second suggestion for making contraceptive-care systems more responsive to risk-takers is to abolish the traditional medical model of the clinic, by which people must telephone weeks in advance for an appointment and must arrive at the specified time. We would suggest instead a "drop-in" or "walk-in" clinic, where no appointments are necessary. This might mean that a woman would have to wait several hours while other women are being taken care of, but it would eliminate the need for a risk-taking woman to plan her intercourse several weeks ahead, then either be abstinent or take contraceptive action on her own initiative in the meantime.

A "drop-in" clinic has several advantages. First, by letting women come in at any time, it takes advantage of any existing motivation to use contraceptives. As we have demonstrated throughout this study, women are not either "risk-takers" or "non-risk-takers," but simply persons engaged in a dynamic human process in which not using contraception sometimes becomes more rational than using it. When the balance is precarious, or when the "cost accounting" is close, readily available contraception may make all the difference between a woman who will subsequently take a risk and one who will not. The pool of potential risk-takers could be significantly diminished by a drop-in clinic ready to help women at critical points along the decision-making chain.

Next, a drop-in clinic can provide "back-up" methods to women who are in the wrong part of their menstrual periods to begin using the pill or an IUD. By providing an interim contraceptive (a diaphragm, foam, condoms, jellies) the chances of pregnancy can be lowered for the period before the woman begins to use "effective contraceptives." Even should the cost accounting change in the interim and the woman not come back for further contraception, she at least has *some* protection against pregnancy.

A third advantage is that a drop-in clinic can effectively translate the "uncertainty" of pregnancy into a concrete probability. As we noted in

Chapter Two, one of the elements of the risk-taking process is that pregnancy is an "uncertainty" (an occurrence with unknown probability) that women "discount" as being unlikely to happen to them. A drop-in contraceptive clinic is an ideal place for a credible source to make clear that over the long run most women having unprotected intercourse will in fact become pregnant. This in itself may alter the "cost accounting" of risk-taking women by demonstrating the high likelihood of a negative outcome to risk-taking.

Lastly, these drop-in clinics should provide their services free, or at least on an unbureaucratic sliding fee scale, so that finances would be no barrier to any woman wanting contraception. Whether the alternatives to contraception are defined as an illegitimate pregnancy, a legitimate but unwanted pregnancy, or a therapeutic abortion, it is clear that in terms of a "cost accounting" for the society as a whole, subsidizing the minimal costs of free or virtually free contraception is less expensive in financial and social terms than subsidizing the costs of the alternatives.

A third suggestion for lowering the social costs attached to contraception, and hence making contraceptive clinics more readily available to risk-taking women, is to change the social definition of contraception as an exclusively female-oriented process, where only female-oriented contraceptives are considered either effective or rational. While changing the social definition of contraception is a massive task, and one obviously beyond the abilities of any one section of the institutional structure, contraceptive clinics could make themselves more effective by refusing to institutionalize the "costly" notion that only women get pregnant and hence only women need to use contraceptives.

This could be done in a variety of ways. First, clinic policy could explicitly be based on the obvious biological fact that it takes two risk-takers to create an unwanted pregnancy, and thus both risk-takers should be the target of concern. As things stand now, half of the people in a position to eliminate unwanted pregnancies (the male partners) are effectively denied any say. "Bringing men back in" from a clinical point of view would mean aiming contraceptive advertising and services at them as well as at women. One example of this is the well-known poster sponsored by the Population Council of Britain, which presents an obviously pregnant young man with the caption, "Would you be more careful if you could get pregnant?"

Examples of contraceptive *services* for men, however, are conspicuously absent except for the sale and advertisement of condoms. The present clinics are structured so as to allow men to come into the clinic for a lecture on the various kinds of contraception, but the actual delivery of those contraceptives usually finds the male in the waiting room while the female makes the actual decision and learns how to use the method. Even should he be permitted to join the intake interview or the pelvic examination, he is still treated as an interested but largely irrelevant bystander.

Two alternative and complementary programs should be created to change this system. First, for men who are in relatively stable, monogamous relationships, the decision about what contraceptive to use and how to use it should be made mutually. Thus both men and women would discuss the alternatives and come to a joint decision in the presence of information about the risks attached to each method. Then both would learn to implement the decision together, and both men and women would receive the medical counseling and advice that goes with contraceptive delivery. For men who are not in stable unions, contraceptive clinics should provide "men only" sessions where male contraception—its meanings, its risks, and its techniques—could be discussed. Just as the sessions for women discuss the likelihood of pregnancy and how to avoid it, these sessions would do exactly the same thing for men, focusing particularly on the "male" and "couple" methods of contraception where male attitudes can play a major part. Needless to say, research to expand the present repertoire of male and "male inclusive" methods is vitally needed.

This leads to a fourth suggestion for putting the findings of this study to work in clinic practice. We have shown that defining as "effective" only the female-oriented contraceptives (the pill and the IUD) imposes a social cost on women, who often resent what they perceive to be an unfair sharing of the less pleasant side of sexual intercourse; and this resentment can decrease a woman's motivation to maintain on-going contraception. Further, we have shown that the so-called effective methods, the pill and the IUD, have such high "drop out" rates that their real-life effectiveness is in serious question.

Thus we suggest that contraceptive clinics look at contraceptive performance in real life rather than in the laboratory for their definition of "effective," and (as a consequence) widen the scope of contraception offered to people coming into contraceptive clinics. Rather than offering only the pill or the IUD (and in some cases the diaphragm), clinics must sensitize themselves to the fact that the social costs to women of using these "effective" contraceptives is often so high that their effectiveness is ephemeral. In pragmatic terms, condoms (or foam, or jellies, or anything else) used consistently are far more effective than pills which are not taken because the social costs are too high. As Tietze has suggested, any method of contraception with a back-up abortion is a "perfect" method in terms of preventing unwanted births.[6] In terms of contraceptive clinics, offering a wide range of contraceptives including the so-called "less effective" methods, in the context of widely available back-up abortion, makes more sense in terms of the expressed goal of reducing unwanted births than insisting on only those contraceptives with a high statistical effectiveness and a low social effectiveness.

Another aspect of this same problem—the tendency of contraceptive clinics to make their own "definition of the situation" which may or may not be similar to that of risk-taking women—is the tendency of these clinics to discount the costs of contraception in what is sometimes a short-sighted commitment to the single goal of fertility control. We demonstrated earlier how clinics and their personnel discount the immediate social situation of a woman which makes contraception personally costly to her. In speaking here of policy, we might ask if they do not also sometimes discount the larger social costs as well. The parallel, in terms of what we have been suggesting so far, is that just as abortion-delivery systems often overrate the risks associated with abortion because the social utility of abortion is perceived as being very low, so contraceptive systems sometimes underrate the risks associated with contraception because its social value is perceived to be so high.

Doctors observed in this study sometimes urged pill use for sexually active women, even when they were very young, on the grounds that whatever the long-term risks of pill use to the very young adolescent, they were less than the risks associated with unwanted pregnancy. A more serious problem is that of prescribing pill use for a population in which gonorrhea is epidemic, as it was and continues to be in the San Francisco Bay Area at the time of the study. Since the use of the pill increases the likelihood of venereal disease directly (by decreasing condom use) and perhaps indirectly as well (by changing the pH of the vaginal mucosa),[7] widespread pill use, although useful in preventing pregnancy, may have long-term costs in terms of the medical consequences of V.D. Thus, in processes very similar to risk-taking women, long-term costs increasing the incidence of venereal disease are discounted in favor of short-term costs reducing unwanted pregnancy.

By now it should be absolutely clear that we are not urging that contraceptive clinics stop prescribing the pill. Rather, we are suggesting that the sometimes single-minded approach that these clinics take toward their stated goals is as "irrational" as the behavior of the risk-taking women in this study has traditionally been thought to be. Just as it is for the risk-taking women, the options are many and varied, and the cost accounting is complex. Both groups could profit from more explicit assessments of how their decisions are made.

A preliminary pragmatic suggestion toward this end would be to urge all family planning clinics to have advisory boards which include people other than the traditional medical and paramedical personnel. Social scientists, for example, might make analyses such as the ones presented in this study. More important, these institutions could and should have representatives from their client populations. It would seem obvious to suggest that agencies like contraceptive clinics and abortion clinics which serve primarily women are unlikely to serve them well, if all (or virtually all) of the decision makers in those clinics are men. But this is only too often the case. Although family planning clinics (and abortion clinics as well) are often liberally staffed with female volunteers, the real policy decisions are usually made by males, and by male professionals, at that. As a first step, then, we might suggest that any abortion agency or family planning agency which does not have a substantial representation of women (including clients and potential clients) among its decision makers should take immediate steps toward changing the situation.

In summary, then, we would suggest that the decision making of institutions should be examined in the same critical way in which we attempted to examine the seemingly "irrational" decision-making of risk-taking women. Just as the decision-making process of risk-taking women could (and should) be studied by institutions dealing with them, so that women and institutions can act more effectively in each other's behalf, so should the decision making of institutions be studied in the interests of the larger society.

1

Methods

Research design: the search for parameters. In beginning this study, I chose to confront a social phenomenon—widespread therapeutic abortion as a primary method of fertility control—which contravened common American social expectations about pregnancy, fertility, contraception, and abortion. This phenomenon was virtually unexplored in the literature, perhaps as a result of its very unexpectedness. The problem was thus to investigate an emergent phenomenon which had virtually no known parameters. Almost all prior work on abortion had been done prior to the spate of liberalized laws which occurred in 1967-1973, and reflected the social fact that abortion prior to liberalization was a scarce resource, differentially distributed. The few women who had successfully obtained abortions in the years prior to liberalization seemed unlikely to be comparable to women in the new situation, where abortions accounted for a significant portion of all pregnancies.

As a preliminary step, the State Department of Public Health (Bureau of Maternal and Child Health) provided unpublished data on the approximately seventy thousand abortions which occurred in 1970 and the approximately fifty thousand which occurred in the first half of 1971 in California. This data, on computer tapes, covered the four variables presented in Appendix Four (age, ethnicity, marital status, prior pregnancies) plus two others—type of hospital where the abortion was performed, and how payment was made. Cross tabulations, not published here, were made in an attempt to sketch out the parameters of abortion in California. As noted in the text, this material, although it covered virtually every abortion in California in the time period under examination, was not sufficiently extensive to warrant drawing any conclusions about the source of what we have called the "abortion revolution." Six variables, even when cross tabulated, do not provide adequate information to do anything but speculate on the etiology of widespread abortion in a contraceptive society. As already noted in the text, the primary function of this material was to demonstrate what abortion was not—or in the terms used so far, to further challenge what Blum and McHugh have called the "laws of plausibility."[1] The cross tabulations showed that abortion was not limited to the poor, the young, the unmarried, the mothers of many children, or the racial minorities who presumably have less access to contraception. But what the real etiology of the "abortion revolution" was remained to be explored.

The second step in exploring this problem was to contemplate a survey research design which would sample two groups of one hundred women each, one group having abortions and one group continuing their pregnancies. These two groups were to be matched on every variable that prior research had suggested was significant: the age, marital status, ethnicity, religion, prior pregnancies, income, and education of the woman, as well as the income, education, and religion of her partner. This survey design was also to take into consideration the effect of the hospital itself (for example, whether it was private, non-profit, proprietary, or county) and of the fact that a pregnancy carried to term lasts nine months, while most pregnancies terminated by abortion last less than three months. To this end, a preliminary survey of all hospitals in the San Francisco Standard Metropolitan Statistical Area was undertaken, and a time lag of six months between interviewing the two groups was arranged, so that women giving birth in a hospital six months later than a similar group of women having abortions in that same hospital would represent similar conception times. A closed-end questionnaire was written, incorporating much of the standard KAP (knowledge, attitude, and practice) material from previous contraceptive studies.

At this point, however, I began to suspect that such a research design could labor mightily and bring forth a mouse. The more preliminary work proceeded, the more it became apparent that a standard research design focusing on one dependent variable (the decision to abort), and "controlling" all the other intervening variables, ran a serious risk of controlling all the interesting data out of existence, particularly since no one knew the weight, importance, and causal strength of those variables in the "open abortion" situation which California was increasingly beginning to represent. On the other hand, increasing familiarity with the field suggested that there were a multitude of variables inherent in the "open abortion" situation that the literature had never discussed, based as that literature was on rare and differentially distributed abortions. As one example, Bracken and Swigar found that women who wait beyond the first trimester to abort tend to be a very different group of women than those who seek their abortions before the end of the first three months.[2] Individual delay in seeking abortion—a non-existent variable in the days when hospital abortion committees were the cause of whatever delay was involved—seemed to be an aspect which should not be overlooked in a survey design. Thus, since open abortion was a new and unanticipated social situation, survey research based on the testing of hypotheses from the classical literature ran the risk of being trivial on the one hand and misleading on the other.

Refocusing the study: the rediscovery of grounded theory. At this point it became apparent that the goals of the study as conceptualized were unrealistic. First, they assumed the presence of a common body of knowledge and literature about the situation, from which hypotheses could be drawn for empirical testing. As noted, this condition was not met, owing to the rapid and unexpected historical changes surrounding abortion in the period under discussion. Second, they assumed more extensive resources available to the researcher than in fact existed. It was estimated by the researcher and by others knowledgeable in the field of survey research that a maximum of seventy-five to one hundred schedules could be administered in the course of this study, based as it was on one researcher working alone without a large research budget. This was clearly far too small a sample to yield significant results (significant at least in terms of sociological theory), especially when the problem was further complicated by the lack of readily available hypotheses which could be tested in a survey research design. Third, and this is a factor rarely mentioned in reviews of methodology, there was the probem of access. Women seeking abortions at the time of the study were compelled by California law to have those abortions in a hospital accredited by the Joint Committee on Accreditation of the American Hospital Association (this section of the law has since been overturned by the recent United States Supreme Court decision). This meant, by extension, that there were no abortions performed in doctors' offices (as in the District of

Columbia) and no free-standing clinics (as in New York). As a consequence, all access to abortion-seeking women would have to be gained through the hospital. It does not overstate the case to note that the doctor-patient relationship is one of the most jealously guarded of professional relationships, and the addition of myriad hospital committees to guard that relationship makes it even more difficult for the social scientist to gain access. When it is remembered that the small body of previous abortion research suggested that abortion clienteles varied significantly by type of hospital, and that a geographic distribution of hospitals in the Bay Area seemed desirable, the problem of access began to seem insurmountable.

As these three factors became clear, the conclusion seemed inescapable. There were no readily agreed-upon hypotheses to be tested, there were not sufficient resources to test such hypotheses even if they did exist, and even if resources and hypotheses had been available, widespread access was not. As a result, hypothesis testing of the kind generally envisioned in survey research was out of the question, and the goals of this study were consequently redefined toward a pilot study, a preliminary investigation aimed at *defining* the relevant parameters, rather than validating them. In other words, it became explicitly designed as an exploratory study, and the goal became what Glaser and Strauss have called hypothesis generating rather than hypothesis testing.[3]

The next problem was to find a sociological method appropriate to a preliminary investigation. Although many excellent exploratory studies have been made in the area of the interrelationships of social variables and fertility behavior (in particular, Blake's *Family Structure in Jamaica* and Rainwater's *And the Poor Get Children*),[4] a common fault of much of the existing exploratory work in this area is that it tends to rely too heavily on description and to ignore analysis. This is particularly true when, as in this case, known parameters do not exist and the decision is made to use qualitative data rather than quantitative data in order to generate preliminary hypotheses. Since hypothesis generating (and eventually substantive theory) were our goal, a method which called for analytical rigor was necessary to avoid the pitfalls of merely recording ethnographic data.

The method which seemed best suited for a preliminary but rigorous investigation of the kind envisioned here was that of the "grounded theoretical'' approach presented by Glaser and Strauss in *The Discovery of Grounded Theory*. This approach, which has its historical roots in the ''rules of evidence'' outlined by Znaniecki and others,[5] uses primarily qualitative data (although the quantifying of qualitative data is always an open option in this method). It is open-ended enough for causally significant variables to emerge in the analysis, a matter of primary concern in an investigation such as this.

At the same time, the process of grounded theory, based as it is on the constant comparison of emerging hypotheses and field data, forces the researcher to reexamine data in the light of emergent theory, and thus leads to analysis which of necessity goes beyond description. As Glaser and Strauss outline grounded theory, each addition of new data must be examined in the light of all analysis which has occurred to date and each analysis must be verified by new data. Cases are selected to fill categories as those categories emerge, and indeed cases are used to define the parameters of those categories. The researcher's task is to define analytical categories which account for all the data. Cases are therefore selected in terms of ''theoretical sampling'' rather than the traditional random sampling: ''Theoretical sampling is the process of data collection for generating theory whereby the analyst jointly collects, codes, and analyzes his data and decides what data to collect next and where to find them, in order to develop his theory as it emerges. This process of data collection is *controlled* by the emerging theory, whether substantive or formal.''[6] ''Theoretical saturation'' is judged to have occurred when the researcher fails to encounter any data which suggest new aspects of the existing categories. The researcher has completed the task of the study when there is a ''parsimony of variables and formulation'' and when there is a scope of applicability to a wide range of situations. (The width of the scope is determined by the empirical research problem at hand.) For a fuller exposition of the grounded theoretical method, the reader is referred to Glaser and Strauss and to the Selected Bibliography in this book.

Refining the focus: the emergence of contraceptive risk-taking. This research, then, was to be a preliminary study, aimed at rigorous hypothesis generating, and eschewing description in favor of analysis. By virtue of the computer tapes supplied by the State Department of Public Health in the survey phase of the study, there existed an overview, albeit skimpy, of the patterns of abortion-seeking women in the state as a whole. With those guidelines in mind, the problem became to find an abortion center or clinic which would provide some comparability to women in the state as a whole, and one which would provide relatively ready access. A survey of local abortion delivery systems (clinics, hospitals, private practitioners using the local hospitals, and abortion referral systems) demonstrated that no one system exactly or even nearly duplicated the overall proportions of the kinds of women who seek abortions. Some clinics served primarily poor women, some private practitioners served almost exclusively older well-to-do women, hospitals in some areas served disproportionate numbers of minority women, and some served Caucasian women exclusively.

Thus investigation of a single abortion system could not hope to cover the whole scope of the abortion situation in California. Further examination of the statewide statistics, however, suggested that, numerically, certain kinds of women were far more typical than other kinds. In the state as a whole, for example, white women accounted for 80 percent of the abortions in 1972, single women accounted for 50 percent, and women aged 20-29 accounted for slightly over 50 percent. Since the rest of the abortions were scattered over other races, ages, parities, and marital statuses, the single, white, young woman having her first pregnancy was statistically the most typical woman having an abortion in California. In a situation where no one abortion delivery system adequately represented all abortion-seeking women, a system which represented these most typical women consequently seemed the best place to begin the study. Additionally, since almost all systems served some range of women, the statewide statistics could be used to show how the chosen clinic differed from the state as a whole.

To this end, access was sought and obtained to an abortion center in metropolitan Northern California through the auspices of Planned Parenthood/World Population. This center saw an average of one hundred women a month and offered services on a clinic basis, at fees lower than the prevailing rates. Women were referred to this clinic from a variety of agencies, including the public media, and all had had a positive pregnancy test before their arival. They were seen in a suburban office for approximately three hours, during which they were asked for their medical histories, given a physical examination, and interviewed by a trained social worker for an hour. This interview had a dual purpose: it served to give the social worker data for a psychiatric diagnosis (legally necessary at that time for an abortion), and it also permitted the women to express their fears and feelings about the pregnancy, the abortion, and surrounding issues. At the end of the session women were scheduled within the following four to six days for a therapeutic abortion in a teaching hospital on the other side of town. Two weeks after the abortion, women returned for a follow-up physical examination, and contraceptive services were offered.

With the cooperation of the agency, I interviewed all the women either before or after their abortion. Although some women were interviewed twice, most were interviewed only once, and the timing of interviews was scattered to randomize the effects of pre- and post-abortion pressures. The interviews were open-ended and relatively unstructured; basically, the woman was asked how she came to be pregnant and how she had decided on an abortion. The interviews were tape recorded and later transcribed, although some were handwritten at the request of the person being interviewed. Fact-sheet data on age, marital status, SES, religion, religiosity, income, and occupation were collected, as were complete sexual, reproductive, and contraceptive histories. The medical case number of the particular woman was also entered on a separate sheet of paper, so that entry to the medical record could be made. (It should be noted that a consent form was used and respondents were told at the beginning of the interview of their rights to confidentiality and anonymity, and of their right to terminate the interview at any time.)

Very early in the interviews a striking anomaly began to emerge from the fact-sheet data and from the verbatim data. All of the women interviewed in the early phase of this investigation presented extensive and effective contraceptive histories, but all had used little or no contraception to avoid this pregnancy. They were all what we later came to call "contraceptive risk-takers." This finding was so striking that when the opportunity became available to survey the medical records of the first five hundred women seen through the clinic, it was quickly seized.

From the medical records of these five hundred women, thirty-three variables were coded and cross tabulated. Since only six hundred and sixty women were eventually seen through this clinic (the clinic closed, for reasons extrinsic to my research, soon after the study was completed), these

TABLE A-1

Cross Tabulation of Two Variables: Most Effective Contraception
Ever Used, and Contraception Used Since Last Menstrual Period.

	Effective contraception	Ineffective contraception	
Ever used	73%	24%	100%
Since last menstrual period	6%	91%[a]	100%

[a]Consists of 67% prior effective users, 24% prior ineffective users.

Note: Column totals do not add up to 100% because of the "no information" category.

five hundred medical records provide not only the sampling frame of the intensive interviews, but also a virtual population of all women seen. A more extensive review of these medical records is available elsewhere.[7] It is significant for this research that two of the variables coded were "most effective contraception every used" and "contraception used since the last menstrual period." By cross tabulating these two variables, the statistical extent of risk-taking could be outlined. A risk-taker in this case was operationally defined as a woman with a history of effective contraception who did not use an effective mothod consistently in the month preceding the pregnancy. (As we shall see below, a more subjective definition of risk-taking was used to define risk-takers in the interviews.) Table A-1 shows the results of the cross tabulations of these two variables.

What this table demonstrates is that in terms of the statistical definition of risk-taking, it was no surprise that all of the early interviews were with risk-taking women, since risk-taking women represented approximately two-thirds of the women whose medical records were examined. Those women (24 percent) who had never used an effective contraceptive method are those women whom we have called "contraceptively ignorant." The remaining 73 percent, who had used an effective method at some point in the past, we defined as contraceptively sophisticated women. (As noted in Appendix Two, 50 percent of these women were one-time pill users.) Of these contraceptively sophisticated women, only 6 percent reported use of an effective, consistent method in the month preceding the pregnancy. (Coding of contraceptive use was based on the woman's report in the medical record; if any discrepancies occurred in the medical record, the woman was coded to the highest reported level of use.) Statistically, then, of the first five hundred women seen at this clinic, erratic or nonexistent use of contraception preceded the pregnancy in 91 percent of the cases; 67 percent of these women, however, had a repertoire of contraceptive skills which belied their non-use and misuse of contraception in the month preceding pregnancy.

This was the preliminary emergence of the phenomenon which we have later elaborated into contraceptive risk-taking, and the research decision was made to interview these "risk-taking women" exclusively. This decision was made for at least two reasons. First, women who have the skills to avoid pregnancy but who do not use them present a much more difficult theoretical and practical problem than women represented by the remaining two categories. The 24 percent of the women who had never used effective contraception are theoretically explicable in terms of their ignorance, and thus can be reached by programs of contraceptive education. Similarly, the 6 percent of women who became pregnant despite the consistent use of effective contraception can be explained in terms of method failure, and they can be dealt with as a technological problem. The unwanted pregnancies in these latter two groups, then, are theoretically explicable and of the type that could be prevented by upgrading current family planning programs. The pregnancies of risk-takers, however, are neither. Second, and most important for a study of abortion, those pregnancies are the majority.

Category emergence: refining the concept of risk-taking. As the interviews with women who were statistical risk-takers continued, several coding categories began to emerge and the concept of risk-taking began to take shape. Almost immediately, however, it became necessary to redefine the operational definition of a risk-taker. As defined above, risk-taking is an objective phenomenon—the non-use of previously demonstrated contraceptive skills. What the interviews rapidly made clear is that risk-taking had a subjective component to it as well. Women whom we would not consider risk-takers in the objective sense defined above sometimes considered themselves to be risk takers; and conversely, women whom we would consider objectively to be risk-takers sometimes did not consider themselves to be so. For example, one woman pregnant with an IUD in place thought of herself as a risk-taker because she had switched from pills (which have an effectiveness rate of approximately 99.9%) to an IUD (which has as effectiveness rate of approximately 97%). She knew she had chosen a very slightly higher level of risk and thus considered herself a risk-taker. As the converse example, we interviewed a woman who was skipping her pills every Friday, Saturday, and Sunday and taking four pills on Monday morning. Every piece of printed information about pill-taking stresses the point that pills must be taken regularly, and at approximately the same time of day, so this woman was unquestionably a risk-taker, objectively speaking. However, she considered herself to be the victim of biological bad luck, and did not see her pregnancy as in any way related to having taken risks with her pills.

As a rule, women whose contraceptive histories showed that they had taken a risk, objectively speaking, usually also thought subjectively that they had taken a risk. (Only two cases in the group showed a discrepancy between objective and subjective definitions.) It was only when we theoretically sampled among the objectively defined non-risk-takers that we came upon a significant number of "false negatives." Women whom we had assumed were contraceptively ignorant or "method failures" often thought that they had not used the most effective contraceptive skills available to them and therefore considered themselves risk-takers.

At various points in the text we have outlined the difficulties involved in separating objective and subjective definitions of contraceptive risk-taking. We have pointed out that historically, the tendency in the literature has been to opt for Type One errors (the risk of including "false positives") and assuming that all women are risk-takers until conclusively proven otherwise. Here we were confronted with the opposite problem: many more women considered themselves to be risk-takers than our strict objective definition of them would include. Since we were interested in explaining the larger phenomenon of risk-taking, and since the slippage in the direction of false positives seemed relatively small, we theoretically sampled among all the objective categories outlined above, but we interviewed only those women who considered themselves risk-takers. As a result, any woman who did not consider herself to be a risk-taker was not interviewed. What this study attempts to discover, then, is how women in one possible subcategory of risk-takers—those who are aborting unwanted pregnancies—account for the subjective risk-taking which led to their pregnancies.

The intensive, open-ended, unstructured interviews with this carefully defined group of risk-takers immediately began to yield data which unfolded into coding categories. It was apparent, for example, that risk-taking women were totally aware of the likelihood of pregnancy and were engaged in constant calculations as to what the exact chances of getting pregnant really were. (This in contrast to the literature which said that these women engaged in "magical thinking," believing that pregnancy could not occur to them.) It was also clear that women found contraception was not the unmitigated boon that family planners like to think it is, and that pregnancy was not the unmitigated disaster that abortion counselors expect. Analysis of the first five interviews demonstrated that every woman interviewed mentioned some of what we were later to call the "costs of contraception" and "the benefits of pregnancy." Coding categories were set up for these two areas and themes within the categories were coded and tabulated. (Later they were reliability-coded by a second coder.) Next was coded the calculation of what we called at that point "awareness of pregnancy." (This emerged somewhat by chance since we were actually testing the idea that women engage in "magical thinking" around pregnancy.) Continuing interviews developed this concept until it became the "subjective probability of pregnancy" variable, and further interviews explored the effects of time on this variable. Thus "awareness of pregnancy" became "subjective probability of pregnancy," which became, in turn, "discounting."

At this point, what was emerging from these interviews was a heuristic model that closely approximated classical decision-making theory. There was a weighing of costs and benefits, an assigning of probabilities, and when the interviews were closely examined, it became clear that the awareness of abortion as an option acted for these women as "likelihood of reversal of consequences" variable, where women estimated how likely it was that they would have to suffer long-term consequences should their "cost accounting" prove wrong. In short, there emerged a paradigm of the "decision making under conditions of risk" model that is discussed in Chapter Two.

At the same time the decision-making model of risk-taking was developed, interviewing continued to strive for theoretical saturation on the variables noted. Because of the nature of the sample of women (and indeed of the universe of abortion-seeking women from whom they were drawn), there was relatively little variation of the awareness of abortion variable. (It is interesting to speculate whether these women are more aware of abortion as an option than non-risk-takers; further research is currently being undertaken to test this statistically with a control group.) The theoretical assumption that these variables do indeed vary was based on earlier non-risk-taking histories and helped account for earlier non-risking. In the two variables of ''utilities of contraception'' and ''utilities of pregnancy,'' however, more themes emerged until all themes covered in this study had been articulated and continued interviewing uncovered no more. Thus, by the end of over fifty interviews, we had theoretical saturation and a tentative theory: the theory of contraceptive risk-taking. Further interviews tested the limits of this theory.

Testing the adequacy of the theory of risk-taking. The most frequent question asked of this theory of risk-taking is whether it is not an over-rationalized model, a product of ad hoc reconstruction by women after they have become pregnant. This criticism has two parts, each we shall deal with separately. First, and to our mind less important theoretically, is the question of whether we are dealing with a reconstruction biased by the effects of the pregnancy and abortion. In part, this is undoubtedly true, if for no other reason than that we could not get access to the ''successful risk-takers''—those who do not get pregnant or whose benefits of pregnancy materialize in such a way that they feel free to continue the pregnancy. Abortion-seeking risk-takers, we cannot emphasize too strongly, are double losers: they have gotten pregnant and they have decided to abort. Thus our theory is explicitly aimed at accounting for only one subgroup of risk takers and for ones with the limitations described in Chapter One. However, although it is true that our data was gathered from women after they had been selected into this group, and some period of time after the decision making which led to the risk taking had occurred, it is important to remember that the women themselves *do not,* as a rule, reconstruct their behavior to themselves at all. In fact, as far as they are concerned, their behavior is inexplicable to them. When interviewed, they uniformly say that they do not understand how this could have happened to them.

We contend that this absence of a reconstruction of their own behavior is due to what Becker has called "the hierarchy of credibility."[8] As we demonstrated throughout the study, women who are cost accounting are doing so before they decide to take a risk. Once they have taken the risk, and particularly once that risk has had negative consequences, they must of necessity reexamine their cost accounting in the light of the actual and actualized present costs of the unwanted pregnancy and subsequent abortion. They are in the position of the automobile drivers noted in the present study who postpone having repairs made to their cars for financial reasons and who subsequently have an accident. Once the accident has occurred, the previous postponing of repairs seems extravagantly foolish, no matter how sensible it seemed before the accident. Unlike drivers, however, risk-taking women who get pregnant face an entire hierarchy of deliverers of social services who assume that women should have known before they engaged in the original cost accounting the real costs of getting pregnant. In other words, these hierarchies, from abortion counselors, to social workers, to doctors to well-meaning friends, assume that women should have known at the beginning of the process information that in fact only becomes available to them at the end, and these people stigmatize abortion-seeking risk-takers for not having had that information. Worse, they try to get risk-taking women who have gotten pregnant to "understand" their "self-destructiveness." In the light of this "hierarchy of credibility," virtually all of the present women subscribe to the prevailing ex post facto assumption that, given the results of their risk-taking (results which up to the present were vague in nature and vague in likelihood), they were irrational to have engaged in that risk-taking to begin with. As a consequence, we are reconstructing past events in a very different way than the women themselves; we are not concerned with the "reconstruction effect" of the women's explanations. True, our construction is based on remembered events, and on the women's accounts of what they did, but then so is virtually all verbatim data about past events which is obtained from respondents. Only written data do not have the effects of memory and reconstruction, and written data have pitfalls of their own.

The second part of the criticism—whether or not this is too rationalistic a model—goes to the basic assumptions of grounded theoretical research. Let us first dismiss one part of this criticism, which is the assumption that the women themselves are portrayed as too "rational." As noted in the text, "rational" is used in the strictly Weberian sense of the word, meaning the use of appropriate means to pursue chosen goals, and in this sense of the word the women are unquestionably rational. If "rational" is in fact a metaphor to suggest that the women are being portrayed as too conscious, as having an implausibly clear series of choices in mind, the reader is referred to the discussion of "tacit bargaining" in Chapter Five.

The other objection raised to the rational decision-making model of contraceptive risk-taking is the issue of how general the model is. In other words, to what extent can this model prove useful for a larger substantive theory of risk-taking, beyond the risk-taking of the women explicitly covered in this study? We have already noted that the model is a heuristic one, analogous to transformational grammars, which account for behavior without directly addressing the question of whether or not the actors carry around such models internally. Once the primary task of this study has been accomplished—the generating of a model to account for seemingly irrational behavior—can it be generalized?

We have reason to believe that it can. Although we have already noted in detail the limits of this clinic in terms of state-wide abortion statistics, and further noted the limitations of the women interviewed within this clinic, several factors lead us to believe that the model may well prove useful as the beginning of a wider substantive theory. First, to check against the possibility that the women in this study were overly aware of the components of tacit bargaining as a result of the two hours of counseling that they received, we interviewed series of women from a private practitioner's office where no counseling was offered. Still the model held up. Within this sample of women from a private practitioner, we selected from wealthy (Hollingshead and Redlich I) and very poor (Hollingshead and Redlich V) women and still the model held true, all responses falling into existing categories. As part of another study, I interviewed unwed mothers and their responses were coded with the coding protocol developed for this study. While a different series of social events were important to these women, and were reflected in their ultimate decisions about what to do with their pregnancies, the model of contraceptive decision making proved valid for them as well.

Although this is a preliminary study and the model which grew from it is still in the exploratory stage, further work can and should be done to extend it into a larger range of populations. When contraceptive risk-taking is assumed to be a social process which is explicable and at times eminently reasonable, the addition of the social categories of other kinds of contraceptive risk-takers not studied here should make this model useful in examining the larger problem of unwanted pregnancies in general.

2

The Women of the Abortion Clinic: Demographic, Referral, and Medical-Contraceptive Information

1. Month Seen

March 29-31	4
April	31
May	72
June	75
July	72
August	99
September	84
October 1-16	63
Total Number	500

2. Age

Under 15 years	1%
15 - 17 years	8%
18 - 20 years	27%
21 - 23 years	24%
24 - 30 years	29%
31 - 35 years	7%
Over 35 years	4%
No information	—
Average age	22 years

3. Educational Background

Some or no high school	10%
High school graduate . .	28%
Part college	41%
College graduate	12%
Graduate work	8%
No information	1%

4. Occupation

(If a client belonged in more than one category the highest one on the list above was given precedence over the others.)

Student (part or fulltime)	23%
Employed	54%
Housewife	10%
Unemployed	10%
No information.	3%

5. Marital Status

Single	64%
Married	22%
Divorced, separated, widowed	13%
No information	1%

6. Religious Background

Catholic	35%
Protestant	50%
Jewish	3%
No religious background	5%
Other	2%
No information	5%

7. Ethnic Background

White	81%
Latin American	7%
Black	4%
Asian, Oriental	7%
No information	1%

8. Social Class

(Five social classes, based on measures developed by Hollingshead and Redlich, *Social Class and Mental Illness,* Chapter 4, Appendix Two.)

I	4%
II	24%
III	50%
IV	13%
V . . . . (only 1 client)	—
No information	9%

9. Birth Control Method Used Since Last Menstrual Period

No method.	39%	A consistent method . .	20%
Rhythm	13%	douche/withdrawal .	1%
Rhythm and an		condom foam. . . .	13%
inconsistent method .	10%	diaphragm	2%
An inconsistent		IUD.	3%
method only	16%	pill	1%
		No information	2%

10. Previous Pregnancies

No	68%
Yes	31%
one	14%
two	9%
three	4%
four	2%
five or more.	2%
No information	1%

Of the 31% who had been pregnant before,
    14% had had previous legal abortions
    12% had had previous illegal abortions
    4% had previously given a child up for adoption

In terms of the total client population,
    4% had had previous legal abortions
    4% had had previous illegal abortions
    2% had previously given a child up for adoption

11. Most Effective Birth Control Method Ever Used

No Method 14%
Douche, rhythm, withdrawal 11%
Condom, foam 20%
Diaphragm, IUD 3%
Pill 50%
No information 2%

12. Psychiatric Diagnoses of Pregnancy Made at the Abortion Clinic

(Nomenclature and numbered diagnostic categories taken from
the *Diagnostic and Statistical Manual of Mental Disorders,*
published by the American Psychiatric Association)

Psychoses (295-298) 1%
    1 case   295.4   Acute schizophrenic episode
    1 case   296.2   Manic-depressive illness, depressed type
    1 case   296.3   Manic-depressive illness, circular type

Neuroses (300) 15%
  19 cases   300.0   Anxiety neuroses
   2 cases   300.1   Hysterical neuroses
   1 case   300.2   Phobic neuroses
  54 cases   300.4   Depressive neuroses
   1 case   300.6   Depersonalization neuroses

Personality disorders (301) 16%
   1 case   301.1   Cyclothymic personality
   3 cases   301.2   Schizoid personality
   2 cases   301.4   Obsessive compulsive personality
   4 cases   301.5   Hysterical personality
   1 case   301.7   Antisocial personality
  60 cases   301.81   Passive-aggressive personality
   6 cases   301.82   Inadequate personality
   1 case   301.9   (Unspecific personality disorder)

Psychophysiologic disorders (305) . . . .   —
   1 case   305.0   Psychophysiologic skin disorder

Transient situational disturbance (307) 65%
 326 cases   307   Transient situational disturbance
                           (adjustment reaction)

Behavior disorders of childhood and adolescence (308) . . . .   –
   1 case   308.3   Runaway reaction of childhood
                    (or adolescence)

Social maladjustments without manifest
psychiatric disorder (316) 1%
   2 cases   316.0   Marital maladjustment
   2 cases   316.1   Social maladjustment

No information 2%

13. Follow-Up Status (Two-Week Follow-Up)

Appointment made and kept 81%
Appointment made and kept, but only with M.D.
  (not counselor) 3%
Appointment made but not kept 13%
Appointment not made, lives out of area 3%
No information . . . .   (only 2 clients)   –

14. Post-Abortion Complications

Minor complications (bleeding, pain, fever) 13 (3.20%)
Retained clots; no hospitalization 7 (1.72%)
Infections 20 (4.92%)
   no hospitalization.   18   (4.43%)
   hospitalized (no operation)   2   (.49%)
Retained products 21 (5.17%)
   no hospitalization.   6   (1.48%)
   repeat operation   15   (3.69%)
Other complications . . . .   2 (.49%)
   (1 anesthetic complication, 1 uterine perforation)
   Total 63 (15.50%)

15. Patient's Reactions to Therapeutic Abortion

Positive 66%
Neutral/ambivalent 27%
Negative 7%

16. Knowledge of Birth Control at First Interview

No knowledge	1%
Little	17%
Some	35%
Much	33%
No information	14%

17. Gestation by Medical Examination at Time of First Appointment

(Halves rounded down; e.g., 8.5 weeks was considered 8 weeks)

Less than 7 weeks pregnant	11%
7 weeks pregnant	17%
8 weeks pregnant	23%
9 weeks pregnant	18%
10 weeks pregnant	18%
11 weeks pregnant	6%
12 weeks pregnant	2%
More than 12 weeks pregnant	1%
No information	4%
Average Gestation	8 weeks pregnant

APPENDIX

3

Abortions in the State of California

1. Percent Distribution of Selected Characteristics of Women Having Abortions in California, 1968-1971

Characteristic	*Year* 1968	1969	1970	1971
Total: Number	5,018	15,339	65,369	116,749
Percent	100.0	100.0	100.0	100.0
Ethnic group				
White	89.1	85.8	81.5	80.0
Black	7.2	9.5	11.8	13.7
Other and not reported	3.6	4.7	6.7	6.3
Marital status				
Married	30.1	25.2	25.4	26.3
Never married	53.0	57.5	55.0	51.0
Other and not reported	16.9	17.2	19.6	22.7
Pregnancy number				
1	51.4	54.5	49.0	47.8
2-3	23.4	24.2	26.8	30.1
4 or more	23.9	20.6	18.4	19.3
Not reported	1.4	0.8	5.8	2.8
Age				
Under 20 years	29.1	31.6	31.7	31.4
20-29	44.4	47.3	49.5	50.9
30-39	21.6	17.8	15.5	15.5
40 and over	4.7	3.1	2.4	2.2
Not reported	0.2	0.2	0.9	0.1
Source of payment				
Medi-Cal	7.8	19.5	35.8	38.5
Other and unknown	92.2	80.5	64.2	61.5
Type of hospital				
County	10.5	14.1	9.4	10.0
Private and other	89.5	84.9	90.6	90.0

Note: Percentages calculated independently and may not total 100.

Source for Tables 1 through 3: *Fifth Annual Report on the Implementation of the California Therapeutic Abortion Act.* A Report to the 1972 Legislature pursuant to Section 25955.5 of the Health and Safety Code. State of California, Human Relations Agency, Department of Public Health, Bureau of Maternal and Child Health, Berkeley.

2. Therapeutic Abortions, Age-Specific Abortion Rates, and Ratios of Abortions per 1,000 Live Births, California, 1969-1971
(by place of residence)

Age of women	Year 1969	1970	1971
	Estimated number of therapeutic abortions		
Total, age 15-44	14,584	59,626	103,678
10-14	329	745	1,166
15-19	4,488	18,634	31,806
20-24	4,770	20,020	35,988
25-34	3,873	16,106	27,940
35-44	1,453	4,866	7,944
	Therapeutic abortion rate, percent		
Total, age 15-44	3.4	13.9	24.2
10-14	0.3	0.8	1.2
15-19	5.1	21.0	35.9
20-24	5.5	23.0	41.4
25-34	2.9	12.0	20.9
35-44	1.2	4.1	6.7
	Therapeutic abortions per 1,000 live births		
Total, age 15-44	41.4	164.9	286.7
10-14	483.1	1,001.3	1,567.2
15-19	76.4	305.4	521.3
20-24	35.8	145.8	262.1
25-34	28.2	113.4	196.7
35-44	65.2	228.6	373.2

3. Therapeutic Abortions and Live Births by Age and Marital Status of Women, California, 1969 and 1970

Abortions, Births, Ratio	All ages		Under 20		20-24		25 and over	
	1970	1969	1970	1969	1970	1969	1970	1969
Therapeutic abortions								
Total number	62,542	15,476	19,839	4,977	20,514	5,930	21,609	5,538
Unmarried	46,316	11,628	18,564	4,764	16,467	4,153	10,807	2,695
Married	15,868	3,753	1,161	185	3,927	751	10,693	2,804
Percent unmarried	74.5	75.6	94.1	96.3	80.7	84.7	50.3	49.0
Live births								
Total number	362,652	352,907	61,757	59,435	137,283	133,399	163,566	160,029
Unmarried	45,593	42,085	19,494	17,908	15,615	14,557	10,469	9,609
Married	317,059	310,822	42,263	41,527	121,668	118,842	153,097	150,420
Percent unmarried	12.6	11.9	31.6	30.1	11.4	10.9	6.4	6.0
Ratio: therapeutic abortions per 1,000								
Live births, total	172.5	43.9	321.2	83.7	149 4	37.0	132.1	34.6
Unmarried	1,015.9	276.3	952.3	266.0	1,054.6	285.3	1,032.3	280.5
Married	50.0	12.1	27.5	4.5	32.3	6.3	69.8	18.6

Note: Totals include women with marital status or age unknown.

4

Direct Comparisons of Women Having Abortions in California and Women Having Abortions in the Abortion Clinic

Comparison	California	The Abortion Clinic
Year	1971	1971-72
Number of abortions	116,749	500
Age distribution		
☐ under 20	31.4%	36%
20-29	50.9%	53%
over 30	17.7%	11%
Marital status		
☐ single	51%	64%
married	26.3%	22%
separated, widowed, divorced	22.7%	13%
Ethnicity		
☐ White	80%	81%
Black	13.7%	4%
Other and not reported	6.3%	15%
Pregnancy number (this pregnancy)		
☐ One	47.8%	68%
Two-Three	30.1%	23%
Four or More	19.3%	8%

DISCUSSION OF APPENDIX FOUR

The State of California tabulates only six variables in its coverage of women having abortions; the current study tabulates thirty-three variables. Of these thirty-three, four (noted here) are roughly comparable to the state variables, although as noted, age ranges were defined slightly differently. (The other two state variables were for type of hospital and source of payment; the women in the present study all paid for the abortion through private means, and had their abortions at the same hospital.)

In examining the four comparable variables, it is evident that the women at the Abortion Clinic were younger, more likely to be single, far less likely to be separated, widowed, or divorced, and far less likely to be Black than their counterparts in the state as a whole. In addition, they were considerably more likely to be primagravidas (pregnant for the first time) and considerably less likely to be having a fourth or higher order pregnancy.

These skews in distribution between the Clinic and the state are most probably the effect of the payment structure of the Clinic and the fact that it was indeed a clinic approach. As noted in some detail in the body of this study, the Clinic offered relatively low-cost abortions by following a clinic approach. The Clinic did not, however, accept Medi-Cal, California's medical care to the indigent. Thus there was a selection factor for women too poor to pay the prevailing private practice fees, yet not poor enough to qualify for Welfare. This probably accounts for the bias toward young, single, white women who were also middle class (see Appendix One). The age and parity biases are probably a product of the fact that women who have been pregnant before tend to have their own private practitioner to go to, and to the fact that higher birth orders are more likely to occur to poorer women, who are in turn more likely to be eligible for Medi-Cal.

Notes

1. A. F. Guttmacher, "Changing Attitudes and Practices Concerning Abortion: A Sociomedical Revolution," *Maryland State Medical Journal*, Vol. 20 (December 1971), pp. 59-63. For the California abortion to live birth ratio: Bureau of Maternal and Child Health, State Department of Public Health, *A Report to the Legislature on the Implementation of the 1967 Therapeutic Abortion Act* (Berkeley, California, 1972, 1973). Figures on California live birth rate prepared by Beth Berkov and June Sklar, in "The Impact of Legalized Abortion on Fertility in California," Preliminary Paper, IPUR (Berkeley, California), Table 1, p. 14.

2. For data on changes in the overall fertility (a necessary part of examining the abortion situation) from 1960-1971, see Beth Berkov and June Sklar, "The Impact of Legalized Abortion on Fertility in California," IPUR Preliminary Paper No. 1 (Berkeley, California, September 1972).

3. Judith Blake, "Abortion and Public Opinion: The 1960-1970 Decade," *Science*, Vol. 171 (12 February 1971), pp. 540-549. Also, see Westoff *et al.*, "The Structure of Attitudes Towards Abortion," *The Milbank Memorial Fund Quarterly*, Vol. 47, No. 1 (Part I, January 1969).

4. Blake, "Abortion and Public Opinion." See also *Current Opinion*, The Roper Public Opinion Research Center, Vol. I, Issue 3, and Vol. I, Issue 6 (Williamstown, Mass., March 1973 and June 1973).

5. Georges Devereux, "A Typological Study of Abortion in 350 Primitive, Ancient, and Pre-Industrial Societies," in Rosen (ed.), *Therapeutic Abortion* (New York: The Julian Press, 1954), p. 97; Kingsley Davis, "The Theory of Change and Response in Modern Demographic History," *Population Index*, Vol. 29 (October 1963).

6. Christopher Tietze and Hans Lehfeldt, "Legal Abortion in Eastern Europe," *Journal of the American Medical Association*, Vol. 175 (April 1, 1961). The exact ratios of abortions per 1,000 live births, from Daniel Callahan, *Abortion: Law, Choice, and Morality* (New York and London: The Macmillan Company, 1970), pp. 242-243, are as follows:

	1965	1966	1967	1968
Bulgaria	750	760	790	600
Czechoslovakia	350	400	440	465
E. Germany	–	61	80	–
Hungary	1,360	1,350	1,260	1,300
Poland	420	420	–	–
Rumania	4,000	–	–	–

7. Minoru Muramatsu, "Effect of Induced Abortion on the Reduction of Fertility in Japan," *Milbank Memorial Fund Quarterly*, Vol. 38 (1960), p. 154.

8. Callahan, *Abortion*, pp. 156-174; Mariano Requena, "Induced Abortion in Latin America," in Hall (ed.), *Abortion in a Changing World* (New York: Columbia University Press, 1970), Vol. 1, pp. 338-352 (Table 1). Cited in Callahan, *Abortion*, p. 172.

9. Calculated by dividing the number of abortions by the number of pregnant women (those having live births and those having abortions).

10. David M. Heer, "Abortion, Contraception, and Population Policy in the Soviet Union," *Demography*, Vol. 2 (1965), pp. 531-539; R. Armijo and T. Monreal, *Components of Population Change in Latin America* (New York: Milbank Memorial Fund, 1965).

11. Minoru Muramatsu, *Japan's Experience in Family Planning: Past and Present* (Tokyo: Family Planning Federation of Japan, 1967), p. 83.

12. Keeping in mind that the 1971 abortion to live birth ratio in California was 286:1000, comparable figures for Scandinavia (also per 1000 live births) are as follows:

	Sweden	Denmark	Finland	Norway
1966	59	67	67	66
1967	79	80	–	–
1968	95	119	241	96

Source: 1966, 1967, Callahan, *Abortion*, p. 193; 1968, *Demographic Yearbook*, 23rd Issue (1968), Tables 25 (legal induced abortions), pp. 656, 23 (live births), and p. 638. These are provisional figures.

13. Callahan, *Abortion*, p. 204.

14. Bureau of Maternal and Child Health, State Department of Public Health (Berkeley, California), unpublished cross tabulations.

15. Only Nevada has a higher suicide rate than California; the rate in Nevada is 24.3 per 100,000 population, in California it is 16.3. The national rate is 10.7. Source: *Vital Statistics of the United States*, Vol. II, "Mortality" (1968), Table 1-14, "Death rates for 69 selected causes, United States, each division and state." The measuring of alcoholism rates are very problematic; until recently the "Jellinek formula" was used to transform the mortality rates from cirrhosis of the liver into alcoholism. Of late, this formula has been discounted: see Robert Popham, "Indirect Methods of Measuring Alcoholism Prevalence: A Critical Evaluation," in *Alcohol and Alcoholism* (Toronto: University of Toronto Press, 1970), pp. 294-306. However, California still has the second highest (again after Nevada) mortality rate from cirrhosis of the liver. For an overview, see Robin Room, *Quarterly Journal of Studies on Alcohol*, Supplement Number 6 (May 1972).

16. In California, for example, the percentage of applications approved were:

	Applications	Approvals	Percent Approved
1969	16,384	15,952	97.4
1970	65,550	65,044	99.2

(More recent data are not available.) For prior years the percent of all applications which resulted in performed abortions were (beginning with November and December of 1967, the first two months the law was in effect):

1967	86.9 performed
1968	88.3
1969	93.5
1970	95.6

(But note that this includes a significant number of women whose applications were approved, but who chose to continue the pregnancy on their own initiative. See Callahan, *Abortion,* p. 204.)

17. Blake, "Abortion and Public Opinion," p. 540.

18. Muramatsu, *Japan's Experience in Family Planning,* p. 59.

19. Mariano Requena, "Social and Economic Correlates of Induced Abortion in Santiago, Chile," *Demography,* Vol. 2 (1965), pp. 37-41.

20. Alan Guttmacher, in Calderone (ed.), *Abortion in the United States* (New York: Hoeber-Harper, 1958), pp. 93-94.

21. M. S. Guttmacher, "The Legal Status of Therapeutic Abortions," in Rosen (ed.), *Therapeutic Abortion.*

22. Blake, "Abortion and Public Opinion," p. 541 (Table 1).

23. Westoff *et al.,* "The Structure of Attitudes Towards Abortion," p. 12.

24. This assertion is based on the fact that except for Catholics educated in Catholic schools, the primary predictor of contraceptive use is education. See Westoff *et al., The Third Child* (Princeton, New Jersey: Princeton University Press, 1963), p. 115. See also Grabill *et al., The Fertility of American Women* (New York: Wiley and Sons, 1958), p. 281. The 1970 census reveals California women to be as educated as the mean, and significantly more so in certain areas of the state.

25. Bureau of Maternal and Child Health, *Report to the Legislature* (1972).

26. National Center for Health Statistics, National Natality Survey Statistics, *Monthly Vital Statistics Report,* Vol. 18, No. 12 Supplement (March 27, 1970).

27. Regarding access to contraception, P. K. Whelpton *et al., Fertility and Family Planning in the United States* (Princeton, New Jersey: Princeton University Press, 1966), pp. 239-242; 248-254; see also Chapter Six. Regarding how abortions are paid for, Bureau of Maternal and Child Health, *Report to the Legislature* (1972), Table 1.

28. Bureau of Maternal and Child Health, *Report to the Legislature* (1972), Table 1.

29. Barney Glaser and Anselm Strauss, *The Discovery of Grounded Theory* (Chicago: Aldine Press, 1967).

30. Raymond Pearl, "Contraception and Fertility in 2,000 Women," *Human Biology,* Vol. 4 (September 1932), pp. 363-407. See also R. G. Potter, "Additional Measures of Use-Effectiveness of Contraception," *Milbank Memorial Fund Quarterly,* Vol. 41 (1963), p. 400, and Potter, "Some Relationships Between Long Range and Short Range Risks of Pregnancy," *Milbank Memorial Fund Quarterly,* Vol. 38 (1960), p. 255.

NOTES TO CHAPTER 2

1. On the American Birth Control League, see David Kennedy, *Birth Control in America: The Career of Margaret Sanger* (New Haven: Yale University Press, 1971). On the Sachs abortion, see Margaret Sanger, *An Autobiography* (New York: Norton, 1938), p. 92.

2. President's Committee on Population and Family Planning, "Population and Family Planning—the Transition from Concern to Action" (Washington, D.C.: Government Printing Office, 1968); Harkavy *et al.*, "Implementing DHEW Policy on Family Planning and Population—A Consultant's Report," Department of Health, Education and Welfre Publication (Washington, D.C.: Government Printing Office, 1967).

3. John T. Noonan, Jr., *Contraception: A History of its Treatment by the Catholic Theologians and Canonists* (Cambridge: Harvard University Press, 1966), p. 413.

4. National Academy of Science, "The Growth of the U.S. Population," National Research Council Publication 1279, p. 22; John Rock, M.D., *The Time Has Come* (New York: Alfred A. Knopf, 1963).

5. Mary Jean Cornish, *Doctors and Family Planning* (New York: National Committee on Maternal Health, 1972).

6. Kennedy, *Birth Control in America,* pp. 15-21.

7. Joseph R. Gusfield, *Symbolic Crusade* (Urbana and London: University of Illinois Press, 1966).

8. Margaret Sanger, *Autobiography* (New York: Norton, 1938), pp. 93-95.

9. United States Army, *Index Catalogue of the Library of the Surgeon General's Office,* 2nd Series, 3 (Washington, D.C.: Government Printing Office, 1898), pp. 800-802.

10. For details about how the birth-control movement achieved this social acceptability and of its flirtation with the Eugenics Movement of the 30's, see Samuel Haber, *Efficiency and Uplift: Scientific Management in the Progressive Era* (Chicago: University of Chicago Press, 1964). See also Margaret Sanger, *Woman and the New Race* (New York: Brentano's, 1922) as well as Kennedy, *Birth Control in America,* pp. 72-107.

11. L. Bumpass and C. Westoff, "The 'Perfect Contraceptive' Population," *Science,* Vol. 169 (1970), pp. 1177-1182.

12. Oscar Harkavy *et al.,* "Implementation of DHEW Policy on Family Planning and Population" (The Ford Foundation, 1967); and also Harkavy *et al.,* "Family Planning and Public Policy: Who is Misleading Whom?" *Science,* Vol. 162, 25 (July 1969), pp. 367-373. The five million figure comes from G. Varky *et al., Five Million Women—Who's Who Among Americans in Need of Subsidized Family Planning Services* (New York: Planned Parenthood/World Population, 1967). (Campbell, in *Journal of Marriage and The Family,* Vol. 30, 1968, estimated the figure to be 4.6 million.)

13. Judith Blake, "Population Policy for Americans: Is the Government Being Misled?" *Science,* Vol. 164, No. 3879 (May 2, 1969), p. 523.

14. This is, of course, a restatement of Merton's classic typology. See Robert K. Merton, *Social Theory and Social Structure* (New York: The Free Press, 1957), pp. 139-160.

15. Blake, "Population Policy for Americans," p. 523.

16. *Fortune*, Vol. 14 (July 1936), p. 158.

17. Ronald Freedman *et al.*, *Family Planning, Sterility, and Population Growth* (New York: McGraw-Hill, 1959), p. 61. This figure has since been replicated by virtually all of the recent KAP studies for married fecund women.

18. Christopher Tietze, "Relative Effectiveness," in Calderone (ed.), *Manual of Family Planning and Contraceptive Practice*, 2nd edition (Baltimore: Williams and Wilkins, 1970), p. 269 (pill effectiveness) and p. 271 (IUD effectiveness).

19. Christopher Tietze, "The Use-Effectiveness of Contraceptive Methods," in Kiser (ed.), *Research in Family Planning* (Princeton, New Jersey: Princeton University Press, 1962), p. 367, Table 6 (based on Family Growth in Metropolitan America data, standardized).

20. Tietze, "Relative Effectiveness," in Calderone (ed.), pp. 271-274, and Tietze, "Use Effectiveness," in Kiser (ed.), pp. 365-368.

21. This was a pre-coded response, coded during the interview by trained social workers. The actual contraceptive histories of the women support this finding. See Appendix Two, Table 11, Most Effective Contraception Ever Used.

22. The median age at first marriage for females is:

1940	22.1	1970	23.2
1950	21.0	1971	23.1
1960	22.8	1972	23.3
1965	22.8		

Sources: *1940 Census of Population*, Differential Fertility, 1940 and 1910, cited in Grabill *et al.*, *The Fertility of American Women* (New York: John Wiley and Sons, 1958), p. 291. *1950 Census of Population*, Vol. IV, Special Reports, Part 2, Chapter E, Table 4, Duration of Current Marital Status. U.S. Bureau of the Census, *Current Population Reports*, "Population Characteristics, Marital Status, and Living Arrangements," March 1972.

23. Grabill *et al.*, *The Fertility of American Women*, pp. 328-329.

24. In the 1960 GAF, for example, P. K. Whelpton *et al.*, (*Fertility and Family Planning in the United States*, Princeton, New Jersey: Princeton University Press, 1965) demonstrate average ideal family size to be about 3.5 (p. 33) for the cohort under discussion here. For comparative data on the birth expectations of the younger cohort, see U.S. Bureau of the Census, *Current Population Reports*, Series P-23, No. 36, "Fertility Indicators: 1970" (Washington, D.C.: U.S. Government Printing Office, 1971), Table 30.

25. See Glaser and Strauss, *The Discovery of Grounded Theory*, and Appendix One for discussion of the sampling method.

26. Eugene Sandberg and Ralph Jacobs, "Psychology of the Misuse and Rejection of Contraception," *American Journal of Obstetrics and Gynecology*, Vol. 110, Number 2 (May 15, 1971), p. 228.

27. Ruth Lidz, "Emotional Factors in the Success of Contraception," *Fertility and Sterility*, 20 (1969), p. 762.

28. Blake, "Population Policy for Americans," pp. 522-529. See also Blake in *Science*, Vol. 165 (19 September 1969), p. 1203, where she points out

that in the 1960 GAF studies in 50 percent of the cases where the couples said the last child was "unwanted," *one* member of the couple "really wanted" the child. See also Westoff *et al., The Third Child: A Study in the Prediction of Fertility* (Princeton, New Jersey: Princeton University Press, 1963), p. 236, where women who had defined their last child as "unwanted" said they would still have the same number of children, if they were to begin over again.

29. Elizabeth Herzog, "Unmarried Mothers: Some Questions to be Answered, Some Answers to be Questioned," *Child Welfare,* 41 (1962). See also Clark Vincent, "The Unwed Mother and Sampling Bias," *American Sociological Review,* Vol. 19, No. 5 (October 1954), pp. 562-567.

30. Sidney Bolter, "The Psychiatrist's Role in Therapeutic Abortion: The Unwitting Accomplice," *American Journal of Psychiatry,* Vol. 119, No. 4 (October 1962), p. 313. Bolter suggests that women may exaggerate psychiatric distress to justify to *themselves* the necessity of the abortion. See also David P. Henry, "Psychological Studies in Abortion," in *Psychological Perspectives on Population* (New York: Basic Books, 1973), pp. 241-273.

31. Jerome D. Pauker, "Girls Pregnant Out of Wedlock: Are They Pregnant Because They Are Different or Are They Different Because They Are Pregnant?" *The Double Jeopardy, The Triple Crisis* (New York: National Council on Illegitimacy, n.d.).

32. Tietze, "Relative Effectiveness," p. 268.

33. Juan Zanartu *et al.,* "Low Dosage Oral Progestogens to Control Fertility: Clinical Investigation," *Obstetrics and Gynecology,* Vol. 43, No. 1 (January 1974), points out that both "low dosage" and regular anovulent pills often act to thin out the endometrium and to change the pH of the cervical mucosa, hence making contraception less likely even should ovulation occur.

34. Edward Pohlman, *The Psychology of Birth Planning* (Cambridge, Mass.: Schenkman Publishing Company, 1969), pp. 382-389. See also Lee Rainwater, *And The Poor Get Children* (Chicago: Quadrangle, 1960).

35. F. Clothier, "Psychological Implications of Unmarried Parenthood," *American Journal of Orthopsychiatry,* Vol. 13, No. 541 (July 1943).

36. Sandberg and Jacobs, "Psychology of the Misuse and Rejection of Contraception," p. 228.

37. Georges Devereux, *A Study of Abortion in Primitive Societies* (New York: The Julian Press, 1955), pp. 89-133. See also Georges Devereux, "A Typological Study of Abortion in 350 Primitive, Ancient, and Pre-Industrial Societies," in Rosen (ed.), *Therapeutic Abortion.*

38. The question has been raised whether or not people are aware of "biological excess" when it comes to children, especially in primitive societies lacking statisticians, economists, demographers, and public media to tell them so. In fact, Himes suggests that primitive societies are often acutely aware of the Malthusian relationship between the production of children and available food supplies. See Norman Himes, *A Medical History of Contraception* (Baltimore: Williams and Wilkins, 1963). See also A. M. Carr-Saunders, *The Population Problem* (Oxford: Clarendon Press, 1922).

39. Bureau of Maternal and Child Health, State Department of Public Health,

A Report to the Legislature on the Implementation of the Therapeutic Abortion Act of 1967 (1972). See also Beth Berkov and June Sklar, "The Impact of Legalized Abortion on Fertility in California," Preliminary Paper (Berkeley, California: International Population and Urban Research).

40. Philip Sarrel and Ruth Lidz, "Contraceptive Failure—Psychosocial Factors: the Unwed," in Calderone (ed.), *Manual of Family Planning and Contraceptive Practice* (Baltimore: Williams and Wilkins Company, 1969), p. 251.

41. In this, we are adhering to Weber's definition of rationality: Max Weber, *Max Weber on the Methodology of the Social Sciences* (Glencoe, Illinois: The Free Press, 1949), p. 53.

42. "Scientific" is Parsons' term. See Talcott Parsons, *Toward a General Theory of Action* (New York: Harper and Row), pp. 48-52.

43. Georges Devereux, "A Psychoanalytic Study of Contraception," *Journal of Sex Research,* Vol. 1 (1965), pp. 105-134. Lehfeldt has used for what we have called "Contraceptive risk-taking" the phrase "Willful Exposure to Unwanted Pregnancy" (WEUP) and adds, "the exposure to pregnancy is called willful rather than accidental, for, in the Freudian sense, it seems to betray an emotional desire for pregnancy that is neither conscious nor rationally sound." See Hans Lehfeldt, "Willful Exposure to Unwanted Pregnancy," *American Journal of Obstetrics and Gynecology,* Vol. 78 (1959), pp. 661-665.

44. For an in-depth presentation of this viewpoint, see "Proceedings of a Conference on Psychological Measurement in the Study of Population Problems" (mimeo, Berkeley: Institute of Personality Assessment and Research, University of California and the American Psychological Association, Task Force on Psychology, Family Planning, and Population Policy). See also the "MacDonald Report," "Internal-External Locus of Control and the Practice of Birth Control," *Psychological Reports,* Vol. 21, p. 206. Chilman also argues that contraceptive use is a matter where "the logic of emotions" outweighs "the logic of the intellect." Catherine Chilman, "Some Psychological Aspects of Fertility, Family Planning, and Population Policy in the U.S.," in Fawcett (ed.).

45. The term is Eugene Sandberg's; see Sandberg and Jacobs, "Psychology of the Misuse and Rejection of Contraception," p. 228.

46. Donald J. Bogue, "Some Tentative Recommendations for a 'Socially Correct' Family Planning Communication and Motivation Program in India," in Kiser (ed.), *Research in Family Planning,* pp. 503-538.

47. On awareness of the process, and for the most cogent review of the literature on "risky choices," see W. Edwards, "Behavioral Decision Theory," *Annual Review of Psychology,* Vol. 12, pp. 473-498; see also von Neumann and Morgenstern, *Theory of Games and Economic Behavior,* 2nd Edition (Princeton: Princeton University Press, 1947) for the classical statement on static and risky decision models. On individual perception of costs and benefits, see A. Iversky, "Additivity, Utility, and Subjective Probability," *Journal of Mathematical Psychology,* Vol. 4, No. 2 (1967), pp. 175-202. See also D. Davidson *et al., Decision Making: An Experimental Approach* (Stanford, Ca.: Stanford University Press, 1957), pp. 49-81, and R. D. Luce and

P. Suppes, "Preference, Utility, and Subjective Probability," in Luce (ed.), *Handbook of Mathematical Psychology* (New York: Wiley and Sons, 1965), pp. 249-441.

48. Jessie Bernard, *The Future of Marriage* (New York: World Publishing, 1972), p. 7.

49. A. Scodel, P. Ratoosh, and J. S. Minas, "Some Personality Correlates of Decision Making Under Conditions of Risk," *Behavioral Sciences,* Vol. 4 (1959), pp. 19-28. For a more general demonstration of the effects of personality variables on risk-taking style, see J. W. Atkinson, "Motivational Determinants of Risk Taking Behavior," *Psychological Review,* Vol. 64 (1957), pp. 359-372. For another exposition of the two main types of risk-taking styles, see W. Edwards, "The Theory of Decision Making," *Psychological Bulletin,* Vol. 51, No. 4, pp. 380-417.

50. David, "Psychological Studies in Abortion," underlines the prevailing ideology of abortion vis-à-vis unwanted pregnancies: he assumes that unwanted conceptions which end in abortion are "hindsight" events, and the product of either poor planning or contraceptive failure (pp. 262-266).

51. W. Edwards, "The Theory of Decision Making," *Psychological Bulletin,* Vol. 51, No. 4, pp. 390-391.

NOTES TO CHAPTER 3

1. Christopher Tietze, "Mortality with Contraception and Induced Abortion," *Studies in Family Planning,* No. 45 (September 1969), pp. 6-8.

2. The actual figures are as follows:

	Total	Mental	Physical	Rape/Incest
Jan.-Dec. 1969				
Number	16.384	13,318	404	662
Percent	100.00	93.5	2.5	4.0
Jan.-Dec. 1970				
Number	65,550	64,343	720	487
Percent	100.00	98.2	1.1	.7

Source: Bureau of Maternal and Child Health, California State Department of Public Health, *Report to the Legislature on the Implementation of the 1967 Therapeutic Abortion Act* (Berkeley, California, 1971).

3. *Ibid.* (1970), p. 6.

4. Allison Davis, *Social Class Influences on Learning* (Cambridge: Harvard University Press, 1948). See also Lee Rainwater, *And The Poor Get Children* (Chicago: Quadrangle, 1960), p. 51.

5. American Psychiatric Association, *Diagnostic and Statistical Manual of Mental Disorders,* Third Edition (Washington, D.C.: 1968). Prepared by the Committee on Nomenclature and Statistics.

6. Edwin Lemert, "Paranoia and the Dynamics of Exclusion," *Sociometry,* Vol. 25 (1962), pp. 2-20. Lemert's article refers to the labeling of paranoids; for

a fuller application of labeling theory in a wider range of social circumstances, see Thomas Scheff, *Being Mentally Ill; A Sociological Theory* (Chicago: Aldine, 1966).

7. For these three theories regarding the origin of social control of sexual activity, see: Claude Lèvi-Strauss, *Structural Anthropology* (Garden City, New York: Anchor Books, 1967), p. 60; Sigmund Freud, *Civilization and its Discontents* (New York: W. W. Norton and Company, 1961), pp. 49-53; and Kingsley Davis and Judith Blake, "Social Structure and Fertility: An Analytic Framework," *Economic Development and Cultural Change,* Vol. 14 (April 1956), pp. 211-235.

8. These data are from the Catholic Social Services and the Catholic *Voice,* who supplied both the *numbers* of nominal Catholics in the area and the *percentage.* When 1970 Census data became available, the percentages given us by these sources were rechecked by independently computing them with fresh population figures as the denominator. (The Census Bureau does not now do surveys on religion, and has not done so since one *Current Population Report* survey in 1958. The author is indebted to Laura Tow for investigative and computational aid for this data.)

9. See Neil Smelser, *A Theory of Collective Behavior* (New York: The Free Press, 1962), pp. 13-14, for an outline of the "value added" process as it applies to social events.

10. See Judith M. Bardwick, "Psychological and Psychosomatic Responses to Oral Contraceptive Use," *Women on Campus: A Symposium* (Ann Arbor: Continuing Education for Women, 1969); and Karen Paige, "The Effects of Contraceptives on Affective Fluctuations Associated with the Menstrual Cycle" (unpublished Ph.D. dissertation, University of Michigan, 1969).

11. Alan Grant, "Infertility due to Anovulation Before and After the 'Pill Era'," *International Journal of Fertility,* Vol. 18, No. 1 (1973), pp. 44-48. D. R. Halbert, "Anovulation Following Use of Oral Contraceptions; A Review," *North Carolina Medical Journal,* Vol. 32 (September 1971), pp. 379-383.

NOTES TO CHAPTER 4

1. That these are traditional virtues into which women are socialized is demonstrated in Inge Broverman *et al.,* "Sex Role Stereotypes and Judgement of Mental Health," *Journal of Consulting Psychology,* Vol. 34, No. 19, pp. 1-7. See also "New Perspectives on Women," *Journal of Social Issues* (special issue), Vol. 28, No. 2 (1972).

2. See Malinowski, "Parenthood—The Basis of Social Structure," in Calverton and Schmalhausen (eds.), *The New Generation,* pp. 129-143.

3. Pearl, "Contraception and Fertility in 2,000 Women," pp. 364-407.

4. See F. Clothier, "Psychological Implications of Unmarried Parenthood," *American Journal of Orthopsychiatry,* Vol. 13 (July 1943); and Peter Gergin *et*

al., "Some Psychiatric Aspects of Illegitimate Pregnancy During Early Adolescence" (paper presented in the 1967 meeting of the American Orthopsychiatric Association); and Louise K. Trout, "Services to the Unmarried Mother," *Child Welfare,* Vol. 30 (February 1956); and Young, *Out of Wedlock.*

5. See Jacob Tuckman, "Attempted Suicide and Family Disorganization," *Journal of Genetic Psychology,* Vol. 105, No. 2 (1964), pp. 187-193; and Schniederman *et al.*, "Separation and Attempted Suicide," *Archives of General Psychiatry,* Vol. 15, No. 2, pp. 158-164.

6. Judith Wallerstein, "Psychosocial Sequelae of Therapeutic Abortion in Young, Unmarried Women," *Archives of General Psychiatry,* Vol. 27 (December 1972).

7. Sandberg and Jacobs, "Psychology of the Misuse and Rejection of Contraception," p. 234.

NOTES TO CHAPTER 5

1. See Max Weber, *Methodology,* p. 55.

2. Thomas C. Schelling, *The Strategy of Conflict* (New York: Oxford University Press, 1963), pp. 5, 21. For a fuller exposition, see pp. 21-52, 54-58.

3. For example, Sandberg and Jacobs, "The Psychology of the Misuse and Rejection of Contraception," pp. 227-241.

4. National Safety Council, Chicago, Illinois; quoted in the *San Francisco Chronicle,* December 31, 1972.

5. On "future time perspectives," see Allison Davis, *Social Class Influences on Learning* (Cambridge: Harvard University Press, 1948); see also Lee Rainwater, *And the Poor Get Children,* p. 51 and *passim.* On psychological differences shown by standardized tests, see C. B. Bakker and C. R. Dightman, "Psychological Factors in Fertility Control," *Fertility and Sterility,* 15 (1964), p. 559; see also J. S. Kutner and T. J. Duffy, "A Psychological Analysis of Oral Contraceptives and the Interuterine Device," *Contraceptions,* 2, pp. 289-296.

6. For more information on the psychology of risk-taking styles, see J. W. Atkinson *et al.*, "The Achievement Motive, Goal Setting, and Probability Preferences," *Journal of Abnormal and Social Psychology,* Vol. 60 (1960), pp. 27-36; J. S. Atkinson, "Motivational Determinants of Risk-Taking Behavior," *Psychological Review,* Vol. 64 (1957), pp. 359-372; and A. Scodel, P. Ratoosh, and J. S. Minas, "Some Personality Correlates of Decision Making Under Conditions of Risk," *Behavioral Science,* Vol. 4 (1959), pp. 19-28.

7. Thomas J. Scheff, *Being Mentally Ill* (Chicago: Aldine Press, 1966), p. 107.

8. U.S. Bureau of the Census, *Current Population Reports;* Series P-28, No. 248, "Birth Expectations and Fertility: June 1972" (U.S. Government Printing Office, Washington, D.C., 1973). U.S. Bureau of the Census, *Current Population Reports,* Series P-20, No. 212, "Marital Status and Family Status: March 1970" (U.S. Government Printing Office, Washington, D.C., 1971).

9. See also Dorothy Nortman, "Parental Age as a Factor in Pregnancy

Outcome and Child Development," *Reports on Population/Family Planning* (The Population Council, August 1974).

10. C. B. Jacobson *et al.*, "Intrauterine Diagnosis and Management of Genetic Defects," *American Journal of Obstetrics and Gynecology,* 99 (November 15, 1967), pp. 796-807. See also H. A. Thiede, "Obstetricians Should Learn the Technique of Amniocentis," *Obstetrics and Gynecology,* 31 (January 1968), pp. 146-148.

11. Judith Blake, "Reproductive Motivation and Population Policy," *Bioscience,* Vol. 31, No. 5 (March 1, 1971), p. 219.

12. U.S. Bureau of the Census, *1970 Census of Population;* Vol. II, 4B Persons by Family Characteristics, Table II; and *1960 Census of Population,* Vol. II, 4B, Persons by Family Characteristics, Table 15.

13. Joseph Rovinsky, "Abortion Recidivism: A Problem in Preventive Medicine," *Journal of Obstetrics and Gynecology,* Vol. 39, No. 5 (May 1972), pp. 649-659. Alan Margolis, "Therapeutic Abortion Follow-Up Study," *American Journal of Obstetrics and Gynecology,* Vol. 110, No. 2 (May 15, 1971), pp. 243-248.

NOTES TO CHAPTER 6

1. On postponing birth of the first child, see U.S. Bureau of the Census, "Previous and Prospective Fertility: 1967," *Current Population Reports,* Series P-20, No. 211 (Washington, D.C.: U.S. Government Printing Office, 1970). See also in the same series: "Birth Expectations and Fertility: June 1972," Series P-20, No. 248 (1973) and "Fertility of the Population: January 1969," Series P-20, No. 203 (Government Printing Office, 1970). On the total number of children women intend to bear, see U.S. Bureau of the Census, "Birth Expectations and Fertility: 1972," *Current Population Reports* (special report), No. 248 (Government Printing Office, June 1972).

2. Willard Waller, *The Family: A Dynamic Interpretation* (New York: The Cordon Company, 1938), Chapter 10.

3. *Ibid.,* p. 240.

4. The term "boarded out" is Alva Myrdal's: *Nation and Family* (London: K. Paul, Trench, Trubner and Company, 1947).

5. Elizabeth Faulkner Baker, *Technology and Women's Work* (New York: Columbia University Press, 1964), Chapter 22.

6. Alice Rossi, paper presented at the Sociologists for Women in Society session of the American Sociological Association Meetings, August 1973.

7. Percent of women experiencing premarital coitus by age 20 in specified years:

1920 and before . . .	8%	1940 - 1949	21%
1920 - 1929	18	1972	46
1930 - 1939	25		

Sources: 1920-1949 adapted from Alfred Kinsey, *Sexual Behavior in the Human Female* (New York: W. B. Saunders, 1953), p. 338, Table 84 (adapted from cohort data). 1972 percentage taken from Melvin Zelnick and John Kantner, "Sexuality, Contraception, and Pregnancy Among Young Unwed Females in the United States," *Demographic and Social Aspects of Population Growth,* U.S. Commission on Population Growth and The American Future (Washington, D.C.: U.S. Government Printing Office, 1972), Volume 1.

8. James McCary, *Human Sexuality: Physiological and Psychological Factors of Human Sexuality* (Princeton, New Jersey: Van Nostrand, 1967).

9. Kinsey, *Human Female,* p. 336, table 78: "Nature and Conditions of Pre-Marital Coitus."

10. Bronislaw Malinowski, "Parenthood—The Basis of Social Structure," in Calverton and Schmalhausen (eds.), *The New Generation* (New York: Macauley Company, 1930), pp. 129-143.

11. Jessie Bernard, *The Future of Marriage* (New York: World Publishing, 1972), pp. 16-17.

12. Leo Srole *et al., Mental Health in the Metropolis* (New York: McGraw Hill, 1962), pp. 177-178.

13. National Center for Health Statistics, 1968 Health Interview Survey, cited in Bernard, *The Future of Marriage,* Table 10; Genevieve Knupfer, Walter Clark, and Robin Room, "The Mental Health of the Unmarried," *American Journal of Psychiatry,* Vol. 122 (February 1966), p. 842; Srole, *Metropolis,* pp. 177-178; National Center for Health Statistics, *Selected Symptoms of Psychological Distress* (Washington, D.C.: U.S. Department of Health, Education, and Welfare, 1970), Table 17, pp. 30-31. For an overview of the male/female/married/unmarried health, demographic, and "happiness" statistics, see Bernard, *The Future of Marriage,* pp. 295-317.

14. U.S. Women's Bureau, *Background Facts on Women Workers in the United States* (September 1968), p. 3.

15. *Ibid.* (September 1970), p. 5.

16. Christopher Jencks *et al., Inequality* (New York: Basic Books, 1972), p. 222. (Table 7-4: "Income of Full-Time, Year Round Workers over 25 with Different Amounts of Schooling, as a Percentage of the 1968 Average.")

17. U.S. Women's Bureau, *Background Facts* (September 1970).

18. Bureau of the Census, U.S. Department of Commerce, "The Social and Economic Status of the Black Population in the United States, 1972," *Current Population Reports* (special studies), Series P-23, Number 46.

19. Evelyne Sullerot, *Women, Society, and Change* (New York: McGraw-Hill, World University Library, 1971), pp. 151-152.

20. Barbara Heyns, "A Socio-Economic Index of Women's Occupations," University of California (forthcoming). See also E. Gross and H. Zellner, "Discrimination Against Women, Occupational Segregation, and the Relative Wage," *American Economic Review: Papers and Proceedings,* Vol. 62 (May 1972), pp. 157-160.

21. Edward Gross, "Plus ça change . . . The Sexual Structure of Occupations Over Time," *Social Problems,* 16 (Fall 1968, 198-208.) See also Cynthia Epstein, "Encountering the Male Establishment: Sex-Status Limits on

Women's Careers in the Professions," *American Journal of Sociology*, Vol. 75, pp. 965-982.

22. Gross, "Plus ça change," pp. 965-982.

23. The term "fantasized realities" is Alice Abarbanel's: "Motherhood, A Mother's Journal," *Women* (Winter 1973).

24. U.S. Bureau of the Census, U.S. Department of Commerce, "Marital Status and Living Arrangements: March 1972," *Current Population Reports*, Population Characteristics, Series P-20, Number 242 (Washington, D.C.: U.S. Government Printing Office, November 1972), p. 3, Table E.

25. Ernest Burgess and Harvey Locke, *The Family* (New York: American Book Company, 1945), pp. 384-385. The term is of course Willard Waller's: "The Rating and Dating Complex," *American Sociological Review*, Vol. 2 (1937), pp. 272-734.

26. Schelling, *The Strategy of Conflict*, pp. 53-67.

27. 1965 was the first year in which more women reported the pill as the "method of contraception used most recently," but the condom was the second most frequently cited method. (Ther percentages here, for 1965, refer to couples who have used contraception at least once.)

Method	Whites	Blacks
pill	23%	21%
condom	19	16
rhythm	14	2
diaphragm	12	5
douche	7	22
withdrawal	6	4

Source: U.S. Bureau of the Census, "Fertilty Indicators: 1970," *Current Population Reports*, Series P-23, No. 36 (Washington, D.C.: U.S. Government Printing Office, 1971), Table 32, p. 53.

28. *Ibid.*, p. 54.

29. See, for example, A. S. Parkes, "Biological Aspects of Fertility Control," *Proceedings of the Seventh Conference of the International Planned Parenthood Federation* (New York: Excerpta Medical Foundation, 1964), p. 307.

30. Kroeber discusses the "couvade" in some detail. A. L. Kroeber, *Anthropology: Race, Language, Culture, Psychology, Prehistory* (New York: Harcourt, 1948), pp. 542-543.

31. Margaret Mead, *Male and Female* (New York: William Morrow and Company, 1949), pp. 79, 104, and *passim*.

32. The finding of the Supreme Court has been embodied in: "La Loi No. 72-73 du 3 Janvier, 1972 (J.C.P. 72, III, 38588)." See Michel Dagot, *Le Nouveau Droit de la Filiation* (Paris: Libraries Techniques, 1972), pp. 33-54.

33. Judith Blake, personal communication.

34. C. Westoff and N. Ryder, "Duration of Use of Oral Contraceptives in the U.S., 1960-1965," *Public Health Reports*, No. 83 (April 1968), pp. 277-287. The authors estimate that 35 to 50 percent of women "drop out" in the first year of pill use.

35. Bureau of Maternal and Child Health, State Department of Public Health, *Report to the Legislature* (1971).

NOTES TO CHAPTER 7

1. Data from unpublished figures supplied by the State Department of Health, New York, and by the Washington, D.C., Department of Public Health.

2. Tietze, "Mortality With Contraception and Induced Abortion," pp. 6-8.

3. K. Shanmugaratanam *et al.*, "Rates per 100,000 Births and Incidence of Choriocarcinoma," *International Journal of Cancer*, No. 8 (1971), pp. 165-175.

4. President's Commission on Population Growth and the American Future, *Demographic and Social Aspects*, edited by Westoff and Parke, Vol. I.

5. Tietze and Lehfeldt, "Legal Abortion in Eastern Europe."

6. Christopher Tietze, "New Estimate of Mortality Associated with Fertility Control," *Family Planning Perspectives*; 1977 (9), pp. 74-76.

7. The exact physiological relationship of pill use to gonorrhea incidence is unknown and under-researched. N. J. Fiumara (*Journal of Reproductive Medicine*, 13 (4): 154-157) argues that pill use means the gonoccoccus can survive throughout the vagina, rather than on the cervix only, thus increasing susceptibility. Other researchers (J. Liden: *British Journal of Venereal Disease* 45: 321-324) dispute this, finding no differences in V.D. rates among pill users and non-users, but the sample is too small to control for behavioral variables. Further research is needed.

NOTES TO APPENDIX 1

1. Alan F. Blum and Peter McHugh, "The Social Ascription of Motives," *American Sociological Review*, Vol. 36, No. 1 (February, 1971), p. 98.

2. Michael Bracken and Mary Swigar, "Psychosocial Factors Associated With Delay in Seeking Induced Abortions," Department of Public Health, Yale University.

3. Barney Glaser and Anselm Strauss, *The Discovery of Grounded Theory* (Chicago: Aldine Press, 1967).

4. Judith Blake, *Family Structure in Jamaica* (New York: Free Press, 1961); Lee Rainwater (assisted by K. K. Weinstein), *And the Poor Get Children* (Chicago: Quadrangle Books, 1960).

5. Florian Znaniecki, *The Method of Sociology* (New York: Octagon Books, 1968).

6. Glaser and Strauss, p. 45.

7. Kristin Luker, "Abortion Histories of Five Hundred Women," Planned Parenthood/World Population, Oakland, California, 1971 (mimeo).

8. Howard Becker, "Whose Side Are We On?" *Social Problems*, 14 (3), Winter, 1967, p. 241.

Bibliography

A selected list of the materials which proved most useful in the writing of this book; also included are all works cited in short form in the Notes.

Armijo, R., and T. Monreal. *Components of Population Change in Latin America*. Milbank Memorial Fund, 1965.

Bakkar, C. B., and C. R. Dightman. "Psychological Factors in Fertility Control." *Fertility and Sterility*, 15, 559-567.

Bates, J. E., and E. S. Zawadski. *Abortion—A Study in Medical Sociology*. Springfield, Illinois: Charles C. Thomas, 1965.

Beck, M. B., S. H. Newman, and S. Lewit. "Abortion: A National Public and Mental Health Problem—Past, Present, and Proposed Research." *American Journal of Public Health*, 59, 2131-2143.

Berelson, B. "KAP Studies on Fertility." *Family Planning and Population Programs: A Review of World Developments*. Edited by B. Berelson. Chicago: University of Chicago Press, 1966, 655-668.

———, R. K. Anderson, O. Harkavy, J. Maier, W. P. Mauldin, and S. J. Segal, eds. *Family Planning and Population Programs*. Chicago: University of Chicago Press, 1966.

———, and R. Freedman. "A Study in Fertility Control." *Scientific American*, 210 (May 1964), 29-37.

Berent, J. "Relationship Between Family Sizes of Two Successive Generations." *Milbank Memorial Fund Quarterly*, 31 (1953), 39-50.

Berkeley-Hill, O. "Unconscious Motives For and Against Birth Control." *Journal of Family Welfre*, 2 (March 1956), 93-97 and 107.

Berkov, Beth, and June Sklar. "The Impact of Legalized Abortion on Fertility in California." *IPUR Preliminary Paper*, No. 1, Berkeley, California, September 1972.

Bernard, Jessie. *The Future of Marriage*. New York: World Publishing, 1972.

Blake, J. *Family Structure in Jamaica: The Social Context of Reproduction*. New York: Free Press of Glencoe, 1961.

———. "Demographic Science and the Redirection of Population Policy." *Public Health and Population Change: Current Research Issues*. Edited by M. C. Sheps and J. C. Ridley. Pittsburgh: University of Pittsburgh Press, 1965, 41-69.

————. "The Americanization of Catholic Reproductive Ideals." *Population Studies*, 20 (1966), 27-43.

————. "Ideal Family Size Among White Americans: A Quarter of a Century's Evidence." *Demography*, 3 (1966), 154-173.

————. "Are Babies Consumer Durables? A Critique of the Economic Theory of Reproductive Motivation." *Population Studies*, 22 (1968), 5-25.

————. "Population Policy for Americans: Is the Government Being Misled?" *Science*, No. 3879 (1969), 522-529.

————. "Abortion and Public Opinion: The 1960-1970 Decade." *Science*, 171 (1971), 540-549.

Blood, R. O. *Marriage*. New York: Free Press of Glencoe, 1962.

————, and D. M. Wolfe, *Husbands and Wives: The Dynamics of Married Living*. New York: Free Press of Glencoe, 1960.

Bogue, D. J. "Hypotheses for Family Planning Derived from Recent and Current Experience in Asia." *Studies in Family Planning* (The Population Council), 3 (1964), 6-8.

Buckley, Walter. *Sociology and Modern Systems Theory*. Englewood Cliffs, New Jersey: Prentice Hall, 1967.

Bumpass, L., and C. Westoff. "The Perfect Contraceptive Population." *Science*, 169 (1970), 1177-1182.

————. "Unwanted Births and U.S. Population Growth." *Family Planning Perspectives*, 2 (1970), 9-11.

Bureau of Maternal and Child Health, State Department of Public Health. *A Report to the Legislature*. Annual Report on the Implementation of the California Therapeutic Abortion Act. Berkeley, California. From 1968 to 1974.

Burgess, E. W., H. J. Locke, and M. M. Thomes. *The Family: From Institution to Companionship*. 3rd ed. New York: American Book Company, 1963.

Calderone, M. S., ed. *Abortion in the United States*. New York: Hoeber-Harper, 1958.

————, ed. *Manual of Contraceptive Practice*. Baltimore: Williams and Wilkins, 1964.

————, ed. *Manual of Family Planning and Contraceptive Practice*. 2nd ed. Baltimore: Williams and Wilkins, 1970.

Callahan, D. *Abortion: Law, Choice, and Morality*. New York: Macmillan, 1970.

Center for Disease Control, U.S. Department of Health, Education and Welfare, Family Planning Evaluation Activity. *Abortion Surveillance Report*. Atlanta, Georgia, 1969, 1970, 1971.

Chandrasekhar, S. *Population and Planned Parenthood in India*. 2nd ed. London: Allen and Unwin, O. P., 1961.

Christensen, H. T. "Cultural Relativism and Premarital Sex Norms." *American Sociological Review*, 25 (1960), 31-39.

Christensen, H. T. "Timing of First Pregnancy as a Factor in Divorce: A Cross-Cultural Analysis." *Eugenics Quarterly,* 10 (1963), 119-130.

Cicourel, Aaron. *The Social Organization of Juvenile Justice.* New York: John Wiley and Sons, 1968.

Cutright, Phillips. "The Teenage Sexual Revolution and the Myth of an Abstinent Past." *Family Planning Perspectives,* 4 (1) (January 1972), 24-31.

David, H. P. *Family Planning and Abortion in the Socialist Countries of Central and Eastern Europe.* New York: The Population Council, 1970.

—————. "Psychological Studies in Abortion." *Psychological Perspectives on Population.* Edited by Fawcett. New York: Basic Books, 1973, pp. 241-273.

—————. "Psychosocial Factors in Transnational Family Planning Research." *Proceedings of the Conference on Psychological Factors in Transnational Family Planning Research.* Edited by H. David and N. Bernheim. Washington, D.C.: American Institutes Research, 1970, 8-15.

—————, ed. *Population and Mental Health.* Berne, Switzerland: Hans Huber, 1964.

Davidson, D. *Decision Making: An Experimental Approach.* Stanford University Press, 1957.

Davis, K., and J. Blake. "Social Structure and Fertility: An Analytical Framework." *Economic Development and Cultural Change,* 4 (1956), 211-235.

Davis, K. "The Sociology of Demographic Behavior." *Sociology Today.* Edited by R. K. Merton, L. Broom, and L. S. Cottrell. New York: Basic Books, 1959, 309-333.

Davis, K. "The Theory of Change and Response in Modern Demographic History." *Population Index,* 29 (1963), 345-366.

—————. "Population Policy: Will Current Programs Succeed?" *Science,* 158 (1967), 730-736.

Day, L. H., and A. Day. *Too Many Americans.* Boston: Houghton Mifflin, 1965.

Devereux, G. *A Study of Abortion in Primitive Societies.* New York: Julian Press, 1955.

—————. "A Psychoanalytic Study of Contraception." *Journal of Sex Research,* 1 (1965), 105-134.

Edwards, W. "Probability Preferences in Gambling." *American Journal of Psychology,* 66 (1953), 349-364.

—————. "Behavioral Decision Theory." *Annual Review of Psychology,* 12, 473-498.

—————, and A. Iversky. *Decision Making.* London: Penguin Books, 1967.

Ehrmann, W. *Premarital Dating Behavior.* New York: Holt, 1959.

Ekblad, M. "Induced Abortion on Psychiatric Grounds: A Followup Study of 479 Women." *Acta. Psychiat. Neurol. Scandinavica,* Supplement 99, 1955.

Fawcett, I. T., ed. *Psychology and Population: Behavioral Research Issues in Fertility and Family Planning*. New York: The Population Council, 1970.

Fleck, S. "Some Psychiatric Aspects of Abortion." *Journal of Nervous and Mental Disease*, 151 (1970), 42-50.

Ford, C. S. *A Comparative Study of Human Reproduction*. Yale University Publications in Anthropology, No. 32. New Haven, Connecticut: Yale University Press, 1945.

————. "Control of Conception in Cross-Cultural Perspectives." *Annals of the New York Academy of Science*, 54 (1952), 763-768.

Freedman, R. "Social Values About Family Size in the United States." *International Population Conference*. Vienna: International Union for the Scientific Study of Popultion, 1959, 173-183.

————. *The Sociology of Human Fertility: A Trend Report and Bibliography*. Oxford: Basil Blackwell, 1963. Appered as *Current Sociology*, 10/11, 1961/1962.

————, and L. Coombs. "Childspacing and Family Economic Position." *American Sociological Review*, No. 31 [5], October, 1966, 631-648.

————, D. Goldberg, and L. Bumpass. "Current Fertility Expectations of Married Couples in the United States: 1963." *Population Index*, 31 (1965), 3-20.

————, P. K. Whelpton, and A. A. Campbell. *Family Planning, Sterility, and Population Growth*. New York: McGraw-Hill, 1959.

Gebhard, P. H., W. B. Pomeroy, C. E. Martin, and C. V. Christenson. *Pregnancy, Birth, and Abortion*. New York: Harper and Brothers, 1958.

Glaser, Barney, and Anselm Strauss. *The Discovery of Grounded Theory*. Chicago: Aldine Press, 1967.

Glass, D. V., and D. E. C. Eversley, eds. *Population in History*. Chicago: Aldine, 1965.

Glass, D. V., and E. Grebenik. *The Trend and Pattern in Family in Great Britain: A Report on the Family Census of 1946*. London: H. M. Stationery Office, 1954.

Gold, Edwin, *et al*. "Therapeutic Abortion in New York City: A Twenty Year Review." *American Journal of Public Health*, 55 (July 1965), 965.

Gold, E. M. "Abortion—1970." *American Journal of Public Health*, 61 (1971), 487-488.

Goldsmith, Sadja, *et al*. "Teenagers, Sex and Contraception." *Family Planning Perspectives*, 4 (1) (January 1972), 32-38.

Grabill, Wilson, *et al. The Fertility of American Women*. New York: Wiley and Sons, 1958.

Gusfield, Joseph. *Symbolic Crusade*. Urbana and London: University of Illinois Press, 1966.

Hall, R. E. "Abortion: Physician and Hospital Attitudes." *American Journal of Public Health*, 61 (1971), 517-519.

————, ed. *Abortion in a Changing World*. New York: Columbia University Press, 1970. 2 vols.

Harkavy, O., *et al.* "Family Planning and Public Policy: Who is Misleading Whom?" *Science*, 162 (25) (July 1969), 367-373.

Harkavy, Oscar, *et al.* "Implementation of DHEW Policy on Family Planning and Population." The Ford Foundation, 1967.

————, *et al.* "Implementing DHEW Policy on Family Planning and Population—A Consultant's Report." Department of Health, Education, and Welfare Publication. Washington, D.C.: Government Printing Office, 1967.

Hart, A. G. "Risk, Uncertainty, and the Unprofitability of Compounding Probabilities." *Studies in Mathematical Economics and Econometrics.* Edited by Lange, *et al.* Chicago: University of Chicago Press, 1962, 110-118.

Hauser, P. M., and O. D. Duncan, eds. *The Study of Population: An Inventory and Appraisal.* Chicago: University of Chicago Press, 1959.

Hauser, P. M., ed. *The Population Dilemma.* Englewood Cliffs, New Jersey: Prentice-Hall, 1963.

Hawthorne, G. *The Sociology of Fertility.* London: Collier-Macmillan, 1970.

Heer, David M. "Abortion, Contraception, and Population Policy in the Soviet Union." *Demography*, 2 (1965), 531-539.

————. "Economic Development and Fertility." *Demography*, 3 (1966), 423-444.

Hill, R., J. M. Stycos, and K. W. Back. *The Family and Population Control: A Puerto Rican Experiment in Social Change.* Chapel Hill, North Carolina: University of North Carolina Press, 1959.

Himes, N. E. *Medical History of Contraception.* Baltimore: Williams and Wilkins, 1936. Reprinted, 1963. New York: Gamut.

Hollingshead, August, and Redlich, Fredrick. *Social Class and Mental Illness.* New York: John Wiley and Sons, 1955.

Jaffe, F. S. "Family Planning, Public Policy, and Intervention Strategy." *Journal of Social Issues*, 1966.

Kantner, J. F., and C. V. Kiser. *The Interrelation of Fertility, Fertility Planning, and Inter-Generational Social Mobility. Milbank Memorial Fund Quarterly*, 22 (1), pp. 69-103.

Kaplan, A., and R. Radner. "A Questionnaire Approach to Subjective Probability—Some Experimental Results." Working Memorandum 41, Santa Monica Conference on Decisions Problems, August 15, 1952. (Mimeographed.)

Kennedy, David. *Birth Control in America: The Career of Margaret Sanger.* New Haven: Yale University Press, 1970.

Kinsey, Alfred, *et al. Sexual Behavior in the Human Male.* Philadelphia: W. B. Saunders Company, 1948.

————, et al. *Sexual Behavior in the Human Female*. Philadelphia: W. B. Saunders Company, 1953.

Kirkendall, L. A. *Premarital Intercourse and Interpersonal Relationships*. New York: Julian Press, 1961.

Kiser, C. V., ed. *Research in Family Planning*. Princeton, New Jersey: Princeton University Press, 1962.

Komarovsky, M. *Women in the Modern World*. Boston: Little, Brown, 1953.

Kummer, Jerome M. "Post-Abortion Psychiatric Illness—A Myth?" *American Journal of Psychiatry*, 119 (April 1963), 981-983.

Lader, L. *Abortion*. Indianapolis: Bobbs-Merrill, 1966.

Lee, N. H. *The Search for an Abortionist*. Chicago: University of Chicago Press, 1969.

Lehfeldt, H. "Willful Exposure to Unwanted Pregnancy (WEUP)." *American Journal of Obstetrics and Gynecology*, 78 (1959), 661-665.

Lehfeldt, H. "Psychological Aspects of Planned Parenthood." *Journal of Sex Research*, 1 (1965), 97-103.

Lehfeldt, H., and Guze, H. "Psychological Factors in Contraceptive Failure." *Fertility and Sterility*, 17 (1966), 110-116.

Levene, H. I., and F. J. Ringney. "Law, Prevention Psychiatry, and Therapeutic Abortion." *Journal of Nervous and Mental Disease*, 151 (1970), 51-59.

Lévi-Strauss, Claude. *Structural Anthropology*. Garden City, New York: Anchor Books, 1967.

Lidz, Ruth. "Emotional Factors in the Success of Contraception." *Fertility and Sterility*, 20 (September-October 1969), 761-771.

Luce, R. D. *Handbook of Mathematical Psychology*. New York: Wiley and Sons, 1965.

Malinowski, Bronislaw. "Parenthood—The Basis of the Social Structure." V. F. Calverton and S. D. Schmalhausen, eds. *The New Generation*. New York: Macauley Company, 1930.

Malthus, T. R. *An Essay on the Principle of Population*. 1798. Available as paperback, New York: Norton, 1976.

Mann, E. C. "The Role of Emotional Determinants in Habitual Abortion." *Journal of Clinics of North America*, 37 (1957), 447.

Mead, M. *Sex and Temperament in Three Primitive Societies*. New York: Morrow, 1935.

————. *Male and Female*. New York: Morrow, 1949.

Menninger, K. "Emotional Factors in Organic Gynecological Conditions." *Bulletin of the Menninger Clinic*, 7 (1943), 47.

————. "Psychiatric Aspects of Contraception." *Bulletin of the Menninger Clinic*, 7 (1943), 36-40.

Milbank Memorial Fund. *Thirty Years of Research in Human Fertility: Retrospect and Prospect*. New York: Milbank Memorial Fund, 1959.

Moore, E. C. "Induced Abortion and Contraception: Theoretical Considerations." *Studies in Family Planning,* 53 (1970), 7-8.

Muramatsu, M., ed. *Japan's Experience in Family Planning—Past and Present.* Tokyo: Family Planning Federation of Japan, 1967.

Myrdal, Alva. *Nation and Family.* London: K. Paul, Trench, Trubner and Company, 1947.

Myrdal, A., and V. Klein. *Women's Two Roles: Home and Work.* London: Routledge and Kegan Paul, 1956.

National Center for Health Statistics. National Natality Survey Statistics, *Monthly Vital Statistics Reports,* 18 (12), Supplement (March 1970).

Niswander, K., M. Klein, and C. Randall. "Changing Attitudes Toward Therapeutic Abortion." *Journal of the American Medical Association,* 196 (1966), 1140-1143.

Noonan, J. T., Jr. *Contraception: A History of its Treatment by the Catholic Theologians and Canonists.* Cambridge, Mass.: Harvard University Press, 1965.

Patt, Stephen L. "Follow-up of Therapeutic Abortion." *Archives of General Psychiatry,* 20 (April 1969), 408-414.

Pearl, R. "Contraception and Fertility in 2,000 Women." *Human Biology,* 4 (1932), 365-407.

———. *The Natural History of Population.* New York: Oxford University Press, 1939.

Pincus, G., J. Rock, and C. R. Garcia. "Field Trials with Norethynodrel as an Oral Contraceptive." *Sixth International Conference on Planned Parenthood.* London: International Planned Parenthood Federation, 1959, 216-230.

Pohlman, E. W. " 'Wanted' and 'Unwanted': Toward Less Ambiguous Definition." *Eugenics Quarterly,* 12 (1965), 19-27.

———. "Unwanted Conceptions: Research on Undesirable Consequences." *Eugenics Quarterly,* 14 (1967), 143-154.

———. *The Psychology of Birth Planning.* Cambridge, Mass.: Schenkman, 1969.

Population Council. "American Attitudes on Population Policy." *Studies in Family Planning,* 9 (1966), 5-8.

Potter, R. G. "Some Relationships Between Short Range and Long Range Risks of Unwanted Pregnancy." *Milbank Memorial Fund Quarterly,* 38 (1960), 225-263.

———. "Additional Measures of Use Effectiveness of Contraception." *Milbank Memorial Fund Quarterly,* 41 (1963).

Potter, R. G., Jr., and Kantner, J. F. "The Influence of Siblings and Friends on Fertility." Whelpton and Kiser, eds., 1946-1958, 1189-1210.

Proceedings of A Conference on Psychological Measurement in the Study of Population Problems. Mimeograph. Berkeley: Institute of Personality

Assessment and Research, University of California and the American Psychological Association Task Force on Psychology, Family Planning, and Population Policy.

Rainwater, L., R. Coleman, and G. Handel. *Workingman's Wife*. New York: Oceana, 1959.

———, assisted by Weinstein, K. K. *And The Poor Get Children*. Chicago: Quadrangle, 1960.

———. *Family Design: Marital Sexuality, Family Size, and Family Planning*. Chicago: Aldine, 1965.

Reiss, I. L. *Premarital Sexual Standards in America*. New York: Free Press of Glencoe, 1960.

———. *The Sociology of Premarital Sexual Permissiveness: An Empirical Study and Theory*. New York: Holt, Rinehart and Winston, 1967.

Requena, Mariano. "Chilean Program of Abortion Control and Family Planning: Present Situation and Forecast for the Next Decade." *Fertility and Family Planning: A World View*. Edited by S. J. Behrman. Ann Arbor: University of Michigan Press, 1969, 478-489.

———. "Abortion in Latin America." *Abortion in a Changing World*. Edited by R. E. Hall. New York: Columbia University Press, 1 (1970), 338-352.

———, and T. Monreal. "Evaluation of Induced Abortion Control and Family Planning Programs in Chile." *Milbank Memorial Fund Quarterly*, 46, Part 2 (1968), 191-218.

Rosen, H., ed. *Therapeutic Abortion*. New York: Julian, 1954.

Sandberg, Eugene, and Jacobs, Ralph. "Psychology of the Misuse and Rejection of Contraception." *American Journal of Obstetrics and Gynecology*, 110 (2) (May 15, 1971).

Sanger, Margaret. *Woman and the New Race*. New York: Brentano's, 1922.

———, ed. *The Sixth International Neo-Malthusian and Birth-Control Conference*. Vol. 4. *Religions and Ethical Aspects of Birth Control*. New York: American Birth Control League, 1926.

———. *An Autobiography*. New York: Norton, 1938.

Sarrel, Phillip, and Ruth Lidz. "Contraceptive Failure—Psychosocial Factors: The Unwed." *Manual of Family Planning and Contraceptive Practice*. Edited by Mary Calderone. Baltimore: Williams and Wilkins.

Scheff, Thomas. *Being Mentally Ill*. Chicago: Aldine Press, 1966.

Schelling, T. *The Strategy of Conflict*. New York: Oxford University Press, 1963.

Schur, E. M. "Abortion and the Social System." *Social Problems*, 3 (1955), 94-99.

Scodel, A., P. Ratoosh, and J. S. Minas. "Some Personality Correlates of Decision Making Under Conditions of Risk." *Behavioral Sciences*, 4 (1959), 19-28.

Shainess, N. "Abortion: Social, Psychiatric, and Psychoanalytic Perspectives." *New York State Journal of Medicine,* 68 (1968), 3070-3073.

Sheps, M. C. "Effects on Family Size and Sex Ratio of Preferences Regarding the Sex of Children." *Population Studies,* 17 (1963), 66-72.

————, and J. C. Ridley, eds. *Public Health and Population Changes: Current Research Issues.* Pittsburgh: University of Pittsburgh Press, 1965.

Simon, Nathan M. "Psychiatric Sequelae of Abortion; Review of the Literature, 1935-1964." *Archives of General Psychiatry,* 15 (October 1966), 378-389.

Sloane, R. B. "The Unwanted Pregnancy." *The New England Journal of Medicine,* 280 (1969), 1206-1213.

Srole, Leo, *et al. Mental Health in the Metropolis.* New York: McGraw-Hill, 1962.

Stycos, J. M. *Family and Fertility in Puerto Rico.* New York: Columbia University Press, 1955.

————. "Obstacles to Programs of Population Control—Facts and Fancies." *Marriage and Family Living,* 25 (1963), 5-13.

Taussig, F. T. *Abortion, Spontaneous and Induced: Medical and Social Aspects.* St. Louis: Mosby, 1936.

Tien, H. Y. "Birth Control in Mainland China: Ideology and Politics." *Milbank Memorial Fund Quarterly,* 41 (1963), 269-290.

Tien, H. Y. *Sterilization, Oral Contraception, and Population Control in Communist China.* Paper presented at the 1964 Convention of the Population Association of America, San Francisco, June 1964. (Mimeographed.)

Tietze, C. "History of Contraceptive Methods." *Journal of Sex Research,* 1 (1965), 69-85.

————. "Induced Abortion as a Method of Fertility Control." *Fertility and Family Planning: A World View.* Edited by S. J. Behrman. Ann Arbor: University of Michigan Press, 1969, 311-337.

————. "Mortality with Contraception and Induced Abortion." *Studies in Family Planning,* 45 (September 1969).

————. "Relative Effectiveness." *Manual of Family Planning and Contraceptive Practice.* 2nd Edition. Edited by Mary Calderone. Baltimore: Williams and Wilkins, 1970.

————, ed. *Selected Bibliography of Contraception: 1940-1960.* New York: National Committee on Maternal Health. Followed by a Supplementary Bibliography.

————, and H. Lehfeldt. "Legal Abortion in Eastern Europe." *Journal of the American Medical Association,* 175 (1961), 1149-1154.

United Nations. *The Determinants and Consequences of Population Trends.* New York: United Nations, 1953.

United States Army. *Index Catalogue of the Library of the Surgeon General's*

Office. 2nd series, 3. Washington, D.C.: Government Printing Office, 1898.

United States Women's Bureau, Department of Labor. *Background Facts on Women Workers in the United States,* September 1968.

Vincent, C. E. *Unmarried Mothers*. New York: Free Press of Glencoe, 1961.

Von Neumann, J., and O. Morgenstern. *Theory of Games and Economic Behavior*. 2nd ed. Princeton: Princeton University Press, 1947.

Walter, G. W. "Psychologic and Emotional Consequences of Elective Abortion." *Obstetrics and Gynecology,* 36 (1970), 482-491.

Weber, Max. *Max Weber on the Methodology of the Social Sciences*. Glencoe, Illinois: The Free Press, 1949.

Westoff, C. F., and C. V. Kiser. "The Interrelation of Fertility, Fertility Planning, and Feeling of Personal Inadequacy." In Whelpton and Kiser, eds., *Social and Psychological Factors Affecting Fertility,* 1946-1958, 741-799.

Westoff, C. F., E. G. Mishler, and E. L. Kelly. "Preferences in Size of Family and Eventual Fertility Twenty Years After." *American Journal of Sociology,* 62 (1957), 491-497.

Westoff, C., and R. Parke, eds. *President's Commission on Population Growth and The American Future,* Vol. I (Demographic and Social Aspects). Washington, D.C.: Government Printing Office, 1972.

Westoff, C. F., E. C. Moore, and N. B. Ryder. "The Structure of Attitudes Towards Abortion." *Milbank Memorial Fund Quarterly,* 47 (1), Part 1 (January 1969).

Westoff, C. F., R. G. Potter, Jr., and P. C. Sagi. *The Third Child*. Princeton, New Jersey: Princeton University Press, 1963.

Whelpton, P. K., and C. V. Kiser. "Differential Fertility Among 41,498 Native White Couples in Indianapolis." In Whelpton and Kiser, eds., *Social and Psychological Factors Affecting Fertility,* 1943, 1946-1958.

―――. "Social and Psychological Factors Affecting Fertility." *Eugenics Review,* 51 (1959), 35-42.

―――, eds. *Social and Psychological Factors Affecting Fertility*. 5 vols. New York: Milbank Memorial Fund 1946-1958. All 33 articles originally appeared in *Milbank Memorial Fund Quarterly,* under same title as the collectin. Original references in *Milbank Memorial Fund,* 1955, 37-39.

Whelpton, P. K., A. A. Campbell, and J. Patterson. *Fertility and Family Planning in the United States*. Princeton, New Jersey: Princeton University Press, 1966.

Williams, J. D. *The Complete Strategyst*. New York: McGraw-Hill, 1954.

World Health Organization. "Report of a Scientific Group on Spontaneous and Induced Abortion." *WHO Technical Report Series,* No. 461. Geneva: World Health Organization, 1970.

Young, Leontine. *Out of Wedlock*. New York: McGraw-Hill Book Company, 1954.

Index